Connected and Associated: Insolvency and Pensions Law

Connected and Associated: Insolvency and Pensions Law

David Pollard
Barrister, Wilberforce Chambers

Bloomsbury Professional
LONDON • DUBLIN • EDINBURGH • NEW YORK • NEW DELHI • SYDNEY

BLOOMSBURY PROFESSIONAL
Bloomsbury Publishing Plc
50 Bedford Square, London, WC1B 3DP, UK
1385 Broadway, New York, NY 10018, USA
29 Earlsfort Terrace, Dublin 2, Ireland

British Library Cataloguing-in-Publication Data

A catalogue record for this book is available from the British Library.

ISBN: HB: 978 1 52651 959 7
ePDF: 978 1 52651 961 0
ePub: 978 1 52651 960 3

Typeset by Compuscript Ltd, Shannon

Preface

The aim of this book is to deal in depth with the tests under the law of England and Wales for persons being 'connected' or 'associated' with another person under insolvency and pensions law. These terms are defined in the Insolvency Act 1986 in section 249 (connected) and section 435 (associated). They are used by reference in the pensions legislation as well.

These relationships (and the linked one of 'control') are complex and yet of immense importance, in particular in relation to occupational pensions.

INSOLVENCY LAW

For insolvency purposes, the original use of the terms was mainly in relation to clawback of pre-insolvency transactions (for example as a transaction at an undervalue). This use now extends to other aspects, including creditor voting majorities for both a company voluntary arrangement (CVA) or for extending a moratorium under Part A1.

A slightly more complex definition of 'connected person' applies for the controls enacted in 2021 on substantial disposals by administrators within the first eight weeks of the administration.

PENSIONS LAW

Pensions legislation uses these terms in the Insolvency Act. The two most important uses are that:

- Limiting those who can be potential targets for the statutory 'moral hazard' powers of the pensions regulator. The Regulator can seek orders (which can be for large amounts) requiring third parties to support or contribute to an occupational pension scheme. Such orders, for a contribution notice (CN) or a financial support direction (FSD), are limited under the Pensions Act 2004 to persons who are connected or associated with an employer.
- the prohibitions and limits under the Pensions Act 1995 on 'employer-related investment' by an occupational pension scheme are framed by

> whether or not the investment is with the employer or an entity which is connected or associated with the employer. In some circumstances, breach of the restriction can be a criminal offence.

These provisions mean that it can be highly important to know if a person is connected (or associated) with another.

I am grateful for comments on a draft of this book (or the predecessor papers) from Dawn Heath, Tim Cox, Philip Bennett, Isabel Carruthers, Tom Robinson, Alison Goudarzi, Harriet Sayer and Katharina Crinson.

The law is stated as at 26 October 2021.

David Pollard
Wilberforce Chambers,
Lincoln's Inn,
London

dpollard@wilberforce.co.uk

About the Author

David Pollard is a barrister, practising since 2017 from Wilberforce Chambers in Lincoln's Inn, London. He previously practised as a solicitor and was for 25 years a partner in Freshfields and then Freshfields Bruckhaus Deringer, based in London in the Employment, Pensions and Benefits department.

He specialises in all aspects of pensions advice, including acquisitions and disposals, joint ventures, terminations, pension scheme reconstructions, the implications of insolvency for employees and pensions, winding up pension schemes and pensions litigation.

David is also the author of the books:

- *Corporate Insolvency: Employment and Pension Rights* (Bloomsbury Professional, 7th edn, 2021, forthcoming)
- *Pensions Contracts and Trusts: Legal Issues on Decision Making* (Bloomsbury Professional, 2020).
- *Employment Law and Pensions* (Bloomsbury Professional, 2016).
- *The Law of Pension Trusts* (Oxford University Press, 2013).

David was a joint general editor of the series of books running from 2012: *Freshfields on Corporate Pensions Law*. The latest *is Freshfields on Corporate Pensions Law 2015* (Bloomsbury Professional, 2015).

- He is a co-editor of the quarterly journal *Trust Law International.*
- He has contributed chapters to three looseleaf books:
  - *Tolley's Pensions Law*;
  - *Tolley's Employment Law*;
  - *Tolley's Insolvency Law.*

David has contributed chapters to various other books, including:

- *Trusts and Private Wealth Management: Developments and Directions* (Cambridge University Press, 2021, forthcoming)
- *Elgar Handbook on Corporate Restructuring* (Edward Elgar, 2021)

- *Pensions – Law, Policy and Practice* (Hart, 2020)
- *Trusts and Modern Wealth Management* (Cambridge University Press 2018).

He was the co-editor of *The Guide to the Pensions Act 1995* (Tolley, 1995).

In 1998 and again in 2015, David was awarded the Wallace Medal by the Association of Pension Lawyers (APL) for excellence in communicating pensions issues.

He was Chairman of the Association of Pension Lawyers (APL) from 2001 to 2003 and has been a vice chair of the Industrial Law Society.

David has (in effect) a mathematics and law degree from St John's College, Cambridge.

Contents

Abbreviations and Glossary

Statutory references are to the Insolvency Act 1986 unless otherwise stated.

Admin Disposal Regs 2021	The Administration (Restrictions on Disposal etc. to Connected Persons) Regulations 2021 (SI 2021/427)
associate	as defined in IA 1986, s 435
CA	Companies Act
CDDA	Company Directors Disqualification Act
CIGA	Corporate Insolvency and Governance Act
company	when used in s 435 includes a body corporate (whether incorporated in the UK or overseas) – IA 1986, s 435(11) – see Chapter 19 below
connected	as defined in IA 1986, s 239
connected person	as defined in IA 1986, Sch B1, para 60A
control or s 435 control	as defined in IA 1986, s 435(10)
CTA	Corporation Tax Act
CVA	company voluntary arrangement (under Part 1 of IA 1986)
CVA company	the company in relation to which the CVA is proposed or has effect
DB	defined benefit (pension)
director	see below
domination	see below
DP	determinations panel (of TPR)
employer	see below
Employer Debt Regulations	the Occupational Pension Schemes (Employer Debt) Regulations 2005 (SI 2005/678, as amended)
ERA	Employment Rights Act
FA	Finance Act
FSMA	Financial Services and Markets Act

IA	Insolvency Act
IA 1986	Insolvency Act 1986
ICTA	Income and Corporation Taxes Act
IP	Insolvency Practitioner (s 388, IA 1986)
IR 1986	Insolvency Rules 1986 (SI 1986/1925)
IR 2016	Insolvency (England and Wales) Rules 2016 (SI 2016/1024)
ITTOIA	Income Tax (Trading and Other Income) Act
IVA	individual voluntary arrangement (under Part 8 of IA 1986)
manager	see below
officer	see below
OPS	occupational pension scheme (as defined in PSA 1993, s 1)
OPS Trustee	a trustee of an occupational pension scheme
PA	Pensions Act
Part A1 moratorium	a moratorium under IA 1986, Part A1 (inserted by CIGA 2020)
PPF	Board of the Pension Protection Fund (established under Part 2 of PA 2004)
PPF assessment period	an assessment period under PA 2004 (see s 132)
PPF Entry Rules	the Pension Protection Fund (Entry Rules) Regulations 2005 (SI 2005/590, as amended)
PPF Multi-employer Regulations	the Pension Protection Fund (Multi-Employer Schemes) (Modification) Regulations 2005 (SI 2005/441, as amended)
PSA	Pension Schemes Act
s 75 debt	a debt on an employer in relation to an OPS arising under PA 1995, s 75 and the Employer Debt Regulations
SBEEA 2015	Small Business, Enterprise and Employment Act 2015
Shadow director	see below
SI	Statutory Instrument
spouse	see below
TCGA	Taxation of Capital Gains Act
TPR	the Pensions Regulator (established under Part 1 of PA 2004)
TULRCA	Trade Union and Labour Relations (Consolidation) Act
TUPE	Transfer of Undertakings (Protection of Employment Regulations

director generally includes (IA 1986, s 251) 'any person occupying the position of director, by whatever name called'. So it covers a '*de facto*' director (see Chapter 21 below). Directors are usually (but not necessarily) individuals, rather than companies or corporations.

'***dominate***' and '***domination***' are not terms used in s 435 (or elsewhere in the legislation), but are used in this book as a shorthand to indicate control under s 435(10)(a) where directors are accustomed to act in accordance with the directions or instructions of the other person – see Part 9 below.

employer and ***employee*** generally probably have their usual meaning – see Chapter 24 below.

However, the term '***employer***' in relation to an occupational pension scheme:

- generally means (under pensions legislation[1]) 'the employer of persons in the description of employment to which the scheme relates' and
- is extended by some regulations (eg the Employer Debt Regulations) to cover some former employers as well.

Such an employer can be called a 'statutory employer'. This can be a difficult test in some cases (eg if there are life members or if a participating company in a scheme has employees, but none is an active member of the scheme).[2]

officer includes a director, manager or secretary – IA 1986, s 251 (see Chapter 25 below).

manager – a rather vague term – see Chapter 25 below.

shadow director in relation to a company means 'a person in accordance with whose directions or instructions the directors of the company are accustomed to act' (but not if the person is a professional advisor, or government entity etc) – IA 1986, s 251 (see Chapter 22 below).

spouse is used as an umbrella term in this book. to mean a husband or wife or civil partner, a former husband or wife or civil partner, and a 'reputed' husband or wife or civil partner (see IA 1986, s 435(8) and 27.3 below). It is not a term used in s 435 (although it is in the equivalent Scottish legislation).

1 PA 2004, s 318 and PA 1995, s 124.

2 See '*Who is the employer under pensions legislation?*', ch 59 in Pollard '*Corporate Insolvency: Employment and Pension Rights*' (7th end, 2021, Bloomsbury Professional). Also *Re Merchant Navy Ratings Pension Fund; Merchant Navy Ratings Pension Trustees Ltd v Stena Line Ltd* [2015] EWHC 448 (Ch), [2015] Pens LR 239 (Asplin J) and *Re G4S Pension Scheme* [2018] EWHC 1749 (Ch), [2019] ICR 141, [2018] Pens LR 16 (Nugee J).
The term 'employer' under PA 2004 can cover a company with just officers: *PI Consulting (Trustee Services) Ltd v Pensions Regulator* [2013] EWHC 3181 (Ch), [2013] Pens LR 433 (Morgan J) and *Board of the Pension Protection Fund v Dalriada Trustees Ltd* [2020] EWHC 2960 (Ch), [2021] ICR 479 (Trower J).

Main Cases

Case	Full reference
Ayerst	*Ayerst (Inspector of Taxes) v C&K (Construction) Ltd* [1976] AC 167, HL (Lord Diplock, Viscount Dilhorne, Lord Kilbrandon and Lord Edmund-Davies).
Box Clever	*Granada UK Rental & Retail Ltd v The Pensions Regulator* [2019] EWCA Civ 1032, [2020] ICR 747, [2019] Pens LR 20 (Patten, Newey and Males LJJ).
Buzzle	*Buzzle Operations Pty Ltd v Apple Computer Australia Pty Ltd* [2011] NSWCA 109, (2011) 250 FLR 242, (2011) 277 ALR 189, (2011) 81 NSWLR 47 (Hodgson, Young and Whealy JJA).
Deverell	*Secretary of State for Trade and Industry v Deverell* [2001] Ch 340; [2000] 2 All ER 365, CA (Morritt, Potter LJJ and Morison J).
Linter Textiles	*Commissioner of Taxation v Linter Textiles Australia Ltd* [2005] HCA 20, 220 CLR 592 (Gleeson CJ, McHugh, Gummow, Kirby, Hayne, Callinan and Heydon JJ).
Unidare	*Re Kilnoore Ltd: Unidare plc v Cohen* [2005] EWHC 1410 (Ch), [2006] Ch 489 (Lewison J).

Courts

CA	Court of Appeal
CJEU	Court of Justice of the European Union
CSIH	Court of Session (Inner House)
CSOH	Court of Session (Outer House)
DC	Divisional Court
EAT	Employment Appeal Tribunal
ECJ	European Court of Justice (now part of the CJEU)
ET	Employment Tribunal
FCA	Federal Court of Australia
HCA	High Court of Australia
HL	House of Lords (Supreme Court from October 2009)
ICC	Insolvency and Companies Court
PC	Privy Council
SC	Supreme Court
UT	Upper Tribunal

Judges

C	Chancellor (replaced the Vice-Chancellor from October 2005)
CJ	Chief Justice (High Court)
DPO	Deputy Pensions Ombudsman
HHJ	Her (or His) Honour Judge
ICC	Insolvency and Companies Court
J	Justice (High Court in England and Wales)
JA	Justice of Appeal (Australia)
LJ	Lord or Lady Justice (Court of Appeal)
MR	Master of the Rolls
P	President
PO	Pensions Ombudsman
V-C	Vice-Chancellor

Other bodies

APL	Association of Pension Lawyers
DWP	Department for Work and Pensions
FMLC	Financial Markets Law Committee
HMRC	Her Majesty's Revenue and Customs
ILA	Insolvency Lawyers Association
PPF	Board of the Pension Protection Fund (established under Part 2 of PA 2004)
R3	The Association of Business Recovery Professionals
TPR	the Pensions Regulator

Table of Statutes

Table of Statutory Instruments

Table of International Legislation

Table of Cases

PARA

D

E

F

PARA

G

H

I

PARA

P

Q

R

PART 1

INTRODUCTION

1

Introduction

1.1 This book looks at the meaning of the 'connected', 'associated' and 'control' tests used in the Insolvency Act 1986 (IA 1986) and incorporated by reference in pensions legislation. This book also looks at the definition of 'connected person' in IA 1986, Sch B1, para 60A used in relation to restrictions on sales by administrators (see Chapters 13 and 20 below).

1.2 Insolvency and pensions legislation has, in a number of areas, sought to include a wide group of broadly 'linked' persons for statutory purposes. In practice, the pensions legislation does not include a completely new definition of such a linked person, but instead uses the existing definitions found in the Insolvency Act 1986.

ENGLAND AND WALES

1.3 This book deals with the legal position in England and Wales. The law on connected and associated looks to be pretty similar in Scotland,[1] Northern Ireland[2] and (in some areas) Singapore (see Chapter 8 below). I have referred to those laws and relevant caselaw and those of other jurisdictions, in particular Australia,[3] as being helpful in construction of the law in England and Wales. But I am not qualified in any of those jurisdictions and this book should not be considered as a guide to those laws.

1 The Insolvency Act 1986 applies to Scotland, but does not cover individual bankruptcy in Scotland. This is now covered by the Bankruptcy (Scotland) Act 2016 (asp 21) – see ch 8 below. An extract is set out in Appendix A.

2 See, eg, the Insolvency (Northern Ireland) Order 1989 (SI 1989/2405) in particular Art 4 defining associate in terms that look to be identical to IA 1986, s 435.

3 On the use of Australian caselaw, see HHJ Matthews in *Sofer v SwissIndependent Trustees SA* [2019] EWHC 2071 (Ch) at [69] and [74].

INSOLVENCY LAW

1.4 These tests are important in insolvency law in relation to issues such as:

- time limits for reversal or clawback of pre insolvency transactions (eg undue preferences or transactions at an undervalue);
- creditor voting in company voluntary arrangements (CVAs)[4] and on Part 1A moratorium extensions (under IA 1986, Part 1A);[5] and
- the new (2021) restrictions on substantial sales of business or assets by an administrator within the first eight weeks of an administration to a 'connected person'[6] – IA 1986, Sch B1, para 60A. The term 'connected person' is not the same as 'connected', but the definition (and the associated regulations) does use the terms 'associated' as well as 'connected'.[7]

PENSIONS LAW

1.5 These terms, 'connected', 'associated' and 'control', in IA 1986 have become of particular importance when used in pensions legislation. The tests are incorporated by reference in various areas of pensions law. The two most important are:

- the moral hazard powers of the Pensions Regulator (TPR) under Part 1 of the Pensions Act 2004 (PA 2004). Broadly the Pensions Regulator has statutory power to issue either contribution notices (CNs)[8] or financial support directions (FSDs)[9] against third parties (ie not just the employer) in certain circumstances. But this power is limited to being only exercised against third parties who are connected or associated with an employer, using the IA 1986 definitions.[10] The connected or associated test is the condition to liability (there are others) that is most objective and easiest to determine.
- Limits are imposed on investment by relevant occupational pension schemes in investment which are 'employer-related' (Pensions Act 1995, s 40 and regulations). These are defined as investments in an employer or any person associated or connected with an employer. In some circumstances investment contrary to the limits is a criminal offence.

The tests appear in other pensions legislation as well.

4 IA 1986, Part 1.
5 As inserted by CIGA 2020.
6 The Admin Disposal Regs 2021: The Administration (Restrictions on Disposal etc. to Connected Persons) Regulations 2021 (SI 2021/427).
7 See chs 13 and 20 below.
8 PA 2004, s 38.
9 PA 2004, s 43.
10 PA 2004, ss 38(10) and 51(3).

CASELAW

1.6 The Insolvency Act definitions of 'connected' and 'associated' do not feature much in caselaw, whether in relation to insolvency or pensions. The main reported case on the 'control' concept in s 435(10) was, until fairly recently, the 2005 decision in *Unidare plc v Cohen*,[11] but parts of this decision were over-ruled on this point in 2019 by the Court of Appeal in *Box Clever.*[12]

1.7 This topic is particularly relevant for insolvency lawyers, pension lawyers, insolvency practitioners, litigators, pension trustees, employers, investors and lenders (and their advisers).

1.8 A similarly worded test also applies in some other legislation.[13]

COMPANIES INCORPORATED IN ENGLAND AND WALES

1.9 In relation to companies, this book is limited to looking at the position in relation to companies incorporated in England and Wales under the Companies Acts. Different issues may well arise if a relevant insolvency is outside England and Wales or if the company is incorporated outside England and Wales.

BANKRUPTCY

1.10 The connected and associated definitions are also used in individual bankruptcy, including:

(a) The provisions dealing with transactions at an undervalue and preferences by an individual are wider in relation to a transaction with an associate of the bankrupt – IA 1986, s 339.

(b) the power of the court to set aside transactions by the trustee in bankruptcy with an associate of him or her – IR 2016, rule 6.147; and

(c) in relation to voting majorities in an IVA – IR 2016, rule 15.34(6).

11 *Re Kilnoore Ltd: Unidare plc v Cohen* [2005] EWHC 1410 (Ch), [2005] 3 All ER 730 (Lewison J). Noted by Look Chan Ho 'Connected Persons and Administrators' Duty to Think: *Unidare v Cohen*' (2005) 20 *Journal of International Banking and Regulation* 11.

12 *Granada UK Rental & Retail Ltd v The Pensions Regulator* [2019] EWCA Civ 1032, [2020] ICR 747, [2019] Pens LR 20.

13 See ch 5 below.

ARTICLES AND COMMENTARY

1.11 This book supplements and builds on three previous articles[14] on the 'connected', 'control' and 'associated' tests in IA 1986:

- 'Who is connected or associated'[15]
- 'Some Tricky Issues on "Control" in Section 435(10) of the Insolvency Act 1986';[16] and
- 'Insolvency and control: the impact of corporate insolvency on "control" under section 435(10) of the Insolvency Act 1986'.[17]

1.12 The law is stated as at 1 October 2021.

14 Other detailed commentary is limited.
For individuals, see Briggs and Tribe *Muir Hunter on Personal Insolvency* (Sweet & Maxwell, Looseleaf, service to March 2021) 3-3074 (discussing s 435).
For companies, see the former chapter by Antony Zacaroli (appointed a High Court Judge in the Chancery Division in November 2017) in Totty, Moss and Segal *Insolvency* (Sweet & Maxwell, looseleaf). There is a discussion of 'associated' in the current edition at F2-24 to F2-33.
See also the short articles (a) by Agnello 'Liability of directors, professional advisors and lenders under the moral hazard provisions' (2016) 9 *JIBFL* 522 and (b) by Griffiths and Clark 'Not so clever? The potential dangers of taking security over shares' (2012) 6 *JIBFL* 351.

15 Pollard 'Who is connected or associated' (2009) 22 *Insolvency Intelligence* 33. A shorter version of a talk at the 2008 Association of Pension Lawyers (APL) Annual Conference. The latest (2016) published version was ch 33 'Who is connected or associated?' in Pollard *Corporate Insolvency: Pension Rights* (6th edn, Bloomsbury Professional, 2016).

16 Pollard and Heath 'Some Tricky Issues on "Control" in Section 435(10) of the Insolvency Act 1986' (2018) 31 *Insolvency Intelligence* 33, based on a talk at the APL Conference in 2017.

17 Pollard (2019) 32(4) *Insolvency Intelligence* 127.

2

Outline: the 'connected' or 'associated' test

2.1 The Insolvency Act 1986 (IA 1986) defines in s 249 (connected) and s 435 (associated) whether a person is 'connected' with a company or 'associated' with another person. These sections are then referred to in various parts of the insolvency and pensions legislation.

2.2 The full text of these sections (and some sections also referred to) are set out in Appendix A to this book.

2.3 These definitions are important because various statutory provisions in IA 1986, and also in other legislation, use them. In a pensions context this is outlined later (see Chapter 3 below), but importantly this includes:

(a) limits on the persons whom the Pensions Regulator can make responsible for pension scheme deficits under the 'moral hazard' powers in the Pensions Act 2004 (PA 2004); and

(b) defining the entities investment in which by an occupational pension scheme can contravene the employer-related investment prohibitions in section 40 of the Pensions Act 1995 (PA 1995).

OVERVIEW OF THE DEFINITIONS

2.4 Pension lawyers mainly deal with situations involving a corporate employer in relation to a pension scheme. A summary of the effect of the 'connected' and 'associated' definitions in relation to companies is:

(a) A company is associated with a person who 'controls' it (and vice versa).

(b) All wholly owned companies in a group are associated with each other.

(c) Directors are associated with the company on whose board they sit, but not necessarily with its subsidiaries. Similarly, an employee is associated with his or her employer (and vice versa).

(d) A company is *associated* with each of its directors, officers and employees.

(e) Significant shareholders (over one-third 'voting power') will have 'control' of the company (and its subsidiaries and other companies it controls) and so are associated with the company (and its subsidiaries and other companies it controls).

(f) The following are each *connected* with a company:

  (i) each of its directors and shadow directors; and

  (ii) any person associated (as defined in s 435) with a director (or shadow director) of the company;[1]

  (iii) all of those who are associated with a company are also connected with the company. But the class of persons connected with a company is wider – it also includes persons who are associated with any of its directors (or shadow directors).

A person (individual or company) can be connected only with a company. The definition does not allow for a person to be connected with an individual.

2.5 The complicated definitions of these terms often refer to other concepts, such as 'director', 'shadow director' and 'officer', which can themselves be problematic (see Part 5 below).

2.6 As the statutory provisions are detailed, at least one case suggests that the courts are unwilling to take a purposive approach when determining whether a person falls within the policy of the voidable preference provisions in IA 1986, s 239(4) which use the definitions – see for example *Re Thirty-Eight Building Limited.*[2]

2.7 In *Box Clever*,[3] the Court of Appeal commented:

> 'Section 435 of the IA 1986 … is an elaborate provision under which a multitude of individuals and companies can potentially be considered to be "associates" simultaneously.'

NO CHAIN

2.8 In general, no 'chain' principle applies: if A is associated with B and B is associated with C, this does not mean (on its own) that A is necessarily associated with C.[4]

1 See, eg: *James Dolman & Company Ltd (In Liquidation) v Treanor* [2010] EWHC 3950 (Ch) (HHJ Cooke): mother of a director connected with a company.
2 [1999] 1 BCLC 416 (Hazel Williamson QC) at [423]: 'part of a scheme of careful and elaborate statutory drafting'. Discussed further in ch 29 (Pension scheme as a trust) below.
3 *Granada UK Rental & Retail Ltd v The Pensions Regulator* [2019] EWCA Civ 1032, [2020] ICR 747.
4 *Re Kilnoore Ltd: Unidare plc v Cohen* [2005] EWHC 1410 (Ch), [2005] 3 All ER 730 (Lewison J) at [35].

2.9 However, there are three exceptions to this:

(a) common s 435(10) control constitutes a chain. If:

- A controls B Co; and
- B Co controls C Co,

then A controls C Co as well[5] (and A is also associated with C Co);

(b) trusts: a trustee is associated both with a beneficiary of the trust and also with an associate of a beneficiary – s 435(5). Certain trusts are excluded from this principle – see Chapters 28 to 30 below; and

(c) the definition of the term 'connected' in s 249 allows one onward link if a person is associated with a director (or shadow director). IA 1986, s 249 provides that in effect if:

- A is associated with B; and
- B is a director (or shadow director) of X Co,

then A is *connected* with X Co (but *not*, by reason of this on its own, *associated* with X Co).

2.10 For the purposes of this test (and the other tests referred to in this book):

(a) a 'person' can be an individual, a company or a body of unincorporated persons;[6]

(b) a person can be *associated* with a company or an individual, but can be *connected* only with a company, not with an individual.

EXAMPLES OF ASSOCIATES AND NON-ASSOCIATES

2.11 Examples of associates:[7]

(a) A lender holds more than one-third of the voting shares in the company following a debt to equity swap. The lender will now be associated with the company as it is has 'control' within s 435(10).

(b) A person holds more than one-third of the voting shares in an intermediate holding company which in turn holds half of the voting shares in a joint venture company with an outside party. The person will have 'control' over the joint venture company.

5 Noted by the Court of Appeal in *Box Clever* [2019] EWCA Civ 1032 at [126]:

> 'a person could be deemed to have control in the context of the IA 1986 if, say, he held just 35% of the shares in a company which in turn held 35% in a company holding 35% in another company with a 35% holding in a yet further company.'

6 Interpretation Act 1978, s 5 and Sch 1. See ch 19 below.

7 See, eg: Beale and Keddie *Insolvency and Restructuring Manual* (3rd edn, Bloomsbury Professional, 2018) at 5.8.

(c) An investor holding less than one-third of the voting shares appoints one of its employees as a director of a company to protect its investment. The investor is connected or associated with the company on at least one, and possibly two bases here. First, the investor will be an associate of its employee, and therefore connected with the company by virtue of being an associate of a director of the company – see Chapter 23 below. Second, if the investor gives instructions to its appointee director, the investor could potentially be associated with the company by virtue of having 'control' – see Part 9 below.

2.12 In contrast, the following are examples where the circumstances concerned do not in themselves mean that the persons are connected or associated:

(a) A lender holds a large number of non-voting preference shares in the company following a debt to equity swap. Preference shares which are non-voting do not contribute towards s 435(10) 'control' of the company, regardless of how many may be held. (In practice the situation is often complicated by the fact that preference shares are in many cases given voting rights in certain circumstances, for example, if a dividend is unpaid – see Part 8 below).

(b) An investor holding less than one-third of the voting shares appoints one of its employees as an observer (not a director) to the company's board (assuming that the observer is careful not to render themselves a shadow director by giving instructions to the board).

3

Why does being 'associated' or 'connected' matter?

3.1 The Insolvency Act 1986 (IA 1986) definitions are used throughout the insolvency legislation and guidance[1] and also used (by cross reference) in the pensions legislation.

INSOLVENCY LEGISLATION

3.2 The insolvency legislation has special rules dealing with situations involving an insolvent body or person and someone who is connected or associated with that person. For example, it is easier for an insolvency officeholder to challenge transactions that took place with an associated person before insolvency as transactions at an undervalue or preference etc.

3.3 These may also be relevant in a pensions context – for example, there will be longer 'hardening' periods for security granted by a company to a pension scheme trustee if it is connected or associated with the company.

PENSIONS LEGISLATION

3.4 Pensions legislation uses these two definitions from IA 1986 in various areas. The three most important are:

- The Pensions Regulator (TPR) can make a moral hazard order (contribution notice or financial support direction) only against a person who is associated or connected with an employer.[2]

1 For example, Statement of Insolvency Practice 16 (SIP 16) on pre-pack administrations.

2 See ch 73 (*TPR: Moral Hazard Powers*) in Pollard '*Corporate Insolvency: Employment and Pension Rights*' (7th edn, forthcoming, Bloomsbury Professional, 2021) and ch 4.1 'Pensions Regulator: moral hazard powers' in *Freshfields on Corporate Pensions Law 2015* (Bloomsbury Professional).

- There are restrictions on 'employer-related investment' by occupational pension schemes. This is defined as investment in an employer or in someone associated or connected with an employer.
- The scheme actuary or auditor must generally not be associated or connected with a trustee.

PENSIONS: MORAL HAZARD POWERS

3.5 An important reason why these definitions have become of particular importance relates to the moral hazard powers given to TPR under Part 1 of the Pensions Act 2004 (PA 2004).

3.6 Broadly, the Pensions Regulator has been given statutory power to issue either:

- contribution notices – CNs (PA 2004, s 38); or
- financial support directions – FSDs (PA 2004, s 43)

against relevant third parties (ie not just the employer) in certain circumstances.

3.7 The moral hazard legislation is important. TPR is able (if various conditions are met[3]) to impose obligations to contribute to a pension scheme on persons (individuals and companies[4]) who are 'connected' or 'associated' with an employer in relation to an occupational pension scheme. For the purposes of the moral hazard provisions, generally the definitions in IA 1986, ss 249 (connected persons) or 435 (associated persons) apply.[5]

3.8 The relevant monetary liability that can be imposed on any one 'target' is limited to the deficiency in the relevant scheme on a buy-out basis[6] (under PA 1995, s 75). In practice this will often mean that the liability could be very high.

3.9 The main objective precondition, before a moral hazard order can be made, is that the 'target' must be or at some stage have been connected with or an associate of an employer in relation to the relevant occupational pension scheme.[7]

3 The Pensions Act 2008 and the Pension Schemes Act 2021 both extended the circumstances in which a CN can be made. The persons against whom CNs can be made are still limited to those who are connected or associated with an employer. The test for FSDs was widened (by PA 2008) to look at the resources available to companies that are connected or associated.

4 See the definition of 'person' in the Interpretation Act 1978.

5 See PA 2004, ss 38(10) and 51(3). These sections also refer to s 229 of the Bankruptcy (Scotland) Act 2016 (asp 21) (formerly s 74 of the Bankruptcy (Scotland) Act 1985) in relation to associated persons.

6 This is a complex area – see *Re Storm Funding Ltd* [2013] EWHC 4019 (Ch) (David Richards J), discussed in ch 74 (Moral hazard and restructuring) in *Corporate Insolvency: Employment and Pension Rights* (fn 2 above).

7 CNs: s 38(3)(b)(ii) and (10), PA 2004; and FSDs: ss 38(6) and 50(3), PA 2004.

3.10 There are other conditions that must be met, but these are less easy to be satisfied about. For example, issue of a contribution notice can only take place if relevant conditions are fulfilled (these are currently, at the time of writing, potentially the subject of retrospective legislation) and if:

> 'the Regulator is of the opinion that it is reasonable to impose liability on the person to pay the sums specified in the notice'.[8]

3.11 The problem with these other conditions is that it is difficult to be certain (even after an extensive factual trawl) whether or not they will be satisfied – ie whether or not a particular connected person is or is not likely to have a contribution notice or financial support direction made against them.

EMPLOYER-RELATED INVESTMENT

3.12 Limits are placed on the extent of employer-related investment[9] that can be made or retained by occupational pension schemes – PA 1995, s 40 and the Investment Regulations 2005.[10]

3.13 These limits include:

- No more than 5% of scheme assets in shares of the employer or an associate/connected person of the employer;
- No loans to an employer or an associate/connected person of an employer.

The definitions in IA 1986, ss 249 and 435 apply for this purpose – PA 1995, s 123(1).

3.14 There is a limited exclusion from the employer-related investment prohibitions where connection is solely by reason of having a common (non-executive?) director (Investment Regulations 2005,[11] reg 10).[12]

3.15 The pensions legislation provides quite severe penalties for a breach of the limits in s 40:

(a) A civil penalty on a trustee who fails to take reasonable steps to secure compliance – PA 1995, ss 10 and 40(4);

8 PA 2004, ss 38(3)(d) and 43(5)(b).
9 These limits are discussed in ch 19, 'Employer-Related Investment', in Pollard *The Law of Pension Trusts* (Oxford University Press, 2013).
10 The Occupational Pension Schemes (Investment) Regulations 2005 (SI 2005/3378, as amended).
11 The Occupational Pension Schemes (Investment) Regulations 2005 (SI 2005/3378, as amended).
12 To be contrasted with the 'non-employee associate' provision in IA 1986, Sch B1, para 60A(4) and (5) applicable to disposals by administrator – see ch 20 below.

(b) If resources are 'invested' in contravention, there is a criminal offence on a 'trustee or manager' who 'agreed in the determination to make the investment' – PA 1995, s 40(5); and

(c) Investment in contravention does not count towards scheme specific funding valuations,[13] nor for s 75 debt calculations.[14]

OTHER USES IN PENSIONS LEGISLATION

3.16 In addition to moral hazard and employer-related investment, the 'connected' and 'associated' tests also crop up in a surprising number of places in pensions legislation. Other examples include:[15]

- Independent trustee on insolvency – person must not be connected or associated with the employer or an insolvency practitioner acting in relation to the employer – PA 1995, s 23(3)(b);
- Scheme actuary or auditor must not be connected or associated with a trustee of the scheme – PA 1995, s 27(1);
- the limits on entities that can give guarantees to pension trustees that the PPF allows to be taken into account by the PPF in assessing its levy;
- lien rules – prescribed transfer credits (see 17.11 below) – PA 1995, s 91(5);
- pension provision following a Tupe transfer – PA 2004, s 257;
- notifiable events – change of control – PA 2004, s 69 (see ch 16 below);
- potentially under the new notification requirements under PA 2004, s 69A (when PSA 2021 comes into force). The detail will be in regulations[16], but PA 2004, s 69A(3), defines an 'appropriate person' (who will be under the relevant duty to notify TPR) as potentially including a person 'connected with' the employer or an 'associate' of the employer;[17]
- section 75 easements (added in 2010) under the Employer Debt Regulations: general and de minimis: the receiving employer must be 'associated';
- fit and proper person checks for master trusts – PSA 2017, s 7 or in relation to collective money purchase schemes – PSA 2021, s 11(5);
- no delegation under the statutory power in the Trustee Act 2000 by trustees of an occupational pension scheme to employer or associate of an employer – Trustee Act 2000, s 36(6)(b).

13 Reg 3(1)(a), Occupational Pension Schemes (Scheme Funding) Regulations 2005 (SI 2005/3377).

14 Reg 5(4)(a), Occupational Pension Schemes (Employer Debt) Regulations 2005 (SI 2005/678).

15 For more detail, see ch 19, 'Employer-Related Investment', in Pollard '*The Law of Pension Trusts*' (OUP, 2013).

16 In September 2021, DWP issued draft regulations for consultation.

17 Applying the definitions in IA 1986, s 249 and 435 – PA 2004, s 69A(14).

USES OF THE CONTROL TEST IN S 435(10)

3.17 Control of a company, as defined in s 435(10), is important in a variety of places:

(a) A person (individual/company) controlling an employer company will be an associate of the employer.

(b) The chain principle (see 2.8 above) applies to control:

    (i) if A controls B; and B controls C; and C controls D; then

    (ii) A controls C and D (and is associated with both C and D) and so on.

(c) Control is not limited to shareholding.

(d) Control is one of the factors to be considered by TPR when looking at reasonableness for a CN – PA 2004, s 37(7)(b).

(e) A decision to relinquish to control is a notifiable event to the Pensions Regulator – PA 2004, s 69 and Notification Regulations 2005,[18] reg 2(2). But this notification obligation does not apply if the scheme is funded to the PPF level and there has been no materially significant failure by the employer to pay contributions in last 12 months.

18 The Pensions Regulator (Notifiable Event) Regulations 2005 (SI 2005/900). It is likely also to be an event within PA 2004, s 69A, when brought into force by PSA 2021.

PART 2

INTERPRETING SECTIONS 239 AND 435

4

Overview of Interpretation Principles

4.1 Legislation must be interpreted in the light of its purpose and context.[1]

4.2 But there are limits as to how far this can be used to override what look to be clear wording in the legislation – in the context of the Insolvency Act 1986 (IA 1986), s 435, see for example *Box Clever*.[2]

CONTEXT

4.3 The context will be very important. In *Daly*[3] Lord Steyn commented in a 'famous phrase' that:

> 'In law, context is everything'.

Lord Nicholls (extra judicially)[4] stated:

> ' ... it is always necessary to know the context in which the words were being used'.

And:

> ' ... context is every bit as important when carrying out this objective exercise as when carrying out the everyday exercise of identifying the meaning intended to be conveyed by the writer of a letter or email'.

1 For example, *R (Westminster City Council) v National Asylum Support Service* [2002] UKHL 38, [2002] 1 WLR 2956 and *Barclays Mercantile Finance Ltd v Mawson* [2004] UKHL 51, [2005] 1 AC 684.

2 *Granada UK Rental & Retail Ltd v The Pensions Regulator* [2019] EWCA Civ 1032, [2020] ICR 747 at [126]. Also *Darty Holdings SAS v Carton-Kelly* [2021] EWHC 1018 (Ch) (Miles J) at [92].

3 *R v Secretary of State for the Home Dept, ex p Daly* [2001] UKHL 26, [2001] 2 AC 532 at [28]. Described as a 'famous phrase' by Lord Clarke at [114] in *Re JR38's Application for Judicial Review (Northern Ireland)* [2015] UKSC 42, [2015] 4 All ER 90. Cited in many later cases.

4 'My kingdom for a horse: The meaning of words' (2005) 121 *LQR* 577, 579 and 580.

DANGEROUS TO INTERPRET ACROSS LEGISLATION?

4.4 Warnings are given in the caselaw about using decisions on similar words in other legislation.[5] For example, in *Hastie & Jenkerson v McMahon*,[6] Woolf LJ commented:

> 'There is always danger in seeking to apply decisions on specific statutory provisions to different situations …'.

4.5 This means that care needs to be taken in looking to interpret the control provisions by looking at similar wording in other Acts (for example the tax legislation mentioned below). This does not, of course, mean that a court will not look carefully at judicial decisions on similar words in other statutes – or even the same statute. But a cautious approach needs to be taken.

4.6 But other statutes can be considered where they 'instructive by way of analogy'. In *R (KBR) v SFO*[7] Lord Lloyd-Jones (with whom the other four JSCs agreed) held:

> '[46] Judicial decisions concerning the effect of different statutory provisions may be instructive by way of analogy but they need to be approached with some caution because they are concerned with entirely different statutory schemes, often enacted for different purposes and operating in different contexts.'

4.7 Lord Lloyd-Jones went on to hold that an extraterritorial ambit for information notices under s 2(3) of the Criminal Justice Act 1987 could not be issued to a person outside the UK with no assets or business in the UK. Lord Lloyd-Jones held that the previous decision of the Supreme Court, *Perry*,[8] on a similar point (but a different statute, the Prevention of Crime Act or POCA) should be followed. He held (emphasis added):

> '[53] In the present case the Divisional Court attempted to distinguish *Perry*. First, *Perry* obviously concerned a different statute and a different issue. The exercise of statutory interpretation must address the specific provisions and context of the statute under consideration. However, as I have already observed, there is a striking similarity between *Perry* and the present case. *While it is not possible simply to read over the conclusion as to the ambit of the legislation in Perry to the circumstances of the present case, the similarity of the provisions and the issues*

5 See Grant 'The rise and potential fall of corrective construction: the implication for pension trusts' (2019) 33 *TLI* 60.

6 [1991] 1 All ER 255, CA per Woolf LJ at [261g]. See also *Walters v Babergh District Council* [1983] 82 LGR 235 (Woolf J) and *Stephens v Cuckfield RDC* [1960] 2 All ER 716, CA per Upjohn LJ at [719G]:

> 'Authorities on rather similar words in other Acts passed for entirely different purposes … do not assist us.'

7 *R (on the application of KBR, Inc) v Director of the Serious Fraud Office* [2021] UKSC 2, [2021] 2 WLR 335.

8 *Serious Organised Crime Agency v Perry* [2012] UKSC 35, [2013] 1 AC 182.

> *under consideration is such that the reasoning of Perry is strongly supportive* of the view that section 2(3) of the 1987 Act was not intended to confer a power to require disclosure by a foreign person abroad.
>
> [54] Secondly, Gross LJ observed that the critical consideration in *Perry* was that the persons to whom the notices were given were outside the jurisdiction and that it can fairly be said that *Perry* was not concerned with the giving of a notice to a person within the jurisdiction, in respect of documents or information held outside the jurisdiction. However, to my mind the fact that in the present case the July notice was served on Ms Akerson when she was induced to travel to the United Kingdom to attend a meeting with the SFO in London is not a material distinction. The intended recipient of the notice was KBR, Inc and it remains the case that the SFO is seeking disclosure of documents situated abroad from a company incorporated in the United States which had no fixed place of business in the United Kingdom and did not carry on business here.'

USUALLY SAME MEANING WITHIN ONE ACT?

4.8 But within the same Act, the presumption is that words and phrases have the same meaning.

> 'It is presumed that a word or phrase is not to be taken as having different meanings within the same instrument unless this fact is made clear. Where therefore the context makes it clear that a term has a particular meaning in one place, it will be taken to have that meaning elsewhere.'[9]

4.9 But this is only a presumption. Sometimes a different interpretation will apply. An example is *Collins v Royal National Theatre Board Ltd*,[10] looking at the Disability Discrimination Act 1995. Sedley LJ held:

> 'In my judgment the only workable construction of s 5(4), in the context of the 1995 Act and its manifest objects, is that it does not permit justification of a breach of s 6 to be established by reference to factors properly relevant to the establishment of a duty under s 6. In other words, the meaning of the closely similar words in the two adjacent subsections is materially different. ….
>
> Such differential construction is no doubt rare and to be avoided – Mr Lissack may therefore be right to call it extraordinary – but it is not impermissible if there is no other way to give effect to Parliament's intention. *Bennion Statutory Interpretation* (4th edn, 2002) pp 992–995 stresses the presumption against holding words in an Act to be idle but also cites judicial decisions which have had to go against the presumption. Some of these contain comments about parliamentary drafting far sharper than anything deserved by the drafter of the 1995 Act which is, as both counsel have stressed, pioneering social legislation

9 Bennion, *Statutory Interpretation*, 4th edn, at p 995. Cited in *R v Bradley* [2005] EWCA Crim at [28]. See also *R (Good Law Project) v Electoral Commission* [2018] EWHC 2414 per Leggatt LJ at [33].

10 [2004] EWCA Civ 144, [2004] 2 All ER 851, [2004] IRLR 395 at [32] and [33].

> always known to be in need of monitoring and review. If absolutely necessary, words may have to be held to be idle.'

4.10 Similarly in *Oxfordshire County Council v Oxford City Council*,[11] Lord Hoffmann construed the word 'locality' used twice in the same sub-section[12] as meaning 'a single locality' when first used and 'locality or localities' when used for the second time.[13]

4.11 A similar approach can apply when construing contracts or trusts. It is not necessary to assume that same words are used in same sense in same document. In *Barnardo's v Buckinghamshire*[14] Lewison LJ held:

> '[73] In construing then the definition of 'Retail Prices Index' in r 53, one should also recall that, whilst words are normally used in the same sense in the same document, that is not always the case. The context will play an important part (see, for example, Lord Hoffmann at para 27 in *Oxfordshire County Council v. Oxford City Council* …).'

DOES THE REST OF THE INSOLVENCY ACT HELP WHEN LOOKING AT SS 249 AND 435 AS USED IN THE PENSIONS LEGISLATION?

4.12 The pensions legislation generally cross refers to IA 1986, ss 249 and 435. So does this mean that those sections should be construed for Pensions Act purposes in the same way as they are for Insolvency Act purposes? For example is it appropriate to look at their Insolvency Act context and the other provisions of the Insolvency Act?

4.13 As a matter of logic the presumptive answer to this should be yes. Parliament should be taken to have intended that the same meaning applied. There is some old authority to this effect. In *Portsmouth Corporation v Smith*[15] Lord Blackburn held:

> 'Where a single section of an Act of Parliament is introduced into another Act, I think it must be read in the sense which it bore in the original Act from which it

11 [2006] UKHL 25, [2006] 2 AC 674 at [27].

12 Commons Registration Act 1965, s 22(1A).

13 Cited by Lewison LJ in *Barnardo's v Buckinghamshire* [2016] EWCA Civ 1064 at [73]. Upheld on appeal, *Barnardo's v Buckinghamshire* [2018] UKSC 55, [2019] UKSC 55, with consistency being mentioned as a principle – see Lord Hodge at [23].

14 [2016] EWCA Civ 1064 per Lewison LJ at [73].

15 (1885) 10 App Cas 364, HL at 371. Cited in *Halsbury's Laws of England* (Vol 96, Statutory Interpretation, 2018) at [1097]. This technique of incorporation has been criticised – see *Knill v Towse* (1889) 24 QBD 186 at [195/6], DC and *Bennion, Bailey and Norbury on Statutory Interpretation* (8th edn, LexisNexis, 2020) section 17.9. *In Re Wood's Estate, ex p Works and Buildings Comrs* (1886) 31 Ch D 607 the Court of Appeal seemed (at 615) to take a different approach, but the wording of the Act being considered used different language, referring to incorporating the sections from the earlier Act on the basis that they 'shall be deemed to be herein repeated'.

is taken, and that consequently it is perfectly legitimate to refer to all the rest of that Act in order to ascertain what the section meant, though those other sections are not incorporated in the new Act. I do not mean that if there was in the original Act a section not incorporated, which came by way of a proviso or exception on that which is incorporated, that should be referred to. But all others, including the interpretation clause, if there be one, may be referred to. It is a dangerous mode of draftsmanship to incorporate a section from a former Act; for unless the draftsman has a much clearer recollection of the whole of the former Act than can always be expected, there is great risk that something may be expressed which was not intended.'

4.14 But context will be relevant – if different words are used in different sections, then the construction may be different.

4.15 More recently, in *Williams v Central Bank of Nigeria*[16] the Supreme Court was looking at the meaning of the term 'trustee' as used in the Limitation Act 1980 (and earlier in the Limitation Act 1939). That term is defined in the Limitation Act by referring to the Trustee Act 1925. The majority in the Supreme Court held that this meant that the term as used in the Limitation Act must have the same meaning as in the Trustee Act 1925. Lord Sumption held at [27]:

> 'By adopting not just the language but the meaning of the ready-made definition in the Trustee Act 1925, Parliament directed the courts to discover its meaning in the latter Act.'

4.16 Lord Neuberger agreed with Lord Sumption and held at [49]:

> 'The proper approach
>
> [49]. The word 'trustee' in section 21(1)(a) is defined in section 38(1) of the 1980 Act, which provides that "trust' and 'trustee' have the same meaning respectively as in the Trustee Act 1925.
>
> [50]. Where a term in a later statute is defined by reference to a definition in an earlier statute, it seems to me self-evident that the meaning of the definition in the later statute must be the same as the meaning of the definition in the earlier statute. Hence, the meaning of the term in the later statute is determined by the definition in the earlier statute. Further, the adoption of the definition in the later statute cannot somehow alter the meaning of the definition in the earlier statute. It accordingly follows that one has to determine the meaning of the term in the later statute simply by construing the definition in the earlier statute. Thus, the meaning of 'trustee' in section 21(1)(a) must be determined by construing the definition of 'trustee' in section 68(1)(17) of the 1925 Act ('section 68(1)(17)'). In the light of Lord Mance JSC's judgment, it is, I think, important to emphasise that the way in which the definition of 'trustee' in section 68(1)(17) is incorporated into

16 [2014] UKSC 10, [2014] AC 1189. Lord Hughes agreed with Lord Sumption, as did Lord Neuberger, although also giving a reasoned judgment. Lord Clark agreed with both Lord Sumption and Lord Neuberger on the interpretation point. Lord Mance dissented, including on this point.

the 1980 Act appears to leave no scope for contending that the meaning of the expression in the 1980 Act can somehow be different from that which it bears in the 1925 Act.'

4.17 Lord Mance dissented and would have held that constructive trustees were covered. He commented (at [161] and [162]):

> '[161]. Lord Neuberger PSC seeks to derive from an examination of the effect of the definition of 'trust' and 'trustee' in the context of the 1925 Act a conclusion that these phrases cannot embrace all express, implied and constructive trusts and trustees in the context of the 1939 Act. I do not agree that the phrases are limited in the context of the 1925 Act in such a way as to exclude a knowing recipient. ...
>
> [162]. I would only add, though not necessary for my decision, that the definitions in both the 1925 and the 1939 Acts are made subject to context. I do not see why the 1925 definition when read into the 1939 Act should not be capable of being shaped in effect by any factors generally admissible to shape the interpretation of the 1939 Act. Those factors include the case law background, the mischief being addressed and Parliament's evident intention when enacting section 21.'

4.18 *Bennion on Statutory Interpretation*[17] cites *Williams*[18] on this cross reference approach commenting:

> 'Where an Act unambiguously states that the meaning of a term is to be determined by reference to the definition in an earlier Act, the courts are likely to give short shrift to any argument that the term should be given a different meaning from that which it has in the earlier Act simply because of the context in which it is used in the later one.'

4.19 This approach was followed in *Box Clever* in relation to construction of s 435 when used in a pensions context. In *Box Clever*, the Court of Appeal upheld a literal view, commenting at [126]:

> 'Plainly, Parliament did not wish section 435(10) (and thus section 435(7)) to bite only on people or entities who control a company in practical terms. It was evidently Parliament's intention that section 435(7), and the term 'associate' more generally, should have a wide meaning for the purposes of, for example, the preference and transaction at an undervalue provisions (see e g sections 239(6), 240(1)(a) and 249(b) of the IA 1986).'

4.20 Similarly in *Darty Holdings SAS v Carton-Kelly*[19] Miles J commented:

> '[91] I am unable to accept [the appellant's] broader submission. In the first place, the Cork Committee report and recommendations do not help. The relevant provisions in the Act go well beyond those recommendations and enact a far

17 *Bennion, Bailey and Norbury on Statutory Interpretation* (8th edn, LexisNexis, 2020) 18.4.
18 *Williams v Central Bank of Nigeria* [2014] UKSC 10, [2014] AC 1189.
19 [2021] EWHC 1018 (Ch) (Miles J).

broader definition of 'control' (via the definition of 'association' in s. 435) than the Committee envisaged. The legislative technique used was therefore quite different from the recommendations.'

…

[94]. Fourthly, as the Court of Appeal said in *Box Clever* at [126] the legislative intent appears to have been to enact a broad concept which does not depend, for instance, on actual, practical control. That is further reason for resisting a restrictive reading based on the ideas of arm's length dealings.

[95]. Fifthly, the definition of associates in s. 435 is a general provision relevant to a number of other provisions of the Act and not merely to the definition of connection for the purposes of preferences (or other impugnable transactions). It covers a broad range of associations (as the Court pointed out in *Box Clever*). It has to be given a uniform reading for all of its statutory purposes.

[96]. [The appellant's] submission is that the court should read s. 435 restrictively for the purpose of a preference claim under ss. 239 and 240 where the purpose of the wider transaction is to sever the relevant connection. But s. 435 is not restricted to preference claims and there is nothing in it which suggests that it does not apply in a case such as the present.

PENAL STATUTE?

4.21 This can be relevant in relation to construction issues – for example should the caselaw on the meaning of 'shadow director' as used in IA 1986 apply when considering the control definition in s 435(10)?

4.22 Is It could be argued to be relevant in relation to its pensions usages given that the moral hazard powers (where the s 435(10) definition is relevant) could be seen to be a penal provision.

4.23 Even more so where the s 435 provision is used in relation to the employer-related investment provisions in and under PA 1995, s 40. Breach of s 40 can give rise to criminal convictions or civil penalties.

CONSTRUING BY LOOKING AT TERMS USED IN THE DEFINITION?

4.24 It may also be relevant to look at what is being defined. For example, s 435(10) deals with defining the term 'control' as used in s 435.

4.25 Clearly the term can be defined as Parliament wishes – so it is noticeable that holding just one third or more of the voting power will give control. But if this had not been expressly stated in the definition, it is likely that the courts would have construed control to require a majority of the voting power.

For example, Employment Rights Act 1996, s 231 refers to employers being associated if 'one is a company of which the other (directly or indirectly) has control'. Rather oddly, the term 'control' is not defined in this legislation, but caselaw has usually applied a voting control test for corporate employers (over 50% of the votes),[20] looking at practical rather than theoretical control – see for example *Tice v Cartwright.*[21]

4.26 A person may be within the s 435(10) definition of control and so have control of a company for s 435 purposes even though he, she or it may not have actual control of the company.

For example if there are two shareholders: A with 40% of the shares (and votes) and B with 60% of the shares (and votes). B clearly has 'control' within s 435(10) and probably has complete control in many senses. But A also has 'control' within s 435(10). It is not relevant that B also has 'control' nor that B has the effective real control.

4.27 The legislation effectively adopts a wide test – presumably to cover other situations, for example where a 40% shareholding may actually give effective control (for example in the case of a public listed company with the remaining 60% held by a diffuse number of small shareholders).

4.28 The clear words used in the definition need to be respected by the courts. But its meaning can be coloured by the words used in the defined term. See also the extensive discussion by Leeming JA in New South Wales (quoting several English cases) in *Singh bhnf Ambu Kanwar v Lynch.*[22]

4.29 But this still leaves open the question of interpretation of s 435(10) where it is not clear. How should the courts approach its interpretation? It seems clear that the concept being defined – here 'control' – can be used as an interpretation factor. The further away from actual real control the situation is the more the courts may be inclined towards the more realistic or consistent construction. This is discussed below in relation to some aspects of the control definition in s 435(10).

4.30 In *MacDonald (Inspector of Taxes) v Dextra Accessories Ltd,*[23] Lord Hoffmann held:

> 'It is true that, as Charles J pointed out, 'potential emoluments' is a defined expression and a definition may give the words a meaning different from their ordinary meaning. But that does not mean that the choice of words adopted by Parliament must be wholly ignored. If the terms of the definition are ambiguous, the choice of the term to be defined may throw some light on what they mean.'

20 See, eg: *Payne v Secretary of State* [1989] IRLR 352, CA and *Secretary of State v Chapman* [1989] ICR 771, CA.

21 [1999] ICR 769 (EAT). See also ch 55 below.

22 [2020] NSWCA 152.

23 [2005] UKHL 47, [2005] 4 All ER 107 at [18].

Bennion on Statutory Interpretation[24] commented:

> 'Potency of the term defined.
>
> Whatever meaning maybe expressly attached to a term, it is important to realise that its dictionary meaning is likely to exercise some influence over the way the definition will be understood by the court. It is impossible to cancel the ingrained emotion of the word merely by an announcement.'

4.31 Lord Scott approved this passage in *Oxfordshire County Council v Oxford City Council*,[25] going on to hold:

> 'The author gives a number of examples from decided cases which illustrate, convincingly in my opinion, his point. The two cases which seem to me particularly pertinent are *British Amusement Catering Trades Association v Westminster City Council* [1989] AC 147, where Lord Griffiths, at p 157, construed the term 'cinematograph exhibition' as excluding video games because the use of the term immediately brought to mind a film show, and *Delaney v. Staples* [1992] 1 AC 687, in which Lord Browne-Wilkinson in construing the definition of "wages" in the Wages Act 1986 said, at p 692, that "it is important to approach such definition bearing in mind the normal meaning of that word".'

4.32 The ordinary meaning of the term defined can assist in the interpretation of a definition in contracts as well – see *Chartbrook v Persimmon Homes Ltd*[26] per Lord Hoffmann:

> 'But the contract does not use algebraic symbols. It uses labels. The words used as labels are seldom arbitrary. They are usually chosen as a distillation of the meaning or purpose of a concept intended to be more precisely stated in the definition. In such cases the language of the defined expression may help to elucidate ambiguities in the definition or other parts of the agreement: compare *Birmingham City Council v Walker* [2007] 2 AC 262, 268.'

4.33 In effect Lord Hoffmann repeated what he had said in the statutory interpretation case, *Birmingham City Council:*[27]

> 'Although successor is a defined expression, the ordinary meaning of the word is part of the material which can be used to construe the definition.'

24 *Bennion, Bailey and Norbury on Statutory Interpretation* (6th edn, Lexis Nexis, 2013) 518 and 519.

25 [2006] UKHL 25, [2006] 2 AC 674 at [82].

26 [2009] UKHL 38, [2009] 1 AC 1101 per Lord Hoffmann at [17]. Followed on this in a pensions case, *Atos IT Services UK Ltd v Atos Pension Schemes Ltd* [2020] EWHC 145 (Ch), [2020] Pens LR 17 (Nugee J) at [59] and by the Court of Appeal in *Revenue and Customs v NCL Investments Ltd* [2020] EWCA Civ 663 at [77].

27 *Birmingham City Council v Walker* [2007] UKHL 22, [2007] 2 AC 262 at [11].
See also the extensive discussion by Leeming JA in New South Wales (quoting several English cases) in *Singh bhnf Ambu Kanwar v Lynch* [2020] NSWCA 15. But contrast *ASIC v King* [2020] HCA 4 at [18] where the High Court criticised the Court of Appeal for what is a basic error of using a word to define itself. The majority noted the 'orthodox view' that one should not attempt to 'construe the words of a definition by reference to the term defined'.

4.34 But this approach of looking at the term defined was not followed in the leading case on the meaning of s 435 In a pensions context. In *Box Clever*[28] the Court of Appeal preferred a literal approach as being mandated by the statute, holding that 'Plainly, Parliament did not wish s.435(10) (and thus s.435(7)) to bite only on people or entities who control a company in practical terms.'

4.35 A fuller excerpt from para [126] is:

> 'Whereas, moreover, a 'controlling interest' presumably had to be one commanding a majority of the votes attaching to a company's shares, someone can be 'taken as having control' under s.435 with no more than a third of the voting power (see s.435(10)(b)). In fact, it would seem that a person could be deemed to have control in the context of IA 1986 if, say, he held just 35% of the shares in a company which in turn held 35% in a company holding 35% in another company with a 35% holding in a yet further company. Plainly, Parliament did not wish s.435(10) (and thus s.435(7)) to bite only on people or entities who control a company in practical terms. It was evidently Parliament's intention that s.435(7), and the term 'associate' more generally, should have a wide meaning for the purposes of, for example, the preference and transaction at an undervalue provisions (see e.g. ss.239(6), 240(1)(a) and 249(b) IA 1986).'

28 *Granada UK Rental & Retail Ltd v The Pensions Regulator* [2019] EWCA Civ 1032, [2020] ICR 747 at [126].

5

Other statutes: defining control or associate?

5.1 Other legislation also uses the concepts of 'control' and 'associated'. But the definition (if there is one) is usually different from that in the Insolvency Act 1986 (IA 1986).

5.2 There can be similarities, for example referring to a percentage of 'voting power at any general meeting' (the term used in one limb of 'control' in s 435(10), discussed in Part 8 below). In practice this can mean that some guidance can be given by decisions on such terms, 'by analogy' with the same term in IA 1986. But care needs to be taken. The definitions may have different purposes and contexts. This issue is discussed further in Chapter 4 above and Chapter 17 below.

COMPANIES ACT 2006

CA 2006, s 252: Payments to directors for loss of office

5.3 Subject to certain exceptions, a company may not make a payment for loss of office to a director unless the payment has been approved by a resolution of the members of the company (CA 2006, s 217).

5.4 Special rules apply in relation to connected persons. The requirements apply also to payments to persons connected with a director – CA 2006, s 215(3)(a). The shareholder resolution must be passed by a majority of the shareholders, sometimes excluding any who are connected.[1]

5.5 A body corporate with which a director is connected is 'connected with' the director (CA 2006, s 252). A director is *connected with* a body corporate if the director and the persons connected with the director are 'entitled to exercise

1 For example, *Lehtimäki v Cooper* [2020] UKSC 33 dealt with a charitable company limited by guarantee needing a resolution under CA 2006, s 217. Two of the three members of the company agreed not to vote in view of their conflict of interest – see Lady Arden at [15].

or control the exercise of more than 20% of the voting power at any general meeting of that body' – CA 2006, s 254.

5.6 A director is taken to *control* voting power held by a body corporate controlled by the director – CA 2006, s 254(4). A director is taken to have control of a company if the director (and any person connected with the director):

> 'is entitled to exercise or control the exercise of more than 50% of' the voting power at any general meeting – CA 2006, s 255(2)'.

5.7 These provisions have some obvious similarities with the 'control' definition in IA 1986, s 435(10) but some differences as well.

CA 2006: ss 823 and 988

5.8 A different definition of associate appears in CA 2006, s 988, in relation to Chapter 3 of Part 28 (Takeover panel; 'squeeze out' and 'sell out'). This includes provision at s 988(3) that defines a substantial interest in a very similar way to 'control' under IA 1986, s 435(10):

> '(3) For the purposes of subsection (1)(c) an offeror has a substantial interest in a body corporate if–
>
> (a) the body or its directors are accustomed to act in accordance with his directions or instructions, or
>
> (b) he is entitled to exercise or control the exercise of one-third or more of the voting power at general meetings of the body.'

5.9 CA 2006, s 988(3) goes on to cross refer to CA 2006, s 823:

> 'Subsections (2) and (3) of section 823 (which contain provision about when a person is treated as entitled to exercise or control the exercise of voting power) apply for the purposes of this subsection as they apply for the purposes of that section.'

5.10 Section 823 deals with persons being 'interested' in shares. It provides:

CA 2006, s 823

Interest in shares: corporate interests

(1) For the purposes of this Part a person is taken to be interested in shares if a body corporate is interested in them and–

(a) the body or its directors are accustomed to act in accordance with his directions or instructions, or

(b) he is entitled to exercise or control the exercise of one-third or more of the voting power at general meetings of the body.

(2) For the purposes of this section a person is treated as entitled to exercise or control the exercise of voting power if–

(a) another body corporate is entitled to exercise or control the exercise of that voting power, and

(b) he is entitled to exercise or control the exercise of one-third or more of the voting power at general meetings of that body corporate.

(3) For the purposes of this section a person is treated as entitled to exercise or control the exercise of voting power if–

(a) he has a right (whether or not subject to conditions) the exercise of which would make him so entitled, or

(b) he is under an obligation (whether or not subject to conditions) the fulfilment of which would make him so entitled.

5.11 These provisions have obvious similarities with the 'control' definition in IA 1986, s 435(10). They use the 'one-third or more of the voting power test', but s 435 does not contain the further provision in CA 2006, s 823(3) dealing with conditional rights.

CA 2006, Part 42

5.12 For the purposes of CA 2006, Part 42 (Statutory auditors) a different definition of 'associate' applies under s 1260. This is similar in some respects to parts of s 435, but does include some differences. For example there is no concept of control and a person is an associate of a company not only if the person is an employee of the company, but also if the person is an employee of another company in the same group – CA 2006, s 1260(3)(c).

PETROLEUM ACT 1998

5.13 The Petroleum Act 1998, ss 30(8), (8A) and (9) deals with 'control' for the purposes of defining persons who may be given notices requiring them to submit abandonment programmes in relation to offshore installations. This is similarly worded to CA 2006, s 988(3)(b) (Associates).

5.14 The 1998 Act refers at s 30(8A)(b) to A controlling B where A:

> 'possesses or is entitled to acquire … such rights as would entitle A to exercise one half or more of the votes exercisable in general meetings of B'.

Voting rights include rights held by a nominee for A or by a company controlled by A – s 30(9)(a).

LEGAL SERVICES ACT 2007

5.15 The Legal Services Act 2007 deals in Schedule 13 with the ownership of licensed bodies. It refers (in para 4) to a percentage of voting rights and then (in para 5) defines associates, parent undertakings and voting power.

CONSUMER CREDIT ACT 1974

5.16 The definition of 'controller' in the Consumer Credit Act 1974, s 189(1):

> '*controller*', in relation to a body corporate, means a person—
>
> (a) in accordance with whose directions or instructions the directors of the body corporate or of another body corporate which is its controller (or any of them) are accustomed to act, or
>
> (b) who, either alone or with any associate or associates, is entitled to exercise, or control the exercise of, one third or more of the voting power at any general meeting of the body corporate or of another body corporate which is its controller;'

5.17 This is similar (but not identical) to the control definition in IA 1986, s 435(10) and to the definitions in CA 2006, ss 252–254 noted above.

5.18 Similarly the definition of 'associate' in s 184 of the 1974 Act is broadly similar to that in IA 1986, s 435, but ignores trustees:

Consumer Credit Act 1974

184. Associates

(1) A person is an associate of an individual if that person is—

- (a) the individual's husband or wife or civil partner,
- (b) a relative of—
  - (i) the individual, or
  - (ii) the individual's husband or wife or civil partner, or
- (c) the husband or wife or civil partner of a relative of—
  - (i) the individual, or
  - (ii) the individual's husband or wife or civil partner.

(2) A person is an associate of any person with whom he is in partnership, and of the husband or wife or civil partner or a relative of any individual with whom he is in partnership.

(3) A body corporate is an associate of another body corporate—

(a) if the same person is a controller of both, or a person is a controller of one and persons who are his associates, or he and persons who are his associates, are the controllers of the other; or

(b) if a group of two or more persons is a controller of each company, and the groups either consist of the same persons or could be regarded as consisting of the same persons by treating (in one or more cases) a member of either group as replaced by a person of whom he is an associate.

(4) A body corporate is an associate of another person if that person is a controller of it or if that person and persons who are his associates together are controllers of it.

(5) In this section 'relative'; means brother, sister, uncle, aunt, nephew, niece, lineal ancestor or lineal descendant, … references to a husband or wife include a former husband or wife and a reputed husband or wife, and references to a civil partner include a former civil partner and a reputed civil partner; and for the purposes of this subsection a relationship shall be established as if any illegitimate child, step-child or adopted child of a person were the legitimate child of the relationship in question.

5.19 *Goode on Consumer Credit Law and Practice*[2] comments on the associate definition in s 184 that it is 'very wide indeed'.

CHARITIES ACT 2011

5.20 The term 'connected person is also used in the charities legislation. For example the Charities Act 2011, ss 117 and 118 (set out in Appendix C to this book) refer to connected persons and trustees for connected persons. Sections 117 and 118 (and ss 350 and 352) are set out in Appendix C.

5.21 The terms have clear similarities with those in IA 1986, although also have many differences.

5.22 Section 352 deals with a substantial interest and contains wording dealing with voting power which is similar to that in s 435(10), although referring to one-fifth (instead of one third in s 435), namely:

> 'is entitled to exercise, or control the exercise of, more than one-fifth of the voting power at any general meeting of that body' – s 352(1)(b).

2 *Goode on Consumer Credit Law and Practice* (Looseleaf, LexisNexis) at [5.364].

BRIBERY ACT 2010

5.23 In the Bribery Act 2010, a relevant commercial organisation (C) is under a duty to prevent a person 'associated' with it from bribing another person (s 7).

5.24 The term associate is defined (s 8) as person who performs services for C. This definition is markedly different from that in s 435.

FINANCIAL SERVICES AND MARKETS ACT 2000

5.25 The Financial Services and Markets Act 2000 ('FSMA 2000'), s 89J states:

> (4) For the purposes of those sections a person ('A') controls another person ('B') if—
>
> (a) A holds a majority of the voting rights in B,
>
> (b) A is a member of B and has the right to appoint or remove a majority of the members of the board of directors (or, if there is no such board, the equivalent management body) of B,
>
> (c) A is a member of B and controls alone, pursuant to an agreement with other shareholders or members, a majority of the voting rights in B, or
>
> (d) A has the right to exercise, or actually exercises, dominant influence or control over B.
>
> (5) For the purposes of subsection (4)(b)—
>
> (a) any rights of a person controlled by A, and
>
> (b) any rights of a person acting on behalf of A or a person controlled by A,
>
> are treated as held by A.

5.26 The term 'controller' is defined in FSMA 2000, ss 422 and 422A. This is an extensive provision (see Appendix C to this book).

5.27 The FSMA 2000 definition is much more sophisticated than the 'control' definition in IA 1986, s 435. Both definitions refer to 'voting power'. Although FSMA 2000, s 422(2)(b) refers to control of just 10% of voting power (contrast IA 1986, s 435(10) referring to one third), there is a much more nuanced definition of what is and is not within 'voting power' – see FSMA 2000, s 422(5). The definition expressly includes voting power of shares held by a person (H) by way of collateral, but only 'provided that H controls the voting power and declares an intention to exercise it'.

EMPLOYMENT LAW

5.28 The terms 'control' (or 'controlling') and 'associated' are used in employment law, but these terms are not defined further.

5.29 The term 'control' is used in ERA 1996, s 231, dealing with the definition of associated employers (relevant for various issues under ERA 1996). The term is undefined further in ERA 1996, but case law indicates that a broad brush basis, usually looking at ownership of a majority of shares in the employer – *South West Launderettes Ltd v Laidler*[3] and *Payne v Secretary of State for Employment*.[4]

5.30 But some cases have extended the concept to look at 'de facto' control (eg by a group acting together or by a 50% shareholder) – *Tice v Cartwright*[5] and *Da Silva Junior v Composite Mouldings & Design Ltd*.[6] In other cases, a 50% shareholder was held not to be enough for control – *Hair Colour Consultants v Mena*.[7] See Chapter 55 below.

5.31 The consultation provisions in TULRCA 1992 and TUPE 2006 refer[8] to the 'person controlling the employer' in relation to aspects of the obligations on an employer to consult or inform about proposals. The concept of control is undefined, but was perhaps likely to be construed in a similar way to that under ERA 1996, s 231. However, the ECJ in *Bichat*[9] interpreted the relevant EU legislation as also catching a 'decisive influence' where there was a 'dispersed capital'.

TAX GROUPS

5.32 The tax legislation uses concepts of association and control, particularly in relation to intra-group transactions.

5.33 Examples are:

(a) Finance Act 1930, s 42: beneficial ownership of 75% or more of the issued ordinary share capital.

(b) Inheritance Tax Act 1984, s 270: Connected persons.

(c) Taxation of Chargeable Gains Act 1992 (TCGA 1992), s 286: Connected persons: interpretation.

(d) Corporation Tax Act 2010, s 1122 to 1124: 'Connected' persons and 'Control' (see Appendix C to this book).

(e) Corporation Tax Act 2010, s 1122 'Control etc. (see Appendix C to this book).

3 [1986] IRLR 305, [1986] ICR 455, CA.
4 [1989] IRLR 352, [1989] ICR 771, CA and the discussion in *Harvey on Industrial Relations and Employment Law* (Butterworths) at [601].
5 [1999] ICR 769, EAT.
6 [2009] ICR 416, EAT.
7 [1984] ICR 671, [1984] IRLR 386.
8 TULRCA 1992, ss 188(7) and 193(7) and TUPE 2006, reg 13(12).
9 *Bichat v Aviation Passage Service Berlin GmbH & Co KG* (C-61/17) EU:C:2018:653, [2018] IRLR 1074 at [41].

5.34 These sections include some wording which is similar to that used in IA 1986, s 435.

5.35 For example, TCGA 1992, s 86 (partly set out below) includes provisions aggregating persons for the purpose of establishing 'control'. The wording is different from that in s 435(10) but could perhaps be a guide (see Chapter 54 below).

TCGA 1992, s 86

(5) A company is connected with another company —

(a) if the same person has control of both, or a person has control of one and persons connected with him, or he and persons connected with him, have control of the other, or

(b) if a group of 2 or more persons has control of each company, and the groups either consist of the same persons or could be regarded as consisting of the same persons by treating (in one or more cases) a member of either group as replaced by a person with whom he is connected.

(6) A company is connected with another person, if that person has control of it or if that person and persons connected with him together have control of it.

(7) Any 2 or more persons acting together to secure or exercise control of a company shall be treated in relation to that company as connected with one another and with any person acting on the directions of any of them to secure or exercise control of the company.

6

Interpreting ss 249 and 435: Hansard

6.1 There was not a huge amount of comment in Parliament when the associated and connected definitions were introduced in the relevant legislation. What there was, was at a high level and pointing out that the definitions are extremely wide.

INSOLVENCY BILL 1985

6.2 The Insolvency Act 1986 (IA 1986) is a consolidating Act, replacing existing legislation in the Companies Acts, the Bankruptcy Act 1914 and the Insolvency Act 1985 (IA 1985). The 1985 Act was a substantial change to insolvency legislation, but had not come into force before it was consolidated into IA 1986. What is now IA 1986, ss 249 and 435 were new provisions in IA 1985. The connected definition was in IA 1985, s 108(5) and the associated definition was in IA 1985, s 233.

6.3 There were extensive parliamentary debates on the Insolvency Bill 1985, but comparatively little was mentioned about the new definitions of connected and associated in the Bill.

6.4 There were various comments made in the debates about the width of the new 'associate' definition. These comments were mainly in the context of the proposed prohibition on an insolvency practitioner acting where he or she was associated with the insolvent company (or bankrupt). These provisions were eventually dropped by the then government and replaced by a separate licensed practitioner regime.[1]

1 See the explanation by Lord Lucas of Chilworth. HL Deb 23 October 1985 vol 467, col 1103.

6.5 The comments made do bring home that the width of the 'associated definition' was fully appreciated. They include a reference by Lord Bruce of Donnington[2] that,

> 'an insolvency practitioner would be disqualified from acting as a trustee, whether he knew of the relevant facts or not, if the divorced former husband of a granddaughter of his owed any money to the common law wife of the bankrupt's grandfather'.

6.6 Lord Bruce of Donnington commented that there could be bizarre results:

> 'Amendment No. 3 seeks to eliminate from the Bill at line 40 on page 2 the words, "or an associate of his", because the associate is referred to twice. It can produce some very bizarre results because this is a criminal clause and it ought to be drawn with very great care. Some of the results that might accrue from this may be stated as follows. For example, a cleaning lady of a firm of insolvent practitioners may have divorced her husband 20 years ago. If the person works for the particular company involved, then the partner could not act as its receiver. Again, an insolvency practitioner would be disqualified from acting as a trustee, whether he knew of the relevant facts or not, if the divorced former husband of a granddaughter of his owed any money to the common law wife of the bankrupt's grandfather. That would tend to be a little bizarre, and I cannot help feeling that when this part of the Bill was originally drawn possibly these very wide concepts had not been taken fully into account.'

6.7 In the House of Commons, similar points were made. Michael Hirst MP commented:[3]

> 'I appreciate that it is essential that a liquidator is shown to have independence and to be a man of professional standards. It is clearly undesirable that there should be any evidence of a conflict of interest. But surely it is somewhat unreasonable that a person should be disqualified from accepting a liquidation appointment merely because he has a partner in Aberdeen whose uncle may owe £3 to the insolvent company.'

6.8 In a rare comment on the definition of associate itself, the Earl of Selkirk moved[4] an amendment to the definition of 'associate' to add the Scottish law concept of a 'conjunct or confident person'. His amendment was resisted by the government on the basis that the term was to be replaced by 'associate'. Lord Wilson of Langdale commented[5] that the Law Society of Scotland had made representations on this. The Earl of Selkirk[6] pointed out that the minister

> 'leaves out cousins, mistresses, persons living together, and, as far as I can see, solicitors themselves'.

2 HL Deb 29 January 1985 vol 459, col 568.
3 HC Deb 30 April 1985 vol 78, col 185.
4 HL Deb 7 February 1985 vol 459, col 1271.
5 HL Deb 7 February 1985 vol 459, col 1271.
6 HL Deb 7 February 1985 vol 459, col 1271.

PENSIONS BILL 2004

6.9 In 2004, a debate in the House of Lords[7] on the Bill which later became the Pensions Act 2004 did include some discussion on the potential width of the moral hazard powers.[8] Lord Skelmersdale wondered if the class was wide enough to catch a nanny:

> 'The full class of connected persons and associates seems very widely drawn and rather oddly random. It would include the company's employees and, in theory, even the nanny of the managing director's children. I know that that is a silliness, but I am advised that, in theory, such a person could be included. It would also include the current business partners of, for example, an ex-wife who divorced the finance director 30 years ago. Yet it might not include a 30 per cent shareholder of the company, and that clearly is important.'

6.10 The Parliamentary Under-Secretary of State, Department for Work and Pensions (Baroness Hollis of Heigham) responded:

> 'I agree with much of what the noble Lord, Lord Skelmersdale, has said. This is clearly not meant to be a clause to catch nannies. In so far as technically it might be read in that way, this is clearly – as with a lot of our discussions at the end of our previous sitting on moral hazard – an issue we shall wish to revisit to clarify the wording and any ambiguity. But, as my noble friend said, it revisits the issue of moral hazard.'

6.11 If any review later occurred, it did not remove a nanny (as an employee of a director and so an associate of the director[9]) from being connected with any company of which the nanny's employer is a director[10]. This means that a nanny would potentially within the net of potential targets for a moral hazard order (ie a CN) in relation to an occupational pension scheme in which the company is an employer. The other conditions for issue of a CN would need to be met.

7 Lords Hansard 13 July 2004, col 1237 on.
8 Tom Robinson pointed this out in the discussion following a talk at the APL Conference.
9 IA 1986, s 435(4).
10 IA 1986, s 249(a). The nanny is connected with the company, but the company is not connected with the nanny – see Part 4 below.

7

Interpreting ss 249 and 435: Cork Report and government response

CORK REPORT

7.1 The definitions in the Insolvency Act 1986 (IA 1986), ss 249 and 435 were inserted into the insolvency legislation by the changes made by the Insolvency Act 1985. The changes in the 1985 Act broadly followed the recommendations made in the 1982 Cork Report[1] on '*Insolvency Law and Practice*'.

7.2 The Cork Report recommended (in chapter 21[2]) that special provisions apply in relation to connected persons and suggested that these be defined to include related individuals and companies with common substantial shareholdings.

7.3 The Cork Report stated (at para 1033):

> 'If the law of insolvency is to reflect the social and economic conditions of modern society and is to be accepted as fair and just by the general public, then it cannot treat husband and wife, or persons living together as man and wife or other closely connected persons, as if they were unrelated parties accustomed to deal with each other at arm's length. Nor can it treat companies which are members of the same group, or other closely associated companies, as if they were wholly unrelated. Special relationships call for special provisions to be made.'

7.4 The suggested test in the Cork Report for a related individual looks similar to that now in s 435 (see below), but the test for associated companies now in s 435 looks wider than that suggested by the Cork Report. Section 435(10)

1 '*Insolvency Law and Practice: Report of the Review Committee*' (June 1982, Cmnd 8558), chaired by Sir Kenneth Cork.
The Cork Report continues to be cited in modern caselaw on issues of policy – eg *Azuonye v Kent* [2019] EWCA Civ 1289, [2019] 4 WLR at [11], *Horton v Henry* [2016] EWCA Civ 989, [2017] 3 All ER 735 at [10] and *Re Nortel GmbH (in administration)* [2013] UKSC 52, [2014] 1 AC 209, per Lord Neuberger at [92].

2 See also chapter 28 'Recovery of Assets Disposed of by the Debtor'. Cited in Briggs and Tribe *Muir Hunter on Personal Insolvency* (Update to March 2021, Thomson Reuters) at 3-3077.

includes a definition of control by reference to one third of the votes in a general meeting. The Cork Report suggested a test of more than half in nominal value of the equity share capital.

7.5 In *Re Thirty-Eight Building Limited*[3] Hazel Williamson QC noted this discrepancy:

> 'Interestingly, both counsel place some reliance on parts of the Report of the Review Committee on Insolvency Law and Practice (Cmnd 8558 (1982), chairman Sir Kenneth Cork), which led to the enactment of the Insolvency Act 1986. However, Mr Goodison did so in support of his purposive construction, in order to emphasise the intention to make it easier to recover assets disposed of to closely connected persons (para 1033) whilst Mr Randall did so in order to show that the Cork proposals were more limited than Parliament had subsequently thought fit to enact, such that no real assistance could be derived from the report itself. This implied that Parliament had carefully considered the extension provisions and intended to go only so far as the provisions themselves clearly laid down. He reminded me that these provisions were an extension of the previous law, and that, therefore, there was nothing surprising, or objectionable, in holding that situations not clearly covered by the new provisions relating to 'connected persons' were intended to continue to be covered by the previous six month time limit.'

GOVERNMENT RESPONSE

7.6 In February 1984, the then government published a command paper in response to the Cork Report: '*A Revised Framework for Insolvency Law*'.[4] This does not give much detail, but commented on the Cork Report proposals in two places:

'(a) The proposed legislation will contain specific provisions defining the term "connected persons"'. This category will include, for example, persons connected by way of family relationship and persons and companies connected through substantial shareholdings.[5]

(b) Discusses voidable preference provisions and makes the point that transactions with connected persons will be conclusively presumed not to be at arm's length.[6] Relevant period for recovery will be two years prior to the relevant date.'

3 [1999] 1 BCLC 416 (Hazel Williamson QC, sitting as a deputy judge of the High Court) at [422]. See also the comments by Millett J (extra judicially) in 'Shadow directorship – a real or imagined threat to the banks' (1991) 14 Insolvency Practitioner commenting on areas in relation to wrongful trading where the Cork Committee's recommendations were not followed in full.

4 Cmnd 9175, February 1984.

5 Footnote on page 28, para 53: Discussing the effect of a disqualification order.

6 Page 33, para 68, in section 'Commencement of Proceedings and antecedent transactions'.

7.7 The command paper does not indicate why the then government chose to put forward, in the Insolvency bill introduced the next year, a wider definition of 'associate' than had been proposed in the Cork Report. In particular the definition of associate refers to a holding of one-third of the voting power, rather than the 'substantial' test suggested in the Cork Report (see **7.3** above).

7.8 There seems to be no report or rationale behind the adoption by the pensions legislation of the Insolvency Act terminology and definitions. This seems to have started with the prohibition on employer-related investment in PA 1995, s 40, (see Chapter 15 below).

7.9 The presumption must be that the drafters of the pensions legislation and Parliament were intending to use a wide definition, one which caught not just real control, but extended to a one-third control (contrast the companies legislation which usually requires 50% voting power). It is tempting to wonder if the draftsperson has a range of definitions that can be used in different circumstances? This must be one of the widest.

7.10 It seems unlikely that the courts would construe the provisions in IA 1986, ss 239 and 435 as having a different meaning when used in the pensions legislation (for example because of the different purpose for their use in the pensions legislation), compared to their meaning in the IA 1986 – see *Williams v Central Bank of Nigeria*[7] and 4.15 above.

7 [2014] UKSC 10, [2014] AC 1189. Lord Hughes agreed with Lord Sumption, as did Lord Neuberger, although also giving a reasoned judgment. Lord Clark agreed with both Lord Sumption and Lord Neuberger on the interpretation point. Lord Mance dissented, including on this point.

8

Interpreting ss 249 and 435: Scots law and laws of other jurisdictions

SCOTLAND

8.1 In 1981, the Scottish Law Commission issued a Report on *Bankruptcy and Related Aspects of Insolvency and Liquidation* (Scot Law Com No 68). This was cited by Lord Hodge in *MacDonald v Carnbroe Estates Ltd.*[1] The SLC report refers to the old Scots law relating to 'gratuitous alienation' (see paras 12.19 to 12.21).

8.2 The report attached a suggested Bill which would include increased time limits etc for challenge of a gratuitous alienation to 'a person who has a family or business relationship with the debtor'.[2] These terms were defined in cl 68(1) of the draft Bill:[3]

> '"A person who has a family or business relationship" with the debtor or the permanent trustee means a person who in relation to the debtor or the permanent trustee –
>
> (a) is the wife or husband, a parent or child, a grandparent or grandchild, or a brother or sister (whether of the full blood or the half blood or by affinity) and 'child' includes an illegitimate child and a wife or husband of an illegitimate child; or
>
> (b) is a partner, employer or employee or a person otherwise standing in a position of trust or confidence in relation to his business or financial affairs.'

8.3 But ultimately as enacted in the Bankruptcy (Scotland) Act 1985, the legislation removed any references to a 'conjunct and confident person' and instead used a term 'associate', defined in s 74 in a very similar way to that in the Insolvency Act 1986 (IA 1986), s 435.[4]

1 [2019] UKSC 57 at [22].
2 Clause 33(1)(a) of the draft Bill.
3 As envisaged in the Scottish Law Commission Report (at 12.20).
4 The Bankruptcy (Scotland) Act 1985 did not, as enacted, include the corporate 'control' provisions in IA 1986, s 435, but the 1985 Act was amended by the Bankruptcy (Scotland) Regulations 1985 (SI 1985/1925), reg 11 (later consolidated in the Bankruptcy (Scotland) Regulations 2008 (SSI 2008/82), reg 8).

8.4 The relevant legislation is now the Bankruptcy (Scotland) Act 2016 (asp 21). Section 229 deals with the meaning of 'associate' (set out in Appendix A below). There is a power given to the Scottish ministers to amend this by delegated legislation – see s 230 (previously in the 1985 Act, s 74(7)). The definition in s 229 looks to be the same as that in s 435, save for various stylistic changes (eg use of letters).

There is not a similar ministerial power in relation to IA 1986.

NORTHERN IRELAND

8.5 The insolvency law in Northern Ireland looks to be very similar to that in England and Wales. A Norther Ireland decision, *Agnew v Moyola Estates Ltd*[5] is cited in Chapter 40 below.

SINGAPORE

8.6 The insolvency law in Singapore in relation to the definition of connected and associate looks to be very similar to that in England and Wales. A decision of the Singapore Court of Appeal, *Show Theatres*[6] is cited in Chapters 23 and 40 below.

AUSTRALIA

8.7 In *MacDonald v Carnbroe Estates Ltd*[7] Lord Hodge noted that counsel had referred 'by way of analogy' to statutory provisions in English law (IA 1986, s 238) and in Australian law (the Corporations Act 2001, ss 588FB, 588FC and 588FF).

8.8 The relevant provisions in the Corporations Act 2001 (Cth) do not look to be very similar to those on 'associate' or 'control' in IA 1986, s 435. The Corporations Act includes in s 588FDA a provision dealing with an 'unreasonable director-related transaction'. One of the conditions for this is that the transaction falls within s 588FDA(1)(b):

> '(b) the payment, disposition or issue is, or is to be, made to:
>
> (i) a director of the company; or
>
> (ii) a close associate of a director of the company; or
>
> (iii) a person on behalf of, or for the benefit of, a person mentioned in subparagraph (i) or (ii)'.

5 [2016] NICh 19 (McBride J).
6 *Show Theatres Pte Ltd v Shaw Theatres Pte Ltd* [2002] SGCA 42, [2002] 4 SLR 145, Singapore CA.
7 [2019] UKSC 57 at [18].

8.9 The term 'close associate' is defined in s 9:

'"close associate" of a director means:

(a) a relative of the director; or

(b) a relative of a spouse of the director'.

8.10 The term 'associate' is also used in the Corporations Act. It is defined in ss 10 to 17 in a way that is significantly different to that in IA 1986, s 435.

9

What do the definitions mean? Who do they apply to?

9.1 Ideally, it would be helpful if the definitions of 'connected', 'associated' and 'control' in the insolvency legislation were themselves fairly clear. As amended to date, they are set out in Appendix A to this book in full.

9.2 They are quite complicated definitions. There is to date very little caselaw on the meaning of the provisions. Until *Box Clever*, there was only one reported case, *Unidare*,[1] on the meaning of the crucial control definition in the Insolvency Act 1986 (IA 1986), s 435(10).

9.3 It is difficult to find much discussion[2] of the definitions in books or publications other than simple repetition of the provisions (without much particular analysis).[3] The Pensions Regulator (TPR) sets out a summary of the provisions at the end of its clearance guidance.[4] But this does not do much more than repeat the wording within the sections.

1 *Re Kilnoore Ltd: Unidare plc v Cohen* [2005] EWHC 1410 (Ch), [2005] 3 All ER 730 (Lewison J). Discussed by Chan Ho 'Connected Persons and Administrators' Duty to Think: Unidare v Cohen' (2005) 20 Journal of International Banking and Regulation, 11.

2 Other detailed commentary is limited. For individuals, Briggs and Tribe *Muir Hunter on Personal Insolvency* (Sweet & Maxwell, Looseleaf, service to November 2020) at 3-3074 (discussing s 435).
For companies, see the former chapter by Antony Zacaroli (appointed a High Court Judge in the Chancery Division in November 2017) in the looseleaf book '*Insolvency*' (edited by Peter Totty, Gabriel Moss and Nick Segal, published by Sweet & Maxwell, looseleaf). There is a discussion of 'associated' in the current edition at F2-24 to F2-33. There are also articles (a) by Agnello 'Liability of directors, professional advisors and lenders under the moral hazard provisions' (2016) 9 JIBFL 522 and (b) by Griffiths and Clark 'Not so clever? The potential dangers of taking security over shares' (2012) 6 JIBFL 351.

3 There was a very useful commentary (dating from 2001) on the provisions by Antony Zacaroli in Chapter H5 of the multi-volume loose leaf work '*Insolvency*' (edited by Peter Totty, Gabriel Moss and Nick Segal, published by Sweet and Maxwell). But this seems to have disappeared from recent updates of that work. Antony Zacaroli is now a justice of the High Court.
There was also an article by Muir Hunter QC in December 1988, but that mainly dealt with the background to the 1986 legislation – Hunter QC, 'Associateship under the Insolvency Act 1986' (1988) 1 Insolvency Intelligence, I10, 73.

4 See Appendix B to the TPR Clearance Guidance (March 2010). On the web at www.thepensionsregulator.gov.uk/guidance/guidance-clearance.aspx#s 1406 (accessed 26 September 2021).

9.4 The definitions used in these sections are complex and not easy to follow. Often they refer to other concepts (eg 'director', 'shadow director', 'officer') which are themselves the source of some difficulty (see the discussion at Part 5 below).

9.5 There is an apt comment in *Palmer's Company Law*[5] that 'It would be an impossible task to make up a complete list of all individuals or companies with which a person is 'associated', let alone expecting to be aware of the relationship in all but the clearest of situations.'

The full passage is:

> 'These provisions are complex and, in many respects, extremely difficult to apply, (e.g. the references to 'reputed husband and wife' and 'reputed father'). It would be an impossible task to make up a complete list of all individuals or companies with which a person is 'associated', let alone expecting to be aware of the relationship in all but the clearest of situations. The statutory consequences, however, mostly flow from the fact of the relationship and not knowledge thereof. If the relationship of 'association' is asserted, however, as the basis of challenge of a transaction, the challenger will require to establish that it exists.'

9.6 The reference in *Palmer* to knowledge of the relationship (by either the associate or the company) not being relevant to the statutory consequences is noteworthy.[6]

9.7 The test for who is a connected or associated party is wide ranging and complex. It extends to parties that may otherwise be considered to be comparatively remote from one another (for example, the ex-wife of the nephew of a former spouse of a person will be connected with each company of which that person is a director).

9.8 Conversely, there are also people who might be expected to be connected, but who do not fall within the definition – for example a fiancée or cohabitee.[7]

9.9 As the statutory provisions are detailed, one case at least (and there are not vast numbers of cases on these provisions) suggests that the courts are unwilling to take a purposive approach when determining whether or not a person falls within the definitions – see *Re Thirty-Eight Building Limited*[8] and *Box Clever*.[9]

5 Smerdon and Morse *Palmer's Company Law* (Sweet & Maxwell, 2000) at para 15.717 in relation to Scotland.

6 But note that some of the insolvency legislation allows an exemption if the liquidator etc can show that he or she did not know or have 'any reason to suppose that the person concerned was an associate' – eg IR 2016, rule 5.15(2)(b), formerly IR 1986, rule 4.149(2)(c).

7 Unless they become a 'reputed' spouse – see IA 1986, s 435(8) and ch 26 below.

8 [1999] 1 BCLC 416 (Hazel Williamson QC, sitting as a deputy High Court judge).

9 *Granada UK Rental & Retail Ltd v The Pensions Regulator* [2019] EWCA Civ 1032, [2020] ICR 747 at [126]: 'an elaborate provision'.

PART 3

USES OF CONNECTION, ASSOCIATION OR CONTROL

10

Insolvency legislation

10.1 Under the Insolvency Act 1986 (IA 1986) transactions involving connected persons or associates can give rise to particular considerations.

REVERSIBLE TRANSACTIONS

10.2 The terms 'connected' and 'associated' are relevant mainly in the insolvency legislation in relation to the question of whether or not antecedent transactions involving an insolvent person can later be challenged or reversed.

10.3 The Insolvency Act 1986 includes provisions that can be used by liquidators or administrators to challenge or reverse transactions which took place before the formal insolvency and which involved the insolvent company. The reversible transactions include transactions at an undervalue (IA 1986, s 238) or preferences (IA 1986, s 239) or floating charges (IA 1986, s 245).[1]

10.4 Generally, if the transaction or payment etc has been from the insolvent company to someone who is a connected party – ie connected or associated, then it is easier for the insolvency practitioner to reverse the transaction. For example, there may be a presumption in favour of the insolvency practitioner and the look-back period (within which transactions can be challenged) can be longer if the transaction involves an associated or connected person.

1 See generally the usual works on insolvency law. In particular: John Armour and Howard Bennett (eds), *Vulnerable Transactions in Corporate Insolvency* (2003, Hart Publishing); and Rebecca Parry, James Ayliffe and Sharif Shivji *Transaction Avoidance in Insolvencies* (3rd ed, 2018, Oxford University Press).

10.5 The reversible transaction provisions are outlined further in Chapter 11 below. Looking at the reversible transaction provisions in slightly more detail:

(a) Voidable transactions

If a transaction is in favour of such a connected party then the onus of proof can be reversed in one of the tests required to void the transaction.[2] Ordinarily the insolvency practitioner would have to show an intention to prefer, but this is presumed (the presumption can be rebutted) if the counterparty is a connected party.

(b) Time limits for challenges under IA 1986

If a person is a connected party, this will extend the time limits for the challenge of an antecedent transaction under IA 1986, ss 239 and 245, and will change the burden of proof required for certain of the elements required to establish an offence under these sections.

CREDITOR VOTING

10.6 *CVAs and IVAs*: In a voluntary arrangement, whether corporate or individual, there are special disclosure requirements (in the proposal and statement of affairs) and special voting majorities taking into account connected creditors in resolutions of creditors.

10.7 *Part A1 moratorium*: Similar voting provisions to a CVA apply to a creditor vote to extend a moratorium under IA 1986, Part A1 (inserted by CIGA 2020).

10.8 The creditor voting provisions are outlined further in Chapter 12 below.

SALES BY ADMINISTRATORS AND PRE PACKS

10.9 There are restrictions on disposals or sales to a 'connected person' of a company in administration by administrators of a substantial part of the company's business or assets within eight weeks of the administration starting.[3] This is not limited to a 'pre-pack' (ie a sale arranged or contemplated before the administration starts).

These provisions are outlined further in Chapter 13 below.

2 For the purposes of IA 1986, ss 238 and 239, certain of the presumptions which arise in respect of connected parties do not arise where a person is connected by reason of only being an employee of the company which has entered into the transaction at an undervalue or given a preference.

3 IA 1986, Sch B1, para 60A and the Admin Disposal Regs 2021.

POST INSOLVENCY TRANSACTIONS

10.10 *Transactions by liquidators and trustees in bankruptcy*:

A transaction entered into by a liquidator with an associate of the liquidator can be set aside by the court.[4] The same applies to a transaction by a trustee in bankruptcy.[5]

In both cases the rules[6] include an exemption if:

> 'it is shown to the court's satisfaction that the transaction was for value and that it was entered into by the [liquidator/trustee] without knowing or having any reason to suppose that the person concerned was an associate'.

This is an indication that the definition of associate is rather wide and the IP may not be aware that a person is an associate.

10.11 A trustee in bankruptcy has to give notice to the creditors' committee (if there is one) if there is to be a disposal of any property to an associate of the bankrupt.[7]

10.12 *Creditors' committees*:

in a liquidation (other than an MVL) or a bankruptcy a member (or member's representative) of a creditors' committee or any associate of a member (or member's representative) must not acquire assets out of the estate or receive any profit from the administration of the insolvent estate or receive out of the debtor's assets any payment for services given or goods supplied.[8] This extends to a person who has been within these categories in the last 12 months. But this does not stop such transactions with a relevant sanction – IR 2016, rule 17.25(3).

10.13 The court can make orders setting aside a transaction or such other order as it considers just (including an order to account for any profit – IR 2016, rule 17.25(5). However, such an order my not be made in respect of an associate of a member of the committee (or an associate of a member's representative) if:

> 'satisfied that the associate or representative entered into the transaction without having any reason to suppose that in doing so the associate or representative would contravene' rule 17.25 – IR 2016, rule 17.25(6).

This is an indication[9] that the definition of associate is rather wide and the party may not be aware that he she or it is an associate of a member of the creditor's committee.

4 IR 2016, rule 5.15. Formerly IR 1986, rule 4.149.
5 IR 2016, rule 10.91. Formerly IR 1986, rule 6.147.
6 IR 2016, rule 5.15(2)(b) and 10.91(2)(b).
7 IA 1986, s 314(6).
8 IR 2016, rule 17.25. Formerly IR 1986, rule 4.170(1)(a) and (c) and rule 6.165(1).
9 Similar to that in IR 2016, rule 5.15(2)(b) – see 10.10 above.

10.14 *All insolvency office holders: SIP 9: payments to associates*

The rules noted above do not extend to transactions by an administrator with associates of an administrator. But the usual fiduciary duties may apply.

10.15 In England and Wales, Statement of Insolvency Practice 9 (SIP 9) deals with 'Payments to insolvency office holders and their associates from an estate'.

SIP 9 provides that the term 'associate' is defined in the insolvency legislation. In practice this is IA 1986, s 435 (although that section is not mentioned). In addition, SIP 9 considers that a wider 'association' may apply, as a matter of substance or likely perception. SIP 9 states:

> 'For the purposes of this statement of insolvency practice, office holders should, in addition to the definition in the insolvency legislation, consider the substance or likely perception of any association between the insolvency practitioner, their firm, or an individual within the insolvency practitioner's firm and the recipient of a payment. Where a reasonable and informed third party might consider there would be an association, payments should be treated as if they are being made to an associate, notwithstanding the nature of the association may not meet the definition in the legislation.'

SIP 9 does not apply to a Part A1 moratorium, nor to an MVL (para 3).

10.16 SIP 9 envisages that:

(a) payments to an associate of an office holder should be fair and reasonable reflections of the work 'necessarily and properly undertaken in an insolvency appointment' (para 7);

(b) all payments to the office holder or their associates should be disclosed by the office holder, together with 'the form and nature of any professional or personal relationships' (para 14); and

(c) expenses payable to an associate of the office holder are 'category 2' expenses requiring approval in the same manner as the office holder's remuneration (para 30).

11

Insolvency: Reversible transactions

11.1 A chart summarising the reversible transaction provisions applicable to companies is below.

SUMMARY OF SS 238, 239 AND 245

	Section 238 – transactions at an undervalue	**Section 239 – preferences**	**Section 245 – floating charges**
Company needs to be 'insolvent' at the transaction date?	Yes	Yes	Chargee connected with the company – no Chargee not *connected* with the company – yes: s 245(4).
Insolvency presumed unless the contrary is shown?	Yes, if transaction with a person who is *connected* with the company – s 240(2).	No	No
Who can claim	Administrators or liquidators.	Administrators or liquidators.	Administrators or liquidators.
Time limit before insolvency process started ('relevant time')	2 years – s 240(1)(a).	2 years if preference is given to a person who is *connected* with the company (otherwise than by reason only of being its employee) – s 240(1)(a). Otherwise, 6 months – s 240(1)(b).	2 years if charge is in favour of a person who is *connected* with the company – s 245(3)(a). Otherwise, 12 months – s 240(3)(b).

	Section 238 – transactions at an undervalue	Section 239 – preferences	Section 245 – floating charges
What transactions?	Transaction at an undervalue in the form of a gift or at significantly less value than consideration provided by the company – s 238(4). Court will not make an order if it considers that: • the company entered into the transaction in good faith and for the purpose of carrying on its business; and • at the time it did so there were reasonable grounds for believing that the transaction would benefit the company – s 238(5).	• puts a creditor in a better position; and • company must be influenced by a desire to prefer. A desire to prefer is presumed unless the contrary is shown, if the preferred person is *connected* with the company (otherwise than by reason only of being its employee) – s 239(6).	Grant of a floating charge The invalidity only applies to the extent that any security exceeds the aggregate of (broadly) the value of the goods or services paid or supplied on or after the creation of the charge – s 245(2).

11.2 Similar provisions to the Insolvency Act 1986 (IA 1986) ss 238 and 239 apply in an individual bankruptcy – IA 1986, ss 339 to 342.

11.3 Conversely, IA 1986, s 423, dealing with transactions at an undervalue if made for the purpose of putting assets beyond reach of a creditor, does not expressly use the terms 'connected' or 'associated'.[1] In practice in an application under s 423 it is likely to be easier for a person to prove an undervalue or an improper purpose where the transaction involving someone who is closely associated (by whatever test).

1 See, eg: Briggs and Tribe *Muir Hunter on Personal Insolvency* (Update to March 2021, Thomson Reuters) at 3-3078.

SECTION 238: TRANSACTION AT AN UNDERVALUE

11.4 A transaction at an undervalue arises where a company makes a gift or otherwise enters into a transaction on terms that the company receives no consideration or enters into a transaction for a consideration the value of which, in money or money's worth, is significantly less than the value, in money or money's worth, of the consideration provided by the company – IA 1986, s 238(4).

11.5 The court can set aside transactions entered into by the company at the 'relevant time' – s 238(2). The 'relevant time' is a period of two years ending with the onset of insolvency, whether or not the party was connected – s 240. The company must be unable to pay its debts at the time of the transaction or become unable to do so as a result – s 240(2). Where the transaction was with a connected person,[2] there will be a presumption of such insolvency (so the burden of proof is reversed).

SECTION 239: PREFERENCES

11.6 A company gives a preference to a person if:

(a) that person is one of the company's creditors or a surety or guarantor for any of the company's debts or other liabilities; and

(b) the company does anything (or suffers anything to be done) which has the effect of putting that person into a position which, in the event of the company going into insolvent liquidation, will be better than the position he would have been in if that thing had not been done – IA 1986, s 239(4).

11.7 The company must have 'desired' to prefer the creditor, surety or guarantor – s 239(5). Where the transaction was with a connected person the burden of proof is reversed: there is a rebuttable presumption that the company intended to put that connected person (other than an employee) in a better position – s 239(6).

11.8 The transaction must have taken place within the 'relevant time'. For a connected person this will be a period of two years ending with the onset of insolvency, for anyone else it will be a period of six months ending with the onset of insolvency – s 240(1).

11.9 As with transactions at an undervalue, the company must be unable to pay its debts at the time of the transaction or become unable to do so as a result – s 240(2). But unlike transactions at an undervalue, there is no presumption of insolvency where the preference was to a connected person.

2 But see 11.14 below where the connection is by reason of being an employee.

SECTION 245: INVALID FLOATING CHARGES

11.10 A floating charge on a company's undertaking or property is invalid if:

(a) it was made within the 12 months ending with the onset of insolvency – s 245(3)(a); and

(b) in the case of a charge to a person connected with the company, at the time the floating charge was created, the company was unable to pay its debts within the meaning of IA 1986, s 123 or becomes unable to pay its debts as a consequence of the charge – IA 1986, s 245(4).

11.11 The invalidity only applies to the extent that any security exceeds the aggregate of (broadly) the value of the goods or services paid or supplied on or after the creation of the charge – s 245(2).

11.12 There are two differences where the charge is created in favour of a person connected with the company:

(a) the invalidity period is extended to two years prior to the onset of insolvency (rather than 12 months) – s 245(3)(a); and

(b) there is no need for the administrator or liquidator challenging the charge to show that the company was insolvent at the time or became insolvent as a result – s245(4).

A floating charge in favour of a person connected with the company (like any other) will still be valid to the extent that any security exceeds the aggregate of (broadly) the value of the goods or services paid or supplied on or after the creation of the charge and interest – IA 1986, s 245(2).

TIME FOR CONNECTION

11.13 In all three cases, the connection test applies as at the time of giving the preference or transaction at an undervalue or creation of the charge. If the counterparty is not connected with the company at the time of the impugned transaction it is irrelevant for this purpose if it becomes connected later.

If the counterparty is connected with the company at the time of the transaction, the differences noted above remain applicable even if the connection is lost later – *Unidare*[3] (charge) and *Darty Holdings*[4] (preference).

3 *Re Kilnoore Ltd: Unidare plc v Cohen* [2005] EWHC 1410 (Ch), [2006] Ch 489 (Lewison J) at [32].

4 *Darty Holdings SAS v Carton-Kelly* [2021] EWHC 1018 (Ch) (Miles J) at [109]. See ch 41 below.

EMPLOYEE AS A CONNECTED PERSON

11.14 Employees are usually connected with their employer (IA 1986, ss 249 and 435(4) and see Chapter 24 below). However, the reversible transactions provisions in ss 238 and 239 (but not s 245) modify their application to a person connected with the company in cases where the only connection of a person is as an employee of the insolvent company. Such employees are not, if that is their only connection:[5]

- subject to the presumption as to the relevant desire under s 239(5) for establishing a preference – s 239(6); or
- subject to the extended two-year preference period before the start of the insolvency process applicable to transactions with other connected person in relation to the giving of an undue preference – s 240(1)(a). Instead the standard six month period applies – s 240(1)(b).

11.15 Perhaps rather oddly, the presumption in s 240(2) that, in the case of a connected person, the company is unable to pay its debts, applies to an employee. There is no modification for employees in s 240(2).

11.16 There is no modification in relation to transactions at an undervalue in s 238 extending the standard two-year time period for transactions with connected persons. And there is no shortening of that period for employees either.

An employee who was 'connected' for some other reason (eg was a director of the insolvent company) is not able to rely on these modifications. There is an example of this in *Katz v McNally*[6] where directors were forced to repay the amount that the company had paid to them in respect of various loan accounts because they could not rebut the presumption that the payments were an undue preference. Similarly *Re Brian D Pierson (Contractors) Ltd.*[7]

11.17 Conversely in *McTear v Eade*[8] the relevant LLP members were able to rebut the presumption.

11.18 Similar rules in relation to employees to those in ss 239(6) and 240(1)(a) apply in an individual bankruptcy: IA 1986 ss 340(5) and 341(2).

5 The employee modifications did not apply in the pre IA 1986 decision in *Re Clasper Group Services Ltd* [1989] BCLC 143 (Warner J) (a case under the Companies Act provisions applicable before IA 1986 came into force). In that case a payment to an employee was reversed as being a preference. The employee was the son of the sole shareholder and director.

6 *Re Exchange Travel (Holdings) Ltd (No.4), Katz v McNally* [1999] BCC 291, CA on appeal from *Re Exchange Travel (Holdings) Ltd (No 3)* [1996] 2 BCLC 579 (Rattee J).

7 [1999] BCC 26 (Hazel Williamson QC, sitting as a deputy High Court judge).

8 [2019] EWHC 1673 (Ch), [2019] BCC 1155 (ICC Judge Jones) at [202].

12

Insolvency: creditor votes in CVAs and IVAs and Part A1 moratorium

12.1 Where there is a voluntary arrangement, whether corporate (Insolvency Act 1986 (IA 1986), Part 1) or individual (IA 1986, Part 8):

(a) The proposal must state how those creditors who are associates of (or connected with) the debtor are to be treated;[1]

(b) The statement of affairs must include details of debts owed to or by associates of (or persons connected with) the debtor;[2] and

(c) Votes of any creditors who are connected with the debtor must be left out of account in counting votes for resolutions of creditors.[3]

12.2 CVAs are discussed further in Part 13 below.

PART A1 MORATORIUM EXTENSION VOTES

12.3 The new free-standing moratorium process in IA 1986, Part A1 was added by the Corporate Insolvency and Governance Act 2020 (CIGA 2020).[4] The Part A1 moratorium can be extended in a variety of circumstances, including with the sanction of a creditor vote.

12.4 The creditor vote is passed if the three tests below are met (CIGA 2020, Sch 4, para 28):

(a) vote in favour of a majority (in value) of the pre-moratorium creditors[5] (PMCs) who are secured; and

1 Insolvency (England and Wales) Rules 2016 (IR 2016), rule 2.3 for a CVA and rule 8.3 for an IVA. Formerly Insolvency Rules 1986 (IR 1986), rule 1.3(2)(c)(ii) for a CVA and rule 5.3(2)(c)(ii) for an IVA.

2 IR 2016, rule 2.6 for a CVA and rule 8.9 for an IVA. Formerly IR 1986, rule 1.5(2)(e) for a CVA, rule 5.8(3)(e) for an IVA.

3 IR 2016, rules 15.34(4) and (5) for a CVA and rules 15.34(6) and (7) for an IVA. Formerly IR 1986, rules 1.19(4) and 5.18(4).

4 For an outline, see ch 13 'Part A1 Moratorium' in Pollard *Corporate Insolvency: Employment and Pension Rights* (7th edn, Bloomsbury Professional, 2021).

5 CIGA 2020, Sch 4, para 28.

(b) vote in favour of a majority (in value) of the PMCs who are not secured; and

(c) a majority of both the unconnected unsecured PMCs and the unconnected secured PMCs did not vote against.

12.5 It is not clear if the 'majority' in the third test is by number or value.

12.6 Whether or not a creditor is connected is to be decided by convenor or chair[6]. The term 'connected' has same meaning as in IA 1986, s 249.[7]

6 IR 2016, rule 15.34(C1) as inserted by CIGA 2020, Sch 4, para 28.
7 IR 2016, rule 1, note.

13

Insolvency: disposals by administrators to connected persons: 2021 Regs

13.1 From April 2021, regulations have imposed limits on administrators making a substantial disposal of a business or assets within the first eight weeks of the start of the administration to a 'connected person'. The regulations are the Administration (Restrictions on Disposal etc. to Connected Persons) Regulations 2021[1] (the Admin Disposal Regs 2021).

13.2 The Admin Disposal Regs 2021 were made under the Insolvency Act 1986 (IA 1986), Sch B1, para 60A[2] and came into force at the end of April 2021. They apply only to administrations that commence on or after 30 April 2021.[3]

13.3 The Admin Disposal Regs 2021 impose requirements in relation to the disposal, hiring out or sale of a company's property by an administrator of that company to a 'connected person'.

13.4 The requirements only apply for disposals in the first eight weeks of the start of the administration, and where the disposal, hiring out or sale involves all or a substantial part of the company's business or assets. This could involve one or more transactions. It is not limited to a 'pre-pack' arrangement which has been agreed or set up in advance of the administration starting.

13.5 Broadly the administrator must not make such a disposal unless the company's creditors have consented or a relevant report from an individual who is an 'evaluator' has been obtained.

1 SI 2021/427. The Regulations came into force on 30 April 2021 – reg 1(1).

2 IA 1986, Sch B1, para 60A added by the Small Business, Enterprise and Employment Act 2015. Para 60A expired at the end of 25 May 2020, but was revived by the Corporate Insolvency and Governance Act 2020 (CIGA 2020), s 8 with effect from 26 June 2020.

3 The day on which the Admin Disposal Regs 2021 come into force – reg 1(2).

CONNECTED PERSON

13.6 The Admin Disposal Regs 2021 uses the term 'connected person', but this is separately defined in para 60A. The definition of 'connected' in IA 1986, s 249 does not apply in this definition.

13.7 The term 'connected person' is defined in IA 1986, Sch B1, para 60A(3) to (6):

> (3) In sub-paragraph (1), 'connected person', in relation to a company, means—
>
> (a) a relevant person in relation to the company, or
>
> (b) a company connected with the company.
>
> (4) For the purposes of sub-paragraph (3)—
>
> (a) 'relevant person', in relation to a company, means—
>
> (i) a director or other officer, or shadow director, of the company;
>
> (ii) a non-employee associate of such a person;
>
> (iii) a non-employee associate of the company;
>
> (b) a company is connected with another if any relevant person of one is or has been a relevant person of the other.
>
> (5) In sub-paragraph (4), 'non-employee associate' of a person means a person who is an associate of that person otherwise than by virtue of employing or being employed by that person.
>
> (6) Subsection (10) of section 435 (extended definition of company) applies for the purposes of sub-paragraphs (3) to (5) as it applies for the purposes of that section.

13.8 Included within the definition of a connected person are specified 'relevant persons' in relation to the company[4] (ie the insolvent company in relation to which the administrator was appointed). These include directors, shadow directors or other officers of the company as well as any 'non-employee associates' of the company or a director, shadow director or other officer.

13.9 A connected person also includes 'companies connected with the company'. A company is connected with another if a relevant person in respect of one of the companies is, or has been, a relevant person in respect of the other. See further Chapter 20 below.

4 IA 1986, Sch B1, para 60A(3)(a).

EVALUATORS: CONNECTED WITH OR ASSOCIATE TESTS

13.10 In addition, elsewhere in the Admin Disposal Regs 2021, the terms 'connected with' and 'associate' are used in:

(a) defining the concept of 'independence' in reg 12, which is one of the requirements for an evaluator (reg 10); and

(b) providing when an individual is excluded from acting as an evaluator (reg 13).

The definitions of those terms in IA 1986, ss 249 and 435 will apply.[5]

13.11 For an evaluator, an individual will meet the independence requirement (reg 12) if he or she:

(i) is not connected with the company or an associate of or connected with the prospective purchaser (called the 'connected person'); and

(ii) does not have reason to think that they have a conflict of interest with respect to the disposal (see reg 12(2)); and

(iii) has not provided relevant insolvency advice in (broadly) the previous 12 months to the company or a connected person in relation to the company.

13.12 The main use of the terms 'connected with' and 'associate of' are in the independence requirement (reg 12) and the exclusion provision (reg 13). The individual acting as evaluator must not be:

(a) connected with the company in administration – reg 12(1)(a); or

(b) an associate of the connected person (ie the prospective recipient of the relevant disposal, probably usually a prospective purchaser) – reg 12(1)(b); or

(c) connected with the connected person (ie the prospective recipient of the disposal) – reg 12(1)(b). This could only apply if the prospective recipient is a company (as, under s 249, it is not possible for a person to be 'connected with' an individual[6]); or

(d) the administrator – reg 13(a)(i); or

5 The Admin Disposal Regs 2021 do not expressly provide for this, but footnotes in the statutory instrument state that '(11) "Connected" (apart from where it is used in the expression "connected person") is defined in section 249 of the Act' and '(12) "Associate" is defined in section 435 of the Act.'
This follows from the basic principle that expressions defined in the authorising statute have the same meaning in subordinate legislation, such as a statutory instrument, 'unless the contrary intention appears' – Interpretation Act 1978, s 11. IA 1986, s 435 applies for the whole of IA 1986. Section 249 only applies for 'this Group of Parts', but this should be taken as including Sch B1 as that Schedule takes effect under IA 1986, s 8, which is in the same Group of Parts in IA 1986 as s 249. See also 65.12 below.

6 See 19.3 below.

(e) an associate of the administrator – reg 13(a)(ii); or

(f) connected with a company with which the administrator is connected – reg 13(1)(iii).

13.13 These all look relatively comprehensible, although there are potential practical problems with identifying when a person is or is not associated or connected with another.

13.14 The most complex exclusion is that in (f) above, under reg 13(1)(iii), which involves two uses of the term 'connected'. Given that the administrator will be an individual who is a licenced insolvency practitioner,[7] this exclusion could not just refer to the evaluator not being connected with the administrator (as, under s 249, it is not possible for a person to be 'connected with' an individual[8]).

13.15 Instead it refers to the evaluator not being 'connected with' any company, where the administrator is also 'connected with' the same company. Given the width of the 'connected with' definition in s 249, it may be no easy task for either the prospective evaluator or the administrator to each produce lists of companies with which they are connected.

13.16 Each will be connected with a particular company if one of the three limbs in s 249 applies – ie if he or she is:

(a) a director or shadow director of the company – s 249(a);

(b) an associate of the company – s 249(b); or

(c) an associate of a director or shadow director of the company – s 249(a).

13.17 Looking at these three limbs in turn:

(a) The individual should be aware of which companies he or she is a director or (although this may be more tricky) a shadow director.

(b) The associate test is wide on its own. An individual will be associated with his or her employer or a company of which he or she is a director or 'officer'. Also of a company where the individual has 'control' of it (alone or together with his or her associates).

(c) The third limb, being an associate of a director, could be very problematic to check. An individual is associated with a large class of relatives (see Chapter 27 below), including spouses (and former spouses), children (and grandchildren), parents (and grandparents) and uncles and aunts, nieces and nephew (but not cousins) and the spouses and former spouses of all of the above. Particularly with a family of any size, it may be very difficult to check if (say) the former spouse of the individual's uncle is also a director or shadow director of a relevant company.

7 IA 1986, s 390(1): 'A person who is not an individual is not qualified to act as an insolvency practitioner'.

8 See 19.3 below.

13.18 The relevant independence and disqualification tests appear to apply only at the relevant time under the Admin Disposal Regs 2021. It does not look back to former connections of associations (both regs 12 and 13 use the present tense only, save for reg 12(10)(d) dealing with relevant advice, which refers to the previous 12 month period). It may be that the test needs to apply only at the time of the relevant qualifying report, but a more cautious approach would be for the administrator to check that the evaluator still complies at the date of the relevant disposal as well.

13.19 Following the Admin Disposal Regs 2021, two relevant Statements of Insolvency Practice (SIP) were re-issued by R3 with effect from 30 April 2021:

- SIP 13 (Disposal of Assets to Connected Parties in an Insolvency Process); and
- SIP 16 (Pre-Packaged Sales in Administrations).

14

Pensions legislation: Moral hazard provisions of the Pensions Act 2004

14.1 The pensions legislation has, in a number of areas, sought to include a wider group of 'linked' persons within a group for statutory purposes. In practice, the pensions legislation did not include a completely new definition of such a linked person, but instead uses the existing definitions found in the Insolvency Act 1986 (IA 1986).

14.2 The terms 'connected' and 'associated', as defined in IA 1986, are, for the purposes of contribution notices (CNs) and financial support directions (FSDs) incorporated into the Pensions Act 2004 (PA 2004).[1]

14.3 The main reason why these definitions have become of particular importance relates to the moral hazard powers given to the Pensions Regulator under Part 1 of the Pensions Act 2004. A CN or FSD may only be issued to an employer or a person[2] who is 'connected' with or 'an associate of' an employer (in relation to the pension scheme) and then only if certain other conditions are met.

14.4 Broadly the Pensions Regulator has statutory powers to issue:

- contribution notices – CNs (PA 2004, s 38) or
- financial support directions – FSDs (PA 2004, s 43),

against third parties that are (or have been) 'connected' or 'associated' with the employer if relevant conditions are fulfilled.

1 PA 2004, ss 38(10) and 51(3).
2 Unlike contribution notices, FSDs can generally only be issued against companies – CNs may be issued against an individual. FSDs can only be issued against an individual if the employer is an individual and the target is an associate of the employer/individual but not 'by reason only of being employed by' the employer/individual – PA 2004, s 43(6)(b).

14.5 There is no cap on the liability which can be imposed, other than the amount of the section 75 deficit in the scheme attributable to the employer[3]. This obviously could, in theory, be fairly high. The main objective restriction is that the person must be connected with or an associate of an employer in relation to the relevant occupational pension scheme.

14.6 There are other conditions that must be met, but these are less easy to be satisfied about. For example, issue of a contribution notice can only take place if relevant conditions are fulfilled and if:

> 'the Regulator is of the opinion that it is reasonable to impose liability on the person to pay the sums specified in the notice'.[4]

14.7 A contribution notice or financial support direction may only be made where the Regulator considers that it is 'reasonable' for the Regulator to do so – PA 2004, s 38(3)(d) and s 43(5)(b). There are a number of factors that the Regulator will, where relevant, consider in deciding this, including the relationship of the party with the employer; the value of any benefits received; the involvement with the pension scheme; and the financial circumstances of the associate – PA 2004, s 38(3)(d)(ii) and (7) and s 43(7).

14.8 In looking at these factors and the relationship of the target person with the employer, s 38(7)(a) and s 43(7)(a) envisage this including whether or not the person had control of the employer, using the definition of control in IA 1986, s 435(10).

14.9 An issue with these other conditions for the issue of a CN or FSD is that it is difficult to be certain (even after an extensive factual trawl) whether or not they will be satisfied – ie whether or not a particular connected or associated person is or is not likely to have a contribution notice or financial support direction made against them.

14.10 For the purposes of the moral hazard provisions, generally the definitions in IA 1986, s 249 (connected persons) or s 435 (associated persons) are applied.[5] The relevant definitions in PA 2004 also refer to the Bankruptcy (Scotland) Act 2016,[6] s 229 in relation to associated persons. But the definition in that legislation looks identical in effect to that in IA 1986, s 435 (see Chapter 8 above).

3 This is the debt that can rise on the employer under PA 1995, s75. See Pollard *Corporate Insolvency: Employment and Pension Rights* (7th edn, 2021, Bloomsbury Professional) at Part 12.

4 PA 2004, ss 38(3)(d) and 43(5)(b).

5 PA 2004, ss 38(10) and 51(3).

6 The Bankruptcy (Scotland) Act 2016 (asp 21), s 229. Formerly the Bankruptcy (Scotland) Act 1985, s 74.

15

Pensions legislation: Employer-related investment – PA 1995, s 40

15.1 Limits are placed on the extent of employer-related investment[1] that can be made or retained by occupational pension schemes – Pensions Act 1995 (PA 1995), s 40 and the Investment Regulations 2005.[2]

15.2 These limits include:

(a) No more than 5% of scheme assets in shares of employer or an associated/connected person of an employer;

(b) No loans to an employer or an associated/connected person of an employer.

15.3 The definitions in the Insolvency Act 1986 (IA 1986), ss 249 and 435 apply for this purpose – PA 1995, s 123(1).

15.4 There is a limited exclusion from the employer-related investment prohibitions where connection is solely by reason of having a common director (Investment Regulations 2005, reg 10). This seems to be limited to non-executive directors (as an executive director will be an employee and so associated with the employer/company by reason of that).

15.5 The term employer-related investment[3] includes shares, land, loans etc of or to:

(a) the employer[4] in relation to the pension scheme; or

(b) any person connected with or an associate of the employer.

1 These limits are discussed in more detail in ch 19, 'Employer-Related Investment', in Pollard *The Law of Pension Trusts* (OUP, 2013).
2 The Occupational Pension Schemes (Investment) Regulations 2005 (SI 2005/3378, as amended).
3 PA 1995, s 40(2).
4 For this purpose, an 'employer' can include a former employer – reg 1(4), Investment Regulations 2005.

15.6 The definition of associate for the purposes of s 40 is modified by the Investment Regulations.[5] The modification is that a company is not treated as connected with another company solely by reason of one or more of its directors being a director of that other company. This is a modification to the 'chain' principle that could otherwise apply – see 2.8 above.

15.7 The pensions legislation provides quite severe penalties for a breach of the limits in s 40:

(a) A civil penalty (under PA 1995, s 10[6]) on a trustee who fails to take reasonable steps to secure compliance – PA 1995, s 40(4);

(b) If scheme resources are 'invested' in contravention, there is a criminal offence on a 'trustee or manager' who 'agreed in the determination to make the investment' – PA 1995, s 40(5); and

(c) Investment not in compliance does not count towards statutory scheme specific funding valuations,[7] nor for the statutory s 75 debt calculations.[8]

15.8 The penalties applicable to breach mean that it is important to be clear what investments by a pension scheme are within the employer-related investment definition. This means that it can be crucial as to whether an entity is connected of an employer.

15.9 Unfortunately, the relevant tests are so wide and potentially vague in application that this can lead to a real risk of inadvertent breach. It seems likely that knowledge that the investee entity is an associate of an employer is not a part of the offence.[9]

15.10 This can be contrasted with the other uses of the tests in IA 1986, ss 249 and 435, such as the pensions moral hazard powers, where connection or association looks to be a gateway and other conditions need to be met before liability can arise (including that the Regulator considers the issue of a CN or FSD to be reasonable).

5 Reg 10, Investment Regulations 2005.

6 The maximum civil penalty is £5,000 for an individual and £50,000 for a company – PA 1995, s 10(2).

7 Reg 3(1)(a), Occupational Pension Schemes (Scheme Funding) Regulations 2005 (SI 2005/3377). See ch 2 of *Freshfields on Corporate Pensions Law* (Bloomsbury Professional).

8 Reg 5(4)(a), Occupational Pension Schemes (Employer Debt) Regulations 2005 (SI 2005/678). See ch 3 of *Freshfields on Corporate Pensions Law* (Bloomsbury Professional).

9 Pollard *The Law of Pension Trusts* (OUP, 2013) at 19.141.

16

Pensions legislation: Notifiable events – PA 2004, ss 69 and 69A

16.1 A duty applies under the Pensions Act 2004 (PA 2004), s 69 on employers and trustees to notify the Pensions Regulator on the occurrence of various specified events.

16.2 The obligations apply to the employer and to the trustees of an occupational pension scheme, but also to 'a person of a prescribed description' – PA 2004, s 69(3)(a)(ii) and (b)(ii). Currently there is no prescribed description that extends the duty (say to cover associates).

16.3 However, one of the prescribed events that requires notification, does refer to the Insolvency Act 1986 (IA 1986), s 435. A notifiable event includes 'a decision by a controlling company to relinquish control of the employer company, or where the controlling company relinquishes such control without a decision to do so having been taken, the relinquishing of control of the employer company by that controlling company'[1].

16.4 For this purpose the term 'control' has the meaning given to it in IA 1986, s 435(10), and 'controlling company' is construed accordingly.[2]

STATEMENT OF INTENT: PA 2004, S 69A

16.5 The Pension Schemes Act 2021 (PA 2021) will (when it comes into force) make various changes to the Pensions Act 2004. These include adding to PA 2004, a new provision, s 69A, for notices and statements to be given to the Pensions Regulator of certain events (as prescribed). This looks likely to be an

1 The Pensions Regulator (Notifiable Events) Regulations 2005 (SI 2005/900), reg 2(2)(f).
2 SI 2005/900, reg 1(2).

enhanced version of the notification obligation under s 69, probably[3] including requirements:

(a) to give notice of any material changes in the event;

(b) for the notices to be given within a prescribed period before the relevant event (or change); and

(c) for the notice to include an accompanying statement containing prescribed information This can include a description of the event, any adverse effects on the scheme, any steps taken to mitigate the adverse effects and any communications with the trustees – s 69A(9).

16.6 The detail will need to be set out in regulations, but the notification obligation applies to each 'appropriate person', defined as including persons connected with or an associate of the employer.[4] For the purposes of s 69A, the definitions in IA 1986, ss 249 and 435 apply.[5]

16.7 It remains to be seen how this obligation will apply in practice, not least because many employer companies are likely to have many persons who are connected with or associated with it (eg all its directors and employees and any other companies in its group). It is not clear if the legislation is envisaging requiring each such person to give a notification, even where this duplicates a notification by the employer or where the associate has no knowledge of the relevant event requiring notification.

3 In September 2021 the government issued a consultation about draft regulations: www.gov.uk/government/consultations/strengthening-the-pensions-regulators-powers-notifiable-events-amendments-regulations-2021.

4 PA 2004, s 69A(3), as to be inserted by PSA 2021, s 109.

5 PA 2004, s 69A(14).

17

Pensions legislation: other provisions

INDEPENDENT TRUSTEE ON INSOLVENCY – S 23(3)(B), PA 1995

17.1 The provisions dealing with appointment of an independent trustee on insolvency of an employer state that a relevant person is independent only if he or she or it is neither connected with nor an associate of the employer or the insolvency practitioner etc – Pensions Act 1995 (PA 1995), s 23(3)(b) (as substituted by Pensions Act 2004 (PA 2004)). Again PA 1995, s 123 applies to incorporate the Insolvency Act definitions.

17.2 This provision is less important than it once was. There is (from 6 April 2005, when the Pensions Act 2004 amendments came into force) no longer any obligation for an independent trustee to be in place on all insolvencies – only a power for the Pensions Regulator to appoint one.[1]

17.3 The definition of independent trustee is used in various other regulations (for example in relation to the 'small scheme' definition in the Investment Regulations 2005[2]).

SCHEME ACTUARY AND AUDITOR – S 27, PA 1995

17.4 A person who is connected with or an associate of a trustee is ineligible to act as an auditor or actuary of the scheme – PA 1995, s 27(1) Some exceptions apply under PA 1995, s 27(2). Again the definitions in the Insolvency Act apply by virtue of PA 1995, s 123.

17.5 There are modifications in reg 7 of the Occupational Pension Schemes (Scheme Administration) Regulations 1996.[3]

1 See ch 61 'Independent Trustee Obligations' in Pollard, *Corporate Insolvency: Employment and Pension Rights* (7th edn, Bloomsbury Professional, 2021).
2 The Occupational Pension Schemes (Investment) Regulations 2005 (SI 2005/3378), reg 1(2).
3 SI 1996/1715.

PPF GUARANTEES

17.6 The Pension Projection Fund (PPF) provides that if various contingent assets are used to support pension schemes, this can operate to reduce the levy payable to the PPF.

17.7 The prescribed form of Type A PPF guarantee is set out on the PPF website. The PPF's requirement is generally that a Type A guarantee is given by an 'associate' of an employer,[4] defined as including an associate within s 435.[5]

17.8 The PPF form only refers to 'associated' employers, not to anyone who is 'connected'.

LIEN RULES – PRESCRIBED TRANSFER CREDITS – S 91, PA 1995

17.9 There are limitations in PA 1995, s 91 on the operation of charges or liens against member's rights under pension schemes. However, under s 91(5)(e), such charges or liens are allowed if they relate to a monetary obligation due to the employer and arise out of a criminal, negligent or fraudulent act or omission.[6]

17.10 This provision does not allow liens to operate against transfer credits (ie credited benefits as a result of a transfer into the scheme). This seems fair enough. If a member has (say) brought a transfer from an entirely unconnected scheme or company, then there is no reason why the current employer should be able to exercise a lien or charge over those benefits (it would not be able to exercise it if the benefits had remained behind in the previous employer's scheme).

17.11 But this exclusion of transfer credits could be seen as operating unfairly where the transfer is from a connected scheme (eg on a scheme merger). So, s 91 envisages that liens and charges etc can still be exercised over 'prescribed transfer credits'. For this purpose, prescribed transfer credits are defined in

4 Para 5.7 in the PPF '*Guidance in relation to Contingent Assets Part 2: Type A Contingent Assets 2020/2021*'.

5 The term 'Employer's Associate' is defined in para 4(7) of the PPF's Contingent Asset Appendix (an Appendix to the Board's Determination under section 175(5) of the Pensions Act 2004 in respect of the 2021/22 Levy Year) as meaning:

'(a) an associate within the meaning of section 435 of the Insolvency Act 1986 of one or more of the Scheme Employers; or

(b) a natural or legal person not falling within (a) above, but which gives a Type A or Type B Contingent Asset or pays for a Type C Contingent Asset by reason of a pre-existing legal or commercial relationship between itself and one or more of the Scheme Employers, where such relationship has not been created for the purpose of enabling that person to give or purchase a Contingent Asset. …..'.

6 See ch 32 'Employer liens and charges over pension benefits' in Pollard *Employment Law and Pensions* (Bloomsbury Professional, 2016).

the relevant regulations.[7] These regulations prescribe[8] transfer credits as being transfer credits attributable to employment 'with the same employer or an associated employer'.

17.12 The term 'associated' is defined[9] to have the same meaning as in the Insolvency Act 1986 (IA 1986), s 435 (or the Scottish legislation).

TUPE TRANSFERS AND FUTURE PENSION PROVISION – S 257, PA 2004

17.13 Sections 257 and 258 of the Pensions Act 2004 deal with the minimum level of pension benefits to be provided by a transferee in some circumstances following a transfer of a business to which the Transfer of Undertakings (Protection of Employment) Regulations 2006[10] (Tupe) apply.[11]

17.14 Broadly, the relevant transferring employees must have been members (or eligible to become members) of an existing occupational pension scheme with the transferor (ie the existing employer). However, PA 2004, s 257 goes on to provide[12] that:

> 'references to the transferor include any associate of the transferor, and section 435 of the Insolvency Act 1986 applies for the purposes of this section as it applies for the purpose of that Act'.

The precise meaning of this provision is somewhat obscure.[13] But it uses the associated definition from IA 1986, s 435.

MASTER TRUSTS AND COLLECTIVE MONEY PURCHASE SCHEMES

17.15 Some pensions legislation envisages that trustees or operators of pensions scheme need to satisfy the Regulator that they are fit and proper persons to act. These provisions include the legislation dealing with:

(a) master trusts (occupational pension schemes established for unconnected employers); and

(b) the new collective money purchase schemes categorisation under Part 1 of the Pension Schemes Act 2021.

7 The Occupational Pension Schemes (Assignment, Forfeiture, Bankruptcy etc.) Regulations 1997 (SI 1997/785).
8 Reg 3.
9 Reg 1(2).
10 SI 2006/246.
11 See ch 53 'Tupe and business transfers: PA 2004' in Pollard *Employment Law and Pensions* (Bloomsbury Professional, 2016).
12 PA 2004, s 257(8).
13 Pollard, *Employment Law and Pensions*, 53.42.

When deciding on this, the relevant legislation allows (but does not require) the Regulator to look at the position of persons connected or associated with the trustee. For this purpose the wide definition of 'associate' under IA 1986, s 435 is used – PSA 2017, s 7 and PSA 2021, s 11(5).

GROUP RESTRUCTURING EASEMENTS

17.16 Two new exemptions to the employer debt (PA 1995, s 75[14]) triggers were added into the Employer Debt Regulations[15] from April 2018 as regulations 6ZB and 6ZC. They are often called the general easement and the de minimis easement. They both involve a 'receiving employer' taking over liabilities from and 'exiting employer'. In order to be a receiving employer, one of the conditions[16] is that it is either:

(a) associated with the exiting employer, or

(b) not associated but falls within reg 2(3B).

The term 'associated' in this context is stated to be within the meaning in IA 1986, s 435 (or the Scottish legislation[17]) – reg 2(3A), Employer Debt Regulations.

14 See *Freshfields on Corporate Pensions Law 2015* (Bloomsbury Professional) at ch 3.

15 Occupational Pension Schemes (Employer Debt) Regulations 2005 (SI 2005/678, as amended).

16 Reg 2(3A).

17 The Employer Debt Regulations still refer to the Bankruptcy (Scotland) Act 1985, s 74.

PART 4

CONNECTED

18

The terms 'connected' and 'associated': general

18.1 The definitions are quite complicated. Often they refer to other concepts (eg 'director', 'shadow director', 'officer') which are themselves the source of some difficulty (see discussion in Part 5 below).

18.2 As the statutory provisions are detailed, one case suggests that the courts are unwilling to take a purposive approach when determining whether or not a person falls within the definitions – see *Re Thirty-Eight Building Limited.*[1]

GENERALLY NO CHAIN PRINCIPLE

18.3 There is, in general, no chain principle: merely because A is associated with B, and B is associated with C, does not necessarily mean that A is associated with C. This is reasonable – otherwise in practice just about everyone one in the world would ultimately end up associated with everyone.

18.4 But there are some exceptions to this:

(a) common control does make a chain: if A controls B and B controls C, then A controls C (and so A is associated with C) – Insolvency Act 1986 (IA 1986), s 435(10) and see Parts 7 to 11 below.

(b) the definition of 'connected' allows an onward link if a person is associated with a director: if A is associated with Mr X and Mr X is a director of C, then A is connected with C (IA 1986, s 249 and see Chapter 23 below).

(c) A trustee is associated with a person if a beneficiary of the trust is an associate of that person – s 435(5) and see Chapter 28 below.

DIFFERENCES BETWEEN CONNECTED AND ASSOCIATED

18.5 A person can be an associate of an individual or a company.

18.6 But a person can only be connected with a company. A person cannot be connected with an individual.

1 [1999] 1 BCLC 416; [1999] OPLR 319 (Hazel Williamson QC). See also 4.73 above.

18.7 All those associated with a company are also connected with it – s 249(b). Not all those connected with a company are also associated with it. For example, an associate of a director is connected with the company, but is not necessarily associated with it.

18.8 The category of connected persons is wider than category of associated persons. The class also includes persons who are associated with any of the company's directors (or shadow directors) – s 249(a).

Examples

18.9 For example, if A is associated with B. This means that B is also associated with A – s 435(1).

18.10 But if Y Co is connected with Z Co, this does not necessarily mean that Z Co is connected with Y Co. For example if D is a director of Z Co and an employee of Y Co, this means that:

(a) Y Co is associated with its employee, D (s 435(4)) and so connected with Z Co (because D is a director of Z Co) – s 249(a); but

(b) Although Z Co is associated with its director, D (ss 435(4) and (9)), Z Co is *not*, just by reason of that association with D alone, connected with Y Co. This is because s 249(a) does not apply to associates of non-directors. (Z Co could be connected with Y Co for some other reason, eg if Z Co and Y Co were otherwise associated).

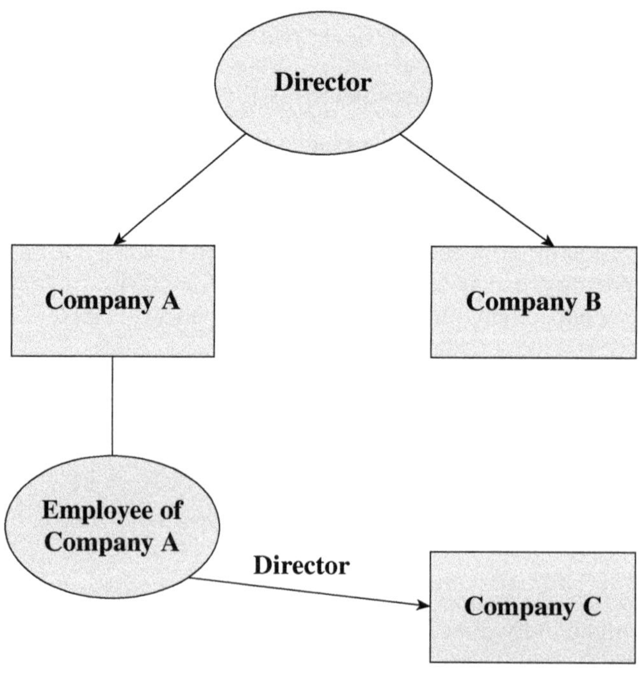

18.11 The director is treated as being an employee of company A, and is therefore an associate of company A. Company A is therefore an associate of a director of company B, so company A is connected with company B. For the same reasons, company B is connected with company A. Companies with common directors are connected to each other (but not, as such, associated). Company A is an associate of its employee. Company A is therefore an associate of a director of company C, so company A is connected with company C. However, company C is not connected with company A.

18.12 If C (an individual) is connected with X Co, this does not mean that X Co is connected with C (as the term 'connected with' can only apply to being connected with a company – s 249).

19

Who is connected?: persons and companies

19.1 The term 'connected' is defined in the Insolvency Act 1986 (IA 1986), s 249:

> **s 249 'Connected' with a company**
>
> For the purposes of any provision in this Group of Parts, a person is connected with a company if—
>
> (a) he is a director or shadow director of the company or an associate of such a director or shadow director, or
>
> (b) he is an associate of the company;
>
> and 'associate' has the meaning given by s 435 in Part XVIII of this Act.

PERSON:

19.2 A person for the purposes of this test (and all of the other tests referred to in this book) can be an individual, a company or a body of unincorporated persons.[1]

19.3 A person can be 'connected' under s 249 only with a company – not with an individual.

19.4 So, for example, if Ms A is an individual who is an associate of a company, XCo, this means that:

- Ms A is connected with XCo; but
- XCo is not connected with Ms A.

1 Interpretation Act 1978, s 5 and Sch 1, applicable 'unless the contrary intention appears'. There seems no contrary intention apparent here.

COMPANY:

19.5 The term 'company' is not defined in s 249.

19.6 IA 1986, s 251 used to state that terms defined in the Companies Act 1985 (CA 1985), Part 26 apply for this purpose (but this provision was repealed from 1 October 2009, with transitional savings).

19.7 Section 735 of the Companies Act 1985 is in Part 26 and defines a company as 'a company formed and registered under this Act or an existing company' (although this does not apply if the contrary intention appears). This suggests, although untested, that the operation of s 249 should be restricted to companies incorporated under the Companies Acts. But it seems more likely that the courts would now construe the term 'company' in s 249 more widely.

19.8 By way of contrast, s 435, which defines 'associate', expressly extends the term 'company' in s 435 to include any body corporate including overseas companies – s 435(11). This wide definition is expressly referenced in some other legislation – for example the Pensions Act 2004 (PA 2004), s 38(7)(b) and IA 1986, Sch B1, para 60A(6).[2]

19.9 The transaction at an undervalue provisions in IA 1986, s 238 apply to overseas transactions (see *Re Paramount Airways Ltd*[3]), so there seems to be no good reason not to extend s 249 similarly.

19.10 Various cases have considered whether other insolvency provisions apply to a corporate body not incorporated under the Companies Acts – including:

- *Re International Bulk Commodities Ltd*[4] (receiver appointed over an overseas company could be an administrative receiver);[5]
- *Re Dallhold Estates (UK) Pty Ltd*[6] (appointment of an administrator following a request from an Australian court);

2 Although there is a cross referencing error in that para 60A(6) refers to s 435(10) instead of s 435(11) – see 20.3 below.

3 [1993] Ch 223, CA.

4 [1993] Ch 77 (Mummery J).

5 But on the particular receivership point, see now the changes made by Companies Act 2006 (Consequential Amendments, Transitional Provisions and Savings) Order 2009 (SI 2009/1941).

6 [1992] BCLC 621; [1992] BCC 394 (Chadwick J).

- *Re Dairy Farmers of Britain Limited*;[7] and
- *Re Rowellian Football Social Club*[8] – a football club is not a company and so an administration order cannot be made.

But none have addressed the question under s 249.

19.11 An associate: the use of the term 'associate' within the definition of connected means that the terms must be considered alongside one another. Associates are considered more fully in Part 6 below.

7 [2009] EWHC 1389 (Ch), [2010] Ch 63, [2009] 4 All ER 241 (Henderson J).
8 [2011] EWHC 1301 (Ch), [2012] Ch 125 (HHJ Behrens, sitting as a judge of the High Court).

20

Connected persons: IA 1986, Sch B1, para 60A

20.1 The term 'connected person' is used in the Admin Disposal Regs 2021[1] dealing with sales by administrators to connected persons within eight weeks of the administration starting.

20.2 Both the terms 'connected person' and 'connected' are used in the Insolvency Act 1986 (IA 1986), Sch B1, para 60A, but they are both separately defined in a way that differs from that used by the rest of IA 1986. The definition of 'connected' in IA 1986, s 249 does not apply in para 60A.[2] But the term 'associate' is also used, and this is defined by reference to IA 1986, s 435.

20.3 The definition of the term 'connected person' is in IA 1986, Sch B1, para 60A(3) to (6) as follows:[3]

> (3) In sub-paragraph (1), 'connected person', in relation to a company, means—
>
> (a) a relevant person in relation to the company, or
>
> (b) a company connected with the company.
>
> (4) For the purposes of sub-paragraph (3)—
>
> (a) 'relevant person', in relation to a company, means—
>
> (i) a director or other officer, or shadow director, of the company;
>
> (ii) a non-employee associate of such a person;
>
> (iii) a non-employee associate of the company;
>
> (b) a company is connected with another if any relevant person of one is or has been a relevant person of the other.

1 The Administration (Restrictions on Disposal etc. to Connected Persons) Regulations 2021 (SI 2021/427). Outlined in ch 13 above.

2 But it is used in the Admin Disposal Regs 2021.

3 Added to IA 1986, Sch B1 by the Small Business, Enterprise and Employment Act 2015 (SBEEA 2015), s 129.

(5) In sub-paragraph (4), 'non-employee associate' of a person means a person who is an associate of that person otherwise than by virtue of employing or being employed by that person.

(6) Subsection (10)[4] of section 435 (extended definition of company) applies for the purposes of sub-paragraphs (3) to (5) as it applies for the purposes of that section.

20.4 A connected person in relation to the company (ie the insolvent company in relation to which the administrator was appointed) is defined as meaning anyone within either or both of the following two wide categories:

(a) a 'relevant person' in relation to the insolvent company;[5] and

(b) a company that is 'connected with' the insolvent company.[6]

20.5 These are quite wide categories. It seems that it will be up to the administrator to verify if a potential purchaser is or is not a connected person. This may not be an easy task, as the definition is both quite wide and fairly complex. In practice the administrator may well ask a purchaser to confirm that he, she or it is not a connected person and probably should attempt some independent due diligence.

20.6 There is no express penalty in the Admin Disposal Regs 2021 on an administrator or avoiding the transaction if they breach the restriction in the Admin Disposal Regs 2021. There could be other sanctions, such a removal as the administrator or a claim for loss by reason of inappropriate actions.

RELEVANT PERSON

20.7 The term 'relevant person' means under para 64(4)(a) anyone who is:

(a) a director or other officer or a shadow director of the insolvent company; or

(b) a 'non-employee associate' of a director or other officer or shadow director; or

(c) a 'non-employee associate' of the insolvent company.

20.8 This is broadly similar in effect to the 'connected with' provision in IA 1986, s 249, save that not all associates are included, only those who are a 'non-employee associate'.

4 This looks to be a cross referencing error. IA 1986, s 435(10) deals with control, whereas s 435(11) has an extended meaning of 'company'. The error looks rather obvious and it is likely that a court would treat the cross reference as being properly to s 435(11). On the potential for such construction, see *Inco Europe Ltd v First Choice Distribution* [2000] 1 WLR 586, HL per Lord Nicholls at 592C.

5 IA 1986, Sch B1, para 60A(3)(a).

6 IA 1986, Sch B1, para 60A(3)(b).

So it seems that a person who is (say) an employee of a company is not, by reason of that alone, a relevant person. However if he or she was also associated with the company not as an employee, but in some other way (eg as a major shareholder), it seems that this would mean that he or she would still be a relevant person.

20.9 The terms 'director', 'officer' and 'shadow director' are defined in IA 1986, s 251 – see Chapters 21, 22 and 25 below.

20.10 The term 'associate' has the meaning given by IA 1986, s 435 – see s 436(1). A 'non-employee associate' of a person means someone who is an associate of that person otherwise than by virtue of employing or being employed by that person.[7]

20.11 The second category, a 'non-employee associate' of a director or other officer or shadow director, is an example of a 'chain' applying.[8]

20.12 The term 'relevant person' seems to look only at current relevant persons – ie presumably at the time of the relevant disposal by the administrator. It does not expressly look at persons who were previously a relevant person (for example former directors or shareholders of the company now in administration).

This seems an odd result, but seems to be mandated by the language of the Admin Disposal Regs 2021 (eg the definition of 'substantial disposal' in reg 3(3)(a) as a disposal 'to one or more connected persons') and the express inclusion of former relevant persons in the connected company definition in para 60A(4)(b).

20.13 A 'relevant person' can clearly include a purchaser/transferee which is a company[9] if it is an associate (under the usual rules in s 435) of the insolvent company[10] or of a director, officer or shadow director of the insolvent company.[11] For example if it 'controls' the insolvent company or is under the control of a person who also controls the insolvent company.

20.14 Besides such association, the category of 'connected company' is potentially wider and could catch a purchaser company even if it is not an associate of the insolvent company under s 435.

CONNECTED COMPANY

20.15 A connected person also includes 'a company connected with the company' – Sch B1, para 60A(3)(b). For this purpose, a company is connected

7 IA 1986, Sch B1, para 60A(3)(b).
8 See 2.9 above on the chain principle.
9 A company is unlikely to be capable of being an employee so cannot be excluded as an employee of the insolvent company – see ch 24 below.
10 Para 60A(4)(a)(iii).
11 Para 60A(4)(a)(ii).

with another if 'any relevant person of one is or has been a relevant person of the other' – Sch B1, para 60A(4)(b).

20.16 Working this out can involve quite a complex process, in particular because of the reference to a person who 'is or has been' a relevant person. By way of contrast, the term 'relevant person' seems to look only at current relevant persons – ie at the time of the relevant disposal.

20.17 There seem to be four main cases here. At the relevant time:

(a) A person (A) *is* a relevant person in relation to the insolvent company and *is* a relevant person in relation to the purchaser company

(b) A person *is* a relevant person in relation to the insolvent company and *was* a relevant person in relation to the purchaser;

(c) A person *was* a relevant person in relation to the insolvent company and *is* a relevant person in relation to the purchaser;

(d) A person *was* a relevant person in relation to the insolvent company and *was* a relevant person in relation to the purchaser.

20.18 The analysis seems to be that in cases (a), (b) and (c) the purchaser company *is* at the relevant time a connected company with the insolvent company. In case (d) it is more likely that it is not.

20.19 Case (a) is fairly obvious. The person is at the relevant time a relevant person in relation to both companies. So they are connected.

20.20 Cases (b) and (c) are both cases where the person *is* a relevant person in relation to one company and *has been* a relevant person in relation to the other. This seems to mean that, in both cases, the purchaser is connected with the insolvent company. The test in para 60(4)(b) applies 'if any relevant person of one is or has been a relevant person of the other'. This wording applies both ways – is there someone who *is* a relevant person of one, who *has been* a relevant person in relation to the other? In both cases (b) and (c) this is met.

20.21 Case (d) is less clear (but could at least have the practical consequence of reducing the prospect of very historic sharing of a relevant person catching a company). The test in para 60(4)(b) of 'if any relevant person of one is or has been a relevant person of the other' seems to require that the person being considered must currently be a relevant person in relation to one of the companies.

If not then the person is not a 'relevant person of one' and so the test in para 60(4)(b) is not met. This seems to flow from the position that in order to be a relevant person in relation to a company, the person must *currently* be such a person. The definition of 'relevant person' in para 60(4)(a) does not (unlike the connected company limb in para 60(4)(b)) refer to persons who were formerly a relevant person.

20.22 The analysis in tabular form is:

Person A as a relevant person. At the relevant time:	**A is a relevant person in relation to purchaser company**	**A was a relevant person in relation to purchaser company**
A is a relevant person in relation to the insolvent company	(a) the purchaser co **is** at the relevant time a connected company with the insolvent co	(b) the purchaser co **is** at the relevant time a connected company with the insolvent co
A was a relevant person in relation to the insolvent company	(c) the purchaser company **is** at the relevant time a connected company with the insolvent co	(d) the purchaser company **is not** at the relevant time a connected company with the insolvent co

20.23 The Insolvency Service guidance to administrators[12] on the Admin Disposal Regs 2021 briefly outlines this issue:

> **3. Connected person**
>
> A connected person is either an individual or a company that is connected to the company entering administration. All references in this guidance to a connected person should be read in this way. Below is a list of those who would fall within the definition of a connected person.
>
> This list is not exhaustive and you may need independent legal advice if there is any doubt about whether a person's relationship to the company makes them a connected person.
>
> A connected person could be:
>
> - director of the company
> - secretary of the company
> - spouse, ex-spouse, child or sibling of a director or any other officer of the company
> - business partner of a director of the company
> - a company that is controlled by any of the above listed individuals
> - any person or company who has control over the company, including shareholders with a third or more voting rights. This could include secured lenders.
>
> It is the responsibility of the insolvency practitioner to establish if a party is connected to the company.

12 Insolvency Service: *Requirements for independent scrutiny of the disposal of assets in administration, including pre-pack sales* (Published 30 April 2021). www.gov.uk/government/publications/requirements-for-independent-scrutiny-of-the-disposal-of-assets-in-administration-including-pre-pack-sales/requirements-for-independent-scrutiny-of-the-disposal-of-assets-in-administration-including-pre-pack-sales.

20.24 The Insolvency Service comments that it is for the administrators to check if the counterparty to the relevant disposal is a connected person. Depending on the circumstances, this can be quite an onerous task, in particular given the width of the 'associate' definition (eg relatives of former spouses of a director) and the difficulty in the administrator being able to work out with certainty whether some of the tests are met – eg a 'reputed' spouse or a shadow director.

INDEPENDENCE AND EXCLUSION

20.25 The individual who acts as the 'evaluator', who is needed to give a report under the Admin Disposal Regs 2021, must be independent and not excluded from acting – regs 12 and 13. This is outlined in Chapter 13 above.

PART 5

DIRECTORS, EMPLOYERS AND EMPLOYEES

21

Directors and de facto directors

21.1 A director (including a de facto director) of a company is connected with the company (s 249) and is an associate of that company – s 435(4) and (9). The term director is defined in the Insolvency Act 1986 (IA 1986), s 251 as:

> '"*director*" includes any person occupying the position of director, by whatever name called;'

21.2 This definition is the same as that applying in the companies legislation[1] – see Companies Act 2006 (CA 2006), s 250[2] and the Company Directors Disqualification Act 1986 (CDDA 1986), s 22(4). The term 'director' is used in the Pensions Act 1995 (PA 1995)[3] and the Pensions Act 2004 (PA 2004),[4] but there is no express definition.

21.3 In practice directors of a UK company are usually individuals.[5]

21.4 See Chapter 23 below on the connection where companies share directors (common directors) and Chapter 46 on the connection and association implications issues for an appointor where it makes an appointment to a board of directors.

1 For the purposes of CA 2006, Pt 42 (Statutory auditors) an expanded definition of director applies under s 1261.
2 Previously CA 1985, s 741(1).
3 For example: PA 1995, s 10(6) (Civil penalties) and s 115 (Offences by bodies corporate).
4 For example: PA 2004, s 242 (Member nominated directors) and s 309 (Offences by bodies corporate).
5 Some jurisdictions (eg Australia and Singapore) provide that only natural persons (ie individuals) may be directors. Currently in the UK the statutory requirement is that at least one director must be a natural person – CA 2006, s 155(1).
A change to this position in the UK (but subject to exceptions) is envisaged. The Small Business, Enterprise and Employment Act 2015 will (when s 87 comes into force) amend CA 2006 to provide that a person may not (subject to exceptions) be appointed a director of a company unless the person is a natural person (CA 2006, s 156A, as to be inserted by the Small Business, Enterprise and Employment Act 2015 (SBEEA 2015), s 87). But these amendments are not, at the time of writing, yet in force. A further government consultation '*Corporate Transparency and Register Reform: Consultation on implementing the ban on corporate directors*' was released in December 2020.

DRAFTING ISSUE: APPLICATION OF IA 1986, S 251

21.5 The definitions in IA 1986, s 251 apply to 'this Group of Parts' – ie including s 249, but *not* s 435. Thus, while de facto directors and shadow directors are clearly connected, it is arguably less clear whether they are associates.

21.6 In IA 1986 itself the fact that s 251 does not apply to s 435 probably does not matter, because the term 'associate' is used in the reversible transaction provisions in ss 238 to 245 (which are in the same Group of Parts as s 251). But this drafting problem could be an issue where (as in pensions legislation[6]) s 435 is being used outside the IA 1986.

21.7 It may be relevant in some places that the pensions legislation incorporating the s 249 definition does this expressly[7] on the basis that it applies 'as it applies for the purposes of any provision of the first Group of Parts' of IA 1986 – for example PA 2004, s 38(10)(a).

21.8 This issue does not seem to have been raised as an issue in any case so far. In practice a judge might decide that this was a drafting slip and construe s 435 as though the interpretation provision in s 251 applied to it as well[8].

21.9 It seems likely that, in construing the definitions of both 'connected' and 'associated', the term 'director' will be construed as if s 251 applies (similarly the term 'officer'). But there is scope for doubt here.

DE FACTO DIRECTOR

21.10 The terms 'director' and 'de facto director' can be difficult. There has been a fair amount of case law on what they actually mean (mainly in contexts other than the connected and associated tests).[9]

21.11 Section 251 defines a director to include any person occupying the position of director, by whatever name called. This means that a person who occupies the relevant position is treated as a director even if:

- he or she is not called a director (eg if the company uses another term); or
- he or she has not been properly appointed.

6 See Part 3 above.

7 Similarly, PA 1995, s 123: 'as they apply for the purposes of that Act'.

8 For an example of construing by reference to different legislation, see *Granada Group Ltd v Law Debenture Pension Trust Corporation plc* at first instance where Andrews J considered the meaning of the term 'pension scheme' as used in CA 1985 and construed it in light of the definitions in the Pension Schemes Act 1993 (PSA 1993). Discussed at 29.6 below.

9 See further *State for Trade and Industry v Deverell* [2001] Ch 340, CA; *Re Mea Corporation Ltd: Secretary of State for Trade and Industry v Aviss* [2006] EWHC 1846 (Ch); [2007] 1 BCLC 618 (Lewison J); *Secretary of State for Trade and Industry v Hollier* [2006] EWHC 1804 (Ch), [2007] BCC 11 (Etherton J) and Noonan and Watson, 'Examining Company Directors through the Lens of De Facto Directorship' [2008] JBL 587.

The term 'de facto director' was originally used to refer to individuals who had been appointed as a director but whose appointment was in some way invalid, or whose appointment had ceased. However, its use has been extended to cover a person who has never been appointed as a director but, in broad terms, assumes that role.[10]

Such a person is called in the caselaw (but not in the legislation) a 'de facto director'.

21.12 Recent cases on de facto directors include:

- *Instant Access Properties Limited (in liquidation) v Rosser:*[11] guidance on the difference between a de facto and a shadow director, and the application of fiduciary duties to a shadow director.
- *Smithton Limited v Naggar:*[12] question of fact and degree. Relevant to look at corporate governance structure.
- *Re Mumtaz Properties Ltd; Wetton (as liquidator of Mumtaz Properties Ltd) v Ahmed:*[13] person who was a 'nerve centre' in a family company held to be a de facto director;
- *Holland:*[14] director of a company (A) acting as a director of another company (B) held not to be a de facto director of B; and
- *Re Keeping Kids Company: Official Receiver v Atkinson:*[15] CEO of large charity not a de facto director.
- *Bishopgate Contracting Solutions Ltd v O'Sullivan*:[16] finance controller not a de facto director.

21.13 In *Keeping Kids Company*,[17] Falk J usefully summarised the key points in relation to de facto directors (in a case relating to disqualification under CDDA 1986):

1. Guidance should be obtained from looking at the purpose of the provision in question (*Holland* at [39]). The primary purpose of the disqualification legislation is the protection of the public. Those who assume the status and functions of a company director should be held to certain minimum standards in the public interest. The legislation has both a deterrent element and serves

10 *Revenue and Customs Comrs v Holland, In re Paycheck Services 3 Ltd* [2010] UKSC 51, [2011] 1 All ER 430 per Lord Collins at [82].
11 [2018] EWHC 756 (Ch) (Morgan J). Noted in ILA Technical Bulletin 834 (Jan 2019).
12 [2014] EWCA Civ 939, [2015] 1 WLR 189, CA.
13 [2011] EWCA Civ 610, [2012] 2 BCLC 109, CA.
14 *Revenue and Customs Comrs v Holland, In re Paycheck Services 3 Ltd* [2010] UKSC 51, [2011] 1 All ER 430.
15 *Re Keeping Kids Company: Official Receiver v Atkinson* [2021] EWHC 175 (Ch) (Falk J), discussing de facto directors at [187] to [201].
16 [2021] EWHC 2103 (QB) (Linden J) at [151] to [174].
17 *Re Keeping Kids Company* [2021] EWHC 175 (Ch) (Falk J) at [201].

as an encouragement to improve standards of behaviour …. I do not think that the purpose of the disqualification legislation is sufficiently different from the purpose of the legislation considered in *Holland* materially to affect the force of the observations in that case in a disqualification context.

2. There is no single test, but an important starting point is the company's corporate governance structure. The court is seeking to identify functions that were the sole responsibility of a director or board of directors, that is, the highest level of management of the company. Those who assume and exercise powers and functions that can only properly be exercised or discharged at that highest level of management will, consistent with the purpose of the disqualification legislation, be within its scope as de facto directors. Those who are subordinate and accountable to that highest level of management will not be.

3. The test has been described as whether the individual was participating, or had the ability to participate, in decision-making as part of the corporate governing structure (which I take to mean the highest level of management decision-making). Another way of putting it is to ask whether the individual was on an 'equal footing' with others in directing the affairs of the company.

4. There is a distinction between being consulted about, advising on or otherwise being involved in, decision-making in some other capacity (even in circumstances where real influence is exerted) and actually participating in making a decision as a director.

5. The question is one of fact and degree. It must be determined objectively, by reference to what the relevant individual actually did (including, for example, whether they were held out as a director and whether they took major decisions), and looking at the cumulative effect of the activities relied on in their overall factual context.

22

Shadow directors

22.1 Unlike a director, a person who is a shadow director of a company is not, just by reason of being a shadow director, as such an associate of the company within IA 1986, s 435 (but a person who is a shadow director is connected with the company within s 249[1]). The term 'shadow director' is not used in s 435 (but s 435(10)(a) arguably has a somewhat similar ambit – see Chapter 42 below).

22.2 The term 'shadow director' can be difficult. There has been a fair amount of case law on what it actually means (mainly in other contexts).[2]

SHADOW DIRECTOR DEFINITION

22.3 The Insolvency Act 1986 (IA 1986), s 251[3] defines a shadow director as a person in accordance with whose directions or instructions the directors of the company are accustomed to act (but a person is not deemed a shadow director by reason only that the directors act on advice given by him in a professional capacity).

22.4 Further exclusions from being a shadow director were added to s 251 in May 2015 by the Small Business, Enterprise and Employment Act 2015 (SBEEA 2015), s 90(1). These exclusions deal with directions or guidance:

(a) given in the exercise of a function under an enactment, or

(b) given by a Minister of the Crown.

1 But the company is not connected with the person (if an individual).

2 See further *State for Trade and Industry v Deverell* [2001] Ch 340, CA; *Re Mea Corporation Ltd: Secretary of State for Trade and Industry v Aviss* [2006] EWHC 1846 (Ch), [2007] 1 BCLC 618 (Lewison J); *Secretary of State for Trade and Industry v Hollier* [2006] EWHC 1804 (Ch), [2007] BCC 11 (Etherton J); and Noonan and Watson, 'Examining Company Directors through the Lens of De Facto Directorship' [2008] JBL 587.

3 The definition in CA 2006, s 251 (previously CA 1985, s 741(2)) is the same, save that it also excludes parent companies.

These additional exclusions also apply to the definition of 'shadow director' in the Companies Act 2006 (CA 2006), s 251 and to that in the Company Directors Disqualification Act 1986 (CDDA 1986), s 22(5).

CASELAW ON THE MEANING OF SHADOW DIRECTOR

22.5 In 2011 in *Buzzle Operations*[4] the New South Wales Court of Appeal held that a parent had not become a shadow director of its subsidiary. The Court of Appeal held that a finding of shadow directorship requires habitual compliance and a causal link must be found between the instructions of the shadow director and the conduct of the board.

22.6 In 2000, the Court of Appeal in *Deverell*[5] considered the statutory definition of shadow director under CDDA 1986 and held[6] that:

- The definition should not be strictly construed.
- The purpose of the legislation was to identify those, other than professional advisers, with real influence in the corporate affairs of the company. But it is not necessary that such influence should be exercised over the whole field of its corporate activities.[7]
- Whether any particular communication from the alleged shadow director, whether by words or conduct, is to be classified as a direction or instruction must be objectively ascertained by the court in the light of all the evidence.
- Non-professional advice may come within that statutory description. The proviso excepting advice given in a professional capacity appears to assume that advice generally is or may be included. Moreover the concepts of 'direction' and 'instruction' do not exclude the concept of 'advice' for all three share the common feature of 'guidance'.
- It is not necessary to show that, in the face of 'directions or instructions' from the alleged shadow director, the properly appointed directors (or some of them) cast themselves in a subservient role or surrendered their respective discretions.

22.7 It seems that a one-off direction is not enough – there must be a course of conduct – Lewison J in *Re Kilnoore: Unidare v Cohen*[8]).

4 *Buzzle Operations Pty Ltd (in liq) v Apple Computer Australia Pty Ltd* [2011] NSWCA 109, (2011) 277 ALR 189, NSW CA.

5 *Secretary of State for Trade and Industry v Deverell* [2001] Ch 340, [2000] 2 All ER 365, CA.

6 [2001] Ch 340, [2000] 2 All ER 365 at pp 375/376 (para 35).

7 Cited by Newey J in *Vivendi SA v Richards* [2013] EWHC 3006 (Ch), [2013] BCC 771 at [125] and by Trower J in *Standish v The Royal Bank of Scotland Plc* [2019] EWHC 3116 (Ch), [2020] 1 All ER (Comm) 814, [2020] 1 BCLC 826 at [54].

8 [2005] 3 All ER 730 at p 739 (para 36). See also the article by Chan Ho 'Connected Persons and Administrators' Duty to Think: Unidare v Cohen' (2005) 20 *Journal of International Banking and Regulation*, 11.

22.8 On advice see the discussion about 'control' through 'domination' at Part 9 below.

22.9 Control (or 'domination') of just one director on a multi-member board does not look to be enough to make a person a shadow director,[9] but control of a majority of the board (or of the active board) may be enough. In *Ultraframe (UK) Ltd v Fielding*,[10] Lewison J held that a person at whose direction a governing majority of the board was accustomed to act was capable of being a shadow director.

22.10 In *Smithton Ltd v Naggar*[11] the Court of Appeal held that Mr Naggar could not be a shadow director if he had only dominated a minority of the board.

22.11 Furthermore in practice a shadow director may well also be at risk of being in 'control' of the company and so be associated with it under the control test in s 435(10)(a) discussed in Part 9 below (if it applies in relation to a single director).

9 *Re Unisoft Group Ltd (No 3)* [1994] 1 BCLC 609, 620 (Harman J) and *Lord v Sinai Securities Ltd* [2004] EWHC 1764 (Ch) at [27], [2005] 1 BCLC 295, 303 (Hart J).

10 *Ultraframe (UK) Ltd v Fielding; Northstar Systems Ltd v Fielding* [2005] EWHC 1638 (Ch), [2005] All ER (D) 397 (Jul), [2007] WTLR 835 (Lewison J) at [1272]. Discussed by Prentice and Payne, 'Directors' fiduciary duties' (2006) 122 LQR 558–565. See also *Lord v Sinai Securities Ltd* [2004] EWHC 1764 (Ch), [2005] 1 BCLC 295 (Hart J) at [27].

11 [2014] EWCA Civ 939, [2015] 1 WLR 189, [2015] 2 BCLC 22 per Arden LJ at [89].

23

Common directorships – connected

23.1 There is a limited chain here. If a company has directors (including non-executive directors) who are also directors of another company, those two companies will be connected with each other under the Insolvency Act 1986 (IA 1986), s 249.

23.2 Thus, for example, if X is a director (or shadow director) of A Co and is also a director of C Co, this will mean that:

(a) A Co is connected with C Co and that C Co is connected with A Co; but

(b) A Co is not (absent some other link) associated with C Co, nor is C Co associated with A Co.

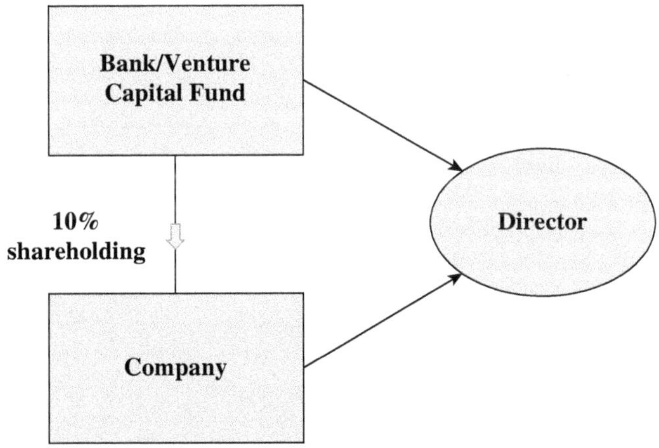

23.3 This has potentially odd results. It means that all companies sharing just one common director are connected for these purposes even though there is no other link (eg common shareholding or transactions etc).

23.4 The Court of Appeal in Singapore (where the statutory provisions are similar) addressed this issue in the context of an unfair preference claim in *Show Theatres Pte Ltd v Shaw Theatres Pte Ltd*[1] and commented:

> '[21]. We were mindful that this ruling could have some repercussions in view of the corporate practice in Singapore, where it is a common phenomenon to see a person sitting on the boards of several companies. We do not, however, see anything seriously objectionable in the construction we have given. All it means is that whenever two companies have a common director or common directors, they are to be treated as 'connected with' each other. In this regard, it is vitally important to bear in mind the clear objective behind ss 98 to 101. What is prescribed in those sections is a scheme for the protection of creditors generally. It underscores the need for transparency. Because of the connection due to common directorship, a payment to a 'connected' company made within the period of two years prior to the liquidation of the company is presumed to be made in unfair preference and it is for the 'connected' company to rebut that presumption. It is right, and not unfair, to assume that a director exercises influence within the company.'

23.5 The Singapore Court of Appeal subsequently noted in *SLR Liquidators of Progen Engineering Pte Ltd v Progen Holdings Ltd*[2] that

> 'it has been unequivocally decided by this court in *Show Theatres Pte Ltd v Shaw Theatres Pte Ltd* [2002] 2 SLR (R) 1143 ('Show Theatres') that where two companies have a common director or common directors, they will be considered to be 'connected with' each other'.

1 [2002] SGCA 42, [2002] 4 SLR 145, Singapore CA.
The judgment is on the web at http://app.supremecourt.gov.sg/default.aspx?pgID=1136.

2 [2010] SGCA 31, [2010] SLR 1104, Singapore CA.

24

Employers and employees

24.1 Persons are connected with a company if they are associates of a director (or shadow director) of the company – Insolvency Act 1986 (IA 1986), s 249(a). Associates include any person whom a person employs or by whom he is employed – IA 1986, s 435(4).

24.2 The term 'employed' or indeed 'employee' is not defined further in IA 1986 (save that directors and officers are treated for the purposes of s 435 as if they were employed by the company – s 435(9)). In practice it seems likely that the usual definition of employee as someone who works under a contract of service or apprenticeship should apply[1]. This will exclude both (a) persons who are self-employed and (b) those who are within the expanded category of "workers" used in some legislation (eg discrimination law, working time, deductions from wages etc[2]) as including those who perform personally work or services[3].

EMPLOYEES AS CONNECTIONS

24.3 An example. If:

(a) a company, A Co, employs someone, Mr X, who is not a director or shadow director of A Co; and

(b) Mr X also is (or becomes) a director of an otherwise unrelated or unconnected company, B Co.

1 See eg *Re CW & CL Hughes Ltd* [1966] 2 All ER 702 (Plowman J) in relation to preferential debts under the insolvency legislation.
2 Equality Act 2010; Working Time Regulations 1998; ERA 1996, Part 2;
3 The line can be difficult to draw in particular cases – *see Pimlico Plumbers v Smith* [2018] *UKSC 29 and Uber BV v Aslam* [2021] UKSC 5.

This means that:

(c) A Co is connected with B Co within s 249 (because A Co is associated with Mr X and Mr X is a director of B Co); but

(d) B Co is *not* (absent anything else) connected with A Co. Although B Co is associated with Mr X (because Mr X is a director of B Co), B Co is not 'connected with' A Co because Mr X is not a director (or shadow director) of A Co.

24.4 The employer of any person who is a director (or shadow director) will, under s 249, be connected with the company or which that person is a director (or shadow director). For example:

(a) If an appointing person (say a bank (or venture capital fund) nominates one of its employees to be a director of a company (perhaps to protect their interests as minority shareholder), this will mean that the appointor will be 'connected with' that company under s 249. The director is also connected (and associated) with the company. Nomination is not necessary for this result. A company (P Co) will be connected with every company which has as one of its directors a person who is an associate of P Co (for example a director or employee of P Co).

(b) If the director nominated by the appointor company was not its associate, the appointor company would not be connected or associated with the company (unless there was another connection – eg it had acted as a shadow director).

24.5 Unlike the definition of associate (see s 435(1), discussed at Part 6 below), there is no reciprocal provision in the connection definition in s 249. Just because A is connected with C does *not* mean that C is connected with A.

24.6 This can be relevant where a connection (or association) is required. For example, in the CVA provisions under Part 1 of IA 1986, special rules apply to creditors of a CVA company who are connected with the CVA company. For example:

(a) A pension trustee company (P Co) may be a creditor of the CVA company (eg for unpaid contributions or by reason of a contingent debt under s 75 of the Pensions Act 1995).

(b) P Co may be a connected creditor of the CVA company (eg if the P Co is a wholly-owned subsidiary of the CVA company and so 'controlled' by it within s 435(10)(b) and hence an associate).

(c) P Co will also be connected with the CVA company if one of the directors of P Co is also a director of the CVA company.

(d) But if neither of these associations or connections applies, what is the position if one of the directors (Ms X) of P Co is also an employee of the CVA company (but not a director or shadow director of the CVA company)?

In this situation, P Co is an associate of Ms X (its director), but, as she is not a director of the CVA company, this means that P Co is not connected with the CVA company under s 249(a).

(e) Conversely the CVA company is also an associate of Ms X (as its employee), meaning that the CVA company is an associate of a director of P Co, meaning that the CVA company is connected with P Co under s 249(a).

24.7 There are some specific modifications of the position of employees in some of the Insolvency Act provisions dealing with reversible transactions. Thus both for corporate insolvencies and for individual bankruptcies, the presumption of a preference being given in favour of an associate does not apply to someone who is only an associate 'by reason of being his employee' – IA 1986, s 340(5). These provisions are discussed in Chapter 11 above.

25

Officers and managers

25.1 The term 'officer' and the linked term 'manager' can be difficult terms to apply. The term 'officer' is used in the Insolvency Act 1986 (IA 1986), s 435 (and IA 1986, Sch B1, para 60A). The term is not expressly defined in s 435, but probably should be interpreted in accordance with IA 1986, s 251 as including a 'manager'. The term 'manager' is used in much legislation, but is not generally defined.

OFFICER

25.2 The term 'officer' is used in IA 1986, s 435(9). This provides that provides that 'any director or other officer' of a company is to be treated as employed by that company and hence will be treated as associated with the company – s 435(4).

25.3 The term 'officer' is not defined in the IA for the purposes of s 435.[1] There is a definition now in IA 2006, s 251. But s 251 states that it only applies for 'this Group of Parts',[2] which does not include s 435.[3] In practice it is likely that the term 'officer' used in s 435 would be treated as having the same meaning as in s 251. This provides:

> '"officer" in relation to a body corporate, includes a director, a manager, a secretary'

The definition in s 251 is similar to the definition in the Companies Act 2006 (CA 2006), s 1173[4] which provides that officer 'includes a director, manager or secretary'.

1 Before October 2009, IA 1986, s 251 used to generally incorporate defined terms from the companies legislation.
2 Ie Pts 1 to 7, ss 1 to 251. It is defined with reference to an insolvent partnership by Art 2(1) of the Insolvent Partnerships Order 1994 (SI 1994/2421).
3 A similar issue arises in relation to directors – see discussion in ch 21 above.
4 Formerly CA 1985, s 744 and before that CA 1948, s 435.

25.4 The term 'officer' is also used in the definition of 'connected person' in IA 1986, Sch B1, para 60A, as used in relation to restrictions on disposals by administrators (see Chapter 20 above). A 'relevant person' is defined to include 'a director or other officer' – para 60A(4)(a)(i).

The definition of officer in s 251 applies to Sch B1 on the basis that Sch B1 applies by virtue of IA 1986, s 8, which forms part of the First Group of Parts to which s 251 applies.

25.5 The companies legislation has various provisions that apply to officers, generally defined as including 'a director, manager or secretary' – CA 2006, s 1173(1).

25.6 There is some difficulty with the s 251 definition: it is inclusive, not exclusive and leaves it open as to who is a 'manager'. At the end of the nineteenth century in *Re Western Counties Steam Bakeries and Milling Co*[5] Lindley LJ held that

> 'to be an officer there must be an office, and an office imports a recognised position with rights and duties annexed to it … it would be an abuse of words to call a person an officer who fills no such position either de jure or de facto, but who happens to do some of the work which he would have to do if he were an officer in the proper sense of the word'.[6]

25.7 Auditors are generally officers (*Re London and General Bank Ltd*[7]), but bankers, solicitors and other professional advisers are not, as such, officers: *Re Imperial Land Co of Marseilles, Re National Bank*[8] (and see also IA 1986, s 219(3), which draws a distinction between an officer and an agent).

25.8 It seems likely that a director (Mr A) of a company (X) which is itself a director of another company (Z) is not an officer of company Z – see the Court of Appeal in *Masri v Consolidated Contractors International (UK) Ltd*[9] discussing the meaning of 'officer' in the context of examination of an officer of a judgment debtor.

INSOLVENCY PRACTITIONERS

25.9 Insolvency practitioners acting in relation to a company are likely to be considered to be officers of that company and hence associated with that company – s 435(4) and (9). Some provisions in the companies legislation

5 [1897] 1 Ch 617, CA.

6 See also *Re London and General Bank* [1895] 2 Ch 166, CA and *Mutual Reinsurance Co Ltd v Peat Marwick Mitchell* [1997] 1 BCLC 1, CA.

7 [1895] 2 Ch 166, CA and *R v Shacter* [1960] 2 QB 252.

8 (1870) LR 10 Eq 298 (Sir R Malins V-C).

9 [2008] EWCA Civ 876; [2009] 2 WLR 699, CA at [20]. Overturned on appeal, but this point not discussed.

expressly provide for an insolvency practitioner to be treated as an officer (for example CA 2006, s 30(4) dealing with the forwarding of copies of resolutions to the registrar[10]). So this could be seen as raising the argument that generally in CA 2006, the term 'officer' may not include an insolvency practitioner.

25.10 In 1955 in *Re B Johnson & Co (Builders) Ltd*[11] the Court of Appeal held that a receiver was not a 'manager' or 'officer' for the purposes of various provisions in what is now the Companies Act 2006 (dealing with liability of a manager or officer for misfeasance). But this could be seen as relating to the different position of a receiver (appointed under a floating charge), compared to a liquidator or administrator (appointed under statutory provisions).

25.11 However in 1991 in *Re Home Treat Ltd*[12] Harman J held that an administrator could be an officer for the purposes of the exoneration provision in what is now s 1157 of the Companies Act 2006 (citing the 1907 decision of Parker J in *Re X Co Ltd*[13] a case on the Stamp Act 1891 in relation to liquidators). This was followed in 2015 by Newey J in *Re Powertrain Ltd*[14] in relation to liquidators and s 1157. Both *Home Treat* and *Powertrain* were unopposed decisions (and so of more limited precedent value[15]) and did not refer to the Court of Appeal decision in *Re B Johnson*.

25.12 There is further doubt as to whether a provision of the kind described above applies to insolvency practitioners because the provision refers to officers of the company whereas in some cases (eg administrators and liquidators in a court winding up) the insolvency practitioner is an officer of the court and not an officer of the company. But in *Re Hartlebury Printers Ltd*[16] Morritt J rejected this argument, albeit in another context entirely. Harman J in *Re Home Treat Ltd*[17] took the same position.

MANAGER

25.13 The term 'manager' in s 251 is not defined. Legislation creating crimes that could apply to a company often extend the potential crime to cover directors and managers as well. Common wording is that the offence applies to

10 See also IA 1986, s 212 referring separately to an 'officer' of the company and to a 'liquidator' or 'administrative receiver'. Discussed in ILA Bulletin 676 (April 2016).
11 [1955] Ch 634, CA.
12 [1991] BCLC 705 (Harman J) at [710].
13 [1907] 2 Ch 92 (Parker J).
14 [2015] EWHC B26 (Ch), [2016] BPIR 456 (Newey J). Not following the doubts expressed in *Rawnsley v Weatherall Green & Smith North Ltd* [2009] EWHC 2482 (Ch), [2010] 1 BCLC 658 (HHJ Behrens). See ILA Bulletin 676 (April 2016).
15 See Practice Direction [2001] 2 All ER 510 at [6].
16 [1993] 1 All ER 470 (Morritt J).
17 [1991] BCLC 705 (Harman J). See generally on this question Hofler 'Elephants and officers: problems of definition' (1996) 17 Company Lawyer, 258.

> 'any director, manager, secretary or other similar officer of the body corporate, or any person who was purporting to act in such capacity'

25.14 The intention of the criminal provisions mentioned above is clearly to impose criminal liability on the persons actually in charge of the running of the company. See, for example, the discussions in *R v Boal*[18] on the Fire Precautions Act 1971, s 23; *Armour v Skeen*[19] on the Health and Safety at Work etc Act 1974, s 37(1); and *Woodhouse v Walsall MBC*[20] on the Control of Pollution Act 1974, s 87.

25.15 In *Re A Company*[21] the Court of Appeal commented that the central administration of a company should not be construed narrowly. Shaw LJ held (at p144):

> 'The expression "manager" should not be too narrowly construed. It is not to be equated with a managing or other director or a general manager. As I see it, any person who in the affairs of the company exercises a supervisory control which reflects the general policy of the company for the time being or which is related to the general administration of the company is in the sphere of management.'

25.16 *Halsbury's Laws*[22] comments:

> '"Manager" means, in every day language, a person who has the management of the whole affairs of the company.[23] It connotes a person holding, whether de jure or de facto, a position in or with the company of a nature charging him with the duty of managing the affairs of the company for the company benefit.[24] It does not include a local manager.'[25]

18 [1992] QB 591, CA.

19 [1977] IRLR 310, Ct of Sess.

20 [1994] 1 BCLC 435; [1994] Env LR 30, DC.

21 [1980] Ch 138 CA. The CA judgment was overturned on appeal, but not on this point. The manager point was not discussed: *Re Racal Communications Ltd* [1981] AC 374. Shaw LJ was cited in Australia in *Commissioner for Corporate Affairs v Bracht* [1989] VR 821, Ormston J commenting:

> 'Whilst it is easy to exclude from the concept of management those activities of a corporation which consist in the carrying out of day to day routine functions in accordance with predetermined policies, whether they be clerical or involve the ordering or supplying of goods or services on its behalf, it is harder to fix on those elements which are critical to management.'

22 *Halsbury's Laws of England*, Vol 15 (2016), *Companies* at para 679.

23 *Gibson v Barton* (1875) LR 10 QB 329, DC at [336] per Blackburn J. Halsbury also cites elsewhere on this: *Tesco Supermarkets Ltd v Nattrass* [1971] 1 QB 133, DC at p 142, per Fisher J (reversed without affecting this point [1972] AC 153, HL).

24 *Re B Johnson & Co (Builders) Ltd* [1955] Ch 634, CA, per Jenkins LJ at [661].

25 *Registrar of Restrictive Trading Agreements v WH Smith & Son Ltd* [1969] 3 All ER 1065, CA, per Lord Denning MR at [1069].

25.17 A hotel front desk employee at a guesthouse was held not to be a manager by the Hong Kong Court of Final Appeal in *HKSAR v Chui Shu Shing.*[26] French NPJ held at [44]:

> '[44] Beginning with the text, the word "manage", according to the Oxford English Dictionary, relevantly means "to conduct or carry on (a war, a business, an undertaking, an operation) …". It may also mean "to control and direct the affairs of (a household, institution, state etc)". It appears in a particular context, namely the collocation "operates, keeps, manages or otherwise has control of". The words "otherwise has control of" suggests that the other terms in the collocation are used as species of the genus "has control of". A wider context is provided by those provisions of the [Ordinance] previously mentioned which contemplate management as conduct of a kind done by the person to whom a certificate of exemption or a licence is issued, or a person doing similar things under the continuous and personal supervision of a licence holder.
>
> [45] The concept of "manage" according to its ordinary meaning read in the context of the [Ordinance] and having regard to its purpose does not extend to a person who carries out essentially non-discretionary functions under the direct supervision of another on the premises. Like each of the terms in the collocation, it incorporates the idea of authority over that which is managed. The precise nature and content of that authority will vary according to the circumstances of the case.'

25.18 In Australia, similar approach to the term 'manager' has been taken. A Station manager was held not an officer in *Windbox Pty Ltd v Daguragu Aboriginal Land Trust (No 3).*[27]

25.19 In *Windbox*, the judge commented (at [228]) that in both *ASIC v Citigroup (No 4)*[28] and *Buzzle Operations Pty Ltd (in liq) v Apple Computer Australia Pty Ltd*[29] the court found against the defendants being 'officers' notwithstanding that the defendants had capacity to significantly affect the corporation's financial standing and made decisions which substantially affected the corporation's business. This was because that capacity to affect was not by reason of the defendants being involved in the management of the corporation in terms of policy formation and significant decision making. in *ASIC v Citigroup (No 4)* Jacobson J observed that both of the categories covered by the Australian statutory definition are concerned with identifying persons who are involved in management of the corporation.

26 [2017] HKCFA 43, (2017) 6 HKC 492.

27 [2020] NTSC 21 (Hiley J).

28 *Australian Securities and Investments Commission (ASIC) v Citigroup Global Markets Australia Pty Ltd (No 4)* [2007] FCA 963, (2007) 160 FCR 35 (Jacobson J).

29 *Buzzle Operations Pty Ltd (in liq) v Apple Computer Australia Pty Ltd.* [2011] NSWCA 109.

PART 6

ASSOCIATES

26

Who is an associate?

26.1 The term 'associate' is defined exhaustively for the purposes of the Insolvency Act 1986 (IA 1986) by the provisions in IA 1986, s 435.[1]

26.2 The associate relationship is reciprocal – s 435(1). Thus if a person (A) is an associate of another (B), then that means that B is also associated with A.[2]

26.3 This is to be contrasted with the definition of 'connected' in s 249, where no such reflexive principle applies (ie if A is connected with company B, that does not necessarily mean that B is connected with A) – see Chapter 18 above.

1 See s 435(1).
2 See the wording in brackets at the end of s 435(1).

27

Associate – individuals

INDIVIDUALS

27.1 An individual is a natural person, and the term will *not* include a company or body corporate. See for example Mann J in *Jasmine Trustees Ltd v Wells & Hind (a firm)*,[1] a decision on s 37 of the Trustee Act 1925.

Conversely the term 'person' usually 'includes a body of persons corporate or unincorporate' (Interpretation Act 1978, Sch 1). This applies 'unless the context otherwise provides', but clear language would be needed to so require.[2]

27.2 A wide range of persons are associated with an individual (and vice-versa):

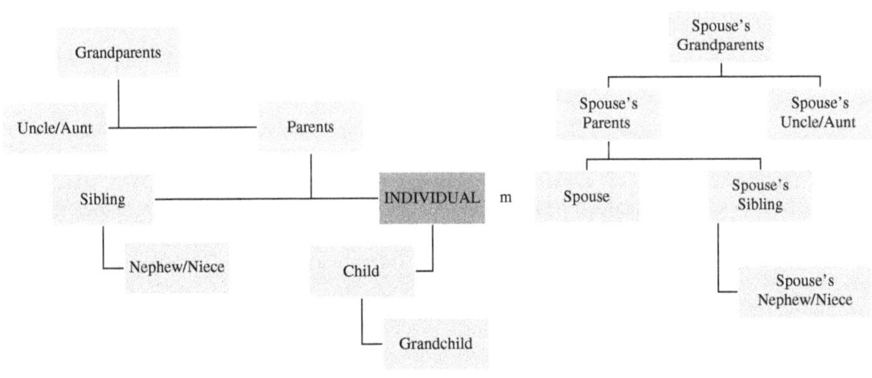

All the persons identified above, plus their current and former 'spouses', would be 'associates' of the individual.

1 [2007] EWHC 38 (Ch); [2007] 1 All ER 1142 (Mann J).
2 *Cosmetic Warriors Ltd v Gerrie* [2017] EWCA Civ 324 at [51] (a case on the Law of Property Act 1925, s 61).

SPOUSES AND REPUTED SPOUSES

27.3 Unsurprisingly, under the Insolvency Act 1986 (IA 1986), s 435(2) a person is treated as associated with his or her spouse, using an expanded meaning of that status, covering:

- a husband or wife[3] or civil partner;[4]
- a former husband or wife or civil partner;[5] and
- a 'reputed' husband or wife or civil partner.[6]

The term *spouse* is not used in s 435, but is used in this book to cover all of these persons.

27.4 The use of the term 'reputed' is quite distinctive (it is also used in s 435(8) in relation to a reputed father of a child).

27.5 The expression 'reputed husband or wife' or 'reputed spouse' is used in various statutes:[7] the Consumer Credit Act 1974, s 184, the Credit Unions Act 1979, s 31, the Estate Agents Act 1979, s 32, and the Pneumoconiosis etc (Workers' Compensation) Act 1979, s 3. Also in the Broadcasting Act 1990, Sch 2, para (2).

27.6 In *Smurthwaite v Simpson-Smith (No 2)*[8] HHJ Rich QC held that something more than living together was needed: there also needed to be a holding out or reputation of marriage. In this case Miss Williams was cohabiting with the bankrupt but had not married him or adopted his name, nor was any of their friends or neighbours under the impression that they were married. Judge Rich held that she was not a reputed wife for the purposes of s 435.

3 Including under a same sex marriage – Marriage (Same Sex Couples) Act 2013, s 11.

4 The sections were amended from December 2005 to include civil partners under the Civil Partnership Act 2004 on the same basis as husbands and wives.
Civil partner means a registered civil partner – Interpretation Act 1978, Sch 1:

> 'Civil partnership' means a civil partnership which exists under or by virtue of the Civil Partnership Act 2004 (and any reference to a civil partner is to be read accordingly).'

5 IA 1986, s 435(8). Absent the express extension in s 435(8) extending the association for s 435 purposes to a former spouse, it is likely that a divorced husband and wife would have no longer been associated under s 435(2), but would have remained associated under s 435(2) until the decree absolute. See on the capital gains tax legislation: *Aspden v Hildesley* [1982] 2 All ER 53 (Nourse J) at p58.

6 IA 1986, s 435(8).

7 *Smurthwaite v Simpson-Smith (No 2)* [2006] BPIR 1483, [2005] All ER (D) 275 (Apr) (HHJ Rich QC) at [37] and [41] discussing how the term is used. Also cited in Briggs and Tribe *Muir Hunter on Personal Insolvency* (Thomson Reuters, update to March 2021) at 3-3074.

8 [2006] BPIR 1483, [2005] All ER (D) 275 (Apr) (HHJ Rich QC, sitting as a deputy High Court Judge). Issue not discussed on appeal: *Smurthwaite v Simpson-Smith* [2006] EWCA Civ 1183, [2006] BPIR 1504.

27.7 Judge Rich commented at [45] that:

> 'I have found no case in which a wife has been held to be a "reputed wife" in circumstances where not only was she not a wife, but neither she nor her reputed husband held her out as such. It may well be that the phrase used in the of 1986 Act is inapt to carry out what one would have expected Parliament's intention to have been, but I cannot find myself justified in attributing to the phrase a meaning which follows neither in the literal meaning of the words, nor any meaning attributed to them, historically in the decided cases.'

27.8 Judge Rich seemingly cited[9] (at [36]) with approval a passage from *Muir Hunter*[10] which now reads:

> 'In the past, there was an established practice of couples living together without being legally married, but with the female partner changing her name to that of the male partner, so as to be known e.g. as "Mr. & Mrs. Brown." In such a case, they might well be described as "reputed husband or wife." Reputation of marriage, in relation to names, was briefly considered in *Fendall v Goldsmid* (1877) 2 P.D. 263.
>
> But there are nowadays many couples who live together as "partners" or "co-habitees", while retaining their own names and not holding themselves out, or purporting to be, or being reputed to be, husband and wife, although they may own "matrimonial homes" in joint names. It would not seem possible to contend that such a couple were "reputed husband or wife," unless evidence was available that, notwithstanding their use of separate names, they had acquired such a reputation among relevant local persons, one class of whom might be creditors of whichever of them was bankrupt. Current expressions used in quasi-matrimonial property cases, such as "a stable union," and "a long-term or settled relationship," or "partners" reflect a degree of permanent association, but do not, it is submitted, create a "reputation of marriage": compare, under the Act of 1914, *Re Meade (A Bankrupt)* [1951] Ch. 774.'

27.9 References to a husband or wife are treated as including a former husband or wife and a reputed husband or wife (and similarly for civil partners) – s 435(8).

27.10 It is not clear if this would include a former reputed husband or wife (or civil partner). Perhaps only for a period while the 'reputation' continued?

9 The BPIR report is incomplete in this area. The report includes an editor's note:

> 'Editor's note: owing to the poor quality of the original transcription, the following judgments contain omissions in some of the quoted material and the main argument, usually identified by "(inaudible)". While considerable effort has been made to complete these where possible, this process has been hindered by the amount of time lapsed since the judgements were handed down and the unavailability of the original documents. As such, the judgments of HHJ Rich are not to be considered as approved in this current form, but are provided solely for the information of the reader in light of the subsequent judgments in the Court of Appeal.'

10 See now Briggs and Tribe *Muir Hunter on Personal Insolvency* (Thomson Reuters, update to March 2021) at 3-3090.

27.11 *Muir Hunter on Personal Insolvency* comments:[11]

> 'Nor is it at all clear what is meant, in the context, by "reputed father." In affiliation law, there is a person described as a "putative father," who is the man alleged by the child's mother to be his father, a fact which is to be determined by litigation and a finding of the court.'

RELATIVES OF INDIVIDUALS AND THEIR SPOUSES

27.12 A person is also an associate of an individual if that person is:

1. a 'relative' of the individual;
2. a relative of the individual's spouse (or former spouse);
3. the spouse (or former spouse) of a 'relative' of the individual; or
4. the spouse (or former spouse) of a 'relative' of the individual's spouse (or former spouse).

27.13 A person is a '*relative*' of an individual if he is that individual's brother, sister, uncle, aunt, nephew, niece, lineal ancestor or lineal descendant – s 435(8). This does not extend to more distant relations than a niece or nephew (eg a cousin or a great niece). But it does extend to lineal ancestors or descendants – eg great grandparents or great grandchildren.

27.14 For an example of a case holding that a man was associated with his mother-in-law, see *Re Yates (a bankrupt).*[12]

27.15 Under s 435(8):

(a) any relationship of half blood is treated as relationship of whole blood;

(b) the stepchild or adopted child of any person is treated as his (or her[13]) child;[14] and

(c) an illegitimate child is treated as the legitimate child of his (or her[15]) mother and *reputed*[16] father.

11 Briggs and Tribe *Muir Hunter on Personal Insolvency* (Sweet & Maxwell, Looseleaf, service to March 2021).

12 *Re Yates (a bankrupt): Carman (trustee of the estate in bankruptcy) v Yates* [2004] EWHC 3448 (Ch), [2005] BPIR 476 (Charles J).

13 Although s 435(8) just refers to 'his', there is no reason not to apply the presumption under Interpretation Act 1978, s 6 of 'words importing the masculine gender include the feminine'.

14 Eg *Bucknall v Wilson* [2021] EWHC 2149 (Ch), Trower J at [21] referring to *Re Fowlds (A Bankrupt)* [2020] EWHC 1200 (Ch) (ICC Judge Jones) at [6](b) in relation to a stepdaughter.

15 Although s 435(8) just refers to 'his', there is no reason not to apply the presumption under Interpretation Act 1978, s 6.

16 For a discussion of the meaning of 'reputed', see 27.4 above.

27.16 The express provisions in relation to an adopted or illegitimate child would presumably not now be needed following the general provisions in the adoption legislation – see the Adoption Act 1976, s 39. The more general provision in the Family Law Reform Act 1987, s 1 does not apply as it is limited to "enactments passed … after the coming into force of this section" and so does not apply to IA 1986.

27.17 It is slightly odd that the section refers only to a 'reputed' father as being associated with an illegitimate child. The legislation does not deal with a 'reputed' mother, nor an actual father. It seems unlikely that as a matter of statutory interpretation these provisions could be construed to apply to the opposite sex as well.[17]

27.18 None of these terms is restricted to persons who are minors. Adult children are within the definition as well as minors (contrast some elements of the Companies Act definition – see Companies Act 2006, s 253(2)(d)).

27.19 The term 'reputed' as used in 'reputed husband or wife' or 'reputed father' is undefined. It does not expressly extend to a 'reputed' mother.

27.20 Questions may arise as to whether a person is the parent of another (or a lineal ancestor or descendent) in the context of trans-gender transition and external fertilisation. See for example McFarlane P on the legal definition of 'mother' in *R (on the application of TT) v The Registrar General for England and Wales*[18] and Munby P in *In Re the Human Fertilisation and Embryology Act 2008 (Cases A, B, C, D, E, F, G and H).*[19]

27.21 Step nephews are included. Contrast the associated persons definition in the Family Law Reform Act 1996, as discussed in *M v D.*[20]

17 In *R v Secretary of State for the Home Department, ex p Crew* [1982] Imm AR 94, a case dealing with the express extension, under the Immigration Act 1971, s 2(3), of the meaning of 'parent' to cover the mother of an illegitimate child, Lord Lane CJ held: 'Under the rule expressio unius exclusio alterius, that express mention of the mother implies that the father is excluded.'
See *Bennion, Bailey and Norbury on Statutory Interpretation* (8th edn, LewisNexis, 2020) at 23.12.

18 [2019] EWHC 2384 (Fam), [2020] Fam 45 (Sir Andrew McFarlane P).

19 [2015] EWHC 2602 (Fam), [2016] 1 All ER 273 (Sir James Munby P)).

20 [2021] EWHC 1351 (Fam) (MacDonald J).

28

Trusts and trustees – s 435(5)

28.1 The Insolvency Act 1986 (IA 1986), s 435(5) provides broadly that a trustee is an associate of any person who is a beneficiary of the trust (or an associate of a beneficiary). This applies vice versa as well[1] (s 435(1)), so that a person who is a beneficiary of a trust (or an associate of a beneficiary) is an associate of the trustee.

28.2 A trustee is associated both with a beneficiary of the trust and also with an associate of a beneficiary – s 435(5). Some trusts are excluded from this principle.

28.3 Section 435(5) provides:

> 435 (5) A person in his capacity as trustee of a trust other than—
>
> (a) a trust arising under any of the second Group of Parts or the Bankruptcy (Scotland) Act 2016, or
>
> (b) a pension scheme or an employees' share scheme …,
>
> is an associate of another person if the beneficiaries of the trust include, or the terms of the trust confer a power that may be exercised for the benefit of, that other person or an associate of that other person.

28.4 A person (in his, her or its capacity as trustee of a trust) is an associate of another person if:

(a) the beneficiaries of the trust include; or

(b) the terms of the trust confer a power that may be exercised for the benefit of,

1 Under the last part of s 435(1), if A is an associate of B, this means that B is an associate of A – see ch 26 above.

that other person or an associate of that other person – s 435(5).[2] This is presumably designed to cover certain trust relationships where the insolvent person (or his or its associates) could benefit from the trust.

28.5 An example would seem to be a discretionary trust where the potential class of persons who may benefit includes a director of the insolvent company. In such a case the trustee would seem to be associated with the director (s 435(5)) and so connected with the company – s 249(a).

28.6 Certain specified types of trusts are excluded. These include pension schemes (undefined[3]) and employees' share schemes (as defined in s 436[4]).

28.7 This means that a trustee is an associate of a company if the beneficiaries include the company or an associate of the company (eg a director, officer or employee of the company). Thus a trustee of (say) a family trust for the benefit of a relative of a director of a company is associated with that director and so connected with that company. Similarly, if the company is a trustee, it is associated with each of the beneficiaries of the trust (and their associates).

28.8 This provision has not been discussed much in the reported caselaw on s 435. It was briefly mentioned in *Kirker v Holyoak Investments*,[5] but is not further discussed in the judgment.

WHO IS A TRUSTEE? WHAT IS A TRUST?

28.9 The terms 'trust' and 'trustee' are not further defined in IA 1986. They are likely to adopt the common meaning.

28.10 As an example of this approach, in *Granada Group Ltd v Law Debenture Pension Trust Corporation plc*[6] at first instance Andrews J considered the meaning of the term 'pension scheme' as used in CA 1985. She noted that there is no definition in CA 1985 of the term 'pension scheme' as used in s 346(3)(b), but considered it 'to be assumed that Parliament intended that expression to be interpreted consistently with other legislation'.

2 There is a similar provision about trusts in the Companies Act 2006 (CA 2006), s 252(2)(c) ('Persons connected with a director') (formerly CA 1985, s 346(2)(c) and (3)(b)).

3 See ch 29 below.

4 The term 'employees' share scheme' is defined in IA 1986, s 436. This definition used to cross refer to the definition in CA 1985, but the definition in IA 1986, s 436 is now free standing. See further ch 30 below.

5 *Kirker (Liquidator of SMU Investments Ltd) v Holyoak Investments Inc* [2020] EWHC 875 (Ch) (ICC Judge Prentis) at [29.3].

6 *Granada Group Ltd v Law Debenture Pension Trust Corporation plc* [2015] EWHC 1499 (Ch), [2015] 2 BCLC 604 (Andrews J) at [86] to [89]. Point not discussed on appeal [2016] EWCA Civ 1289. The CA decision is discussed at 29.6 below.

CONSTRUCTIVE/RESULTING TRUSTEE/

28.11 A person holding funds may become a trustee in favour of a third party if it undertakes only to use the funds for a specific purpose – see *Quistclose*[7] and *Twinsectra v Yardley.*[8]

28.12 In *Paragon Finance Plc v Thakerar & Co*[9], Millett LJ distinguished two classes of constructive trusts. In the first, the defendant was not expressly appointed as a trustee, but he assumed the duties of a trustee in a lawful transaction. In the second, the trust obligation arose out of the unlawful transaction which was impeached by the claimant, and the constructive trust was nothing more than a formula for equitable relief.

28.13 A person may be liable as a constructive trustee if he, she or it knowingly assists in a dishonest breach of trust – *Royal Brunei Airlines v Tan*[10] and *Twinsectra v Yardley.*[11] Similarly a resulting trustee may well not owe the full range of trustee or fiduciary duty.[12]

28.14 In *Williams v Central Bank of Nigeria*[13] the Supreme Court that the words 'trust' and 'trustee' in the Limitation Act 1980, s 21(1)(a) had their usual bore their meaning and so, for the purposes of that section, a 'trust' did not include a constructive trust of the kind alleged against the bank and a 'trustee' did not include a party who was liable to account in equity simply because he was a dishonest assister in a breach of trust and/or a knowing recipient of trust assets.

28.15 Lord Sumption held at [26]:

> 'The Trustee Act 1925 is concerned with the administration of true trusts. It is not concerned with constructive trusts imposed by equity on strangers to the trust in the exercise of its remedial jurisdiction. As Millett LJ observed when making this point in the *Paragon case* [1999] 1 All ER 400, 412, constructive trustees required to account in the exercise of equity's remedial jurisdiction,
>
>> "have no trust powers or duties; they cannot invest, sell or deal with the trust property; they cannot retire or appoint new trustees; they have no trust property in their possession or under their control, since they became accountable as

7 *Quistclose Investments Ltd v Rolls Razor Ltd* [1970] AC 567.

8 [2002] UKHL 12, [2002] 2 AC 164.

9 [1999] 1 All ER 400, CA at 408–409.

10 [1995] 2 AC 378, PC.

11 [2002] UKHL 12, [2002] 2 AC 164. See Yeo and Tjio, 'Knowing what is dishonesty' (2002) 118 LQR 502.

12 See Lord Browne-Wilkinson in *Westdeustche* [1996] AC 669 at [705]; *Port of Brisbane Corp v ANZ Securities* [2002] QCA 158; *Lonrho v Fayed (No 2)* [1992] 1 WLR 1 (Millett J); *Tan Yok Koon v Tan Choo Suan* [2017] SGCA 13, [2017] 1 SLR 654; cited in Collings, '*The duties of a resulting trustee*' (2020) 26 Trusts and Trustees 746.

13 [2014] UKSC 10, [2014] AC 1189.

> constructive trustees only by parting with the trust property. They are in reality neither trustees nor fiduciaries, but merely wrongdoers."
>
> All of these considerations apply equally to section 21 of the Limitation Act 1980, which is in the same terms.'

28.16 It may be arguable that a resulting or constructive trust does not fall within s 435(5) at least before the trustee is aware of the relevant trust status.

BARE TRUSTS OR CUSTODIANS: CONTROL

28.17 A bare trust[14] or custodian arrangement seems less likely to be outside s 435(5). Both *Unidare* and *Box Clever* were concerned with the position of a quasi trustee holder of shares (either as part of a sale or as part of security arrangements) and the question was whether or not this was enough to confer control (see Part 8 below). The question of association under s 435(5) was not discussed.

28.18 Bare trusts were treated differently in relation to 'control' issues in three tax cases: *IRC v Silverts Ltd;*[15] *IRC v J Bibby & Sons Ltd*[16] and *S Berendsen Ltd v IRC.*[17]

28.19 All three cases are discussed by the Court of Appeal in *Box Clever* at [122] to [126], but the Court ultimately held that the three cases did not cast 'any real light' on how s 435 should be interpreted as the 'statutory provisions and contexts are too different' – at [126].

OTHER LEGISLATION AND TRUSTS

28.20 Other legislation makes specific provision for trusts. An example is CA 2006, Sch 1, para 6(3) which excludes bare trustees and custodian trustees 'under the law of any part of the United Kingdom'.

28.21 In addition, CA 2006, Sch 1A deals with references to people with significant control over a company for the purposes of the PSC register provisions in CA 2006, s 790A to 790V.[18] Para 14 deals with voting rights 'at general meetings of the entity on all or substantially all matters'. Para 19 excludes nominees and paras 20 to 23 deal with rights held by persons who control their exercise and rights only exercisable in certain circumstances.

14 On bare trusts see Flannigan, 'Resolving the status of a bare trust' [2019] Conv, 207 and Matthews, 'All about bare trusts' (2005) PCB, 266 (Part 1) and (2005) PCB, 366 (Part 2). See also Pawlowski and Brown, 'Trusts: what is a bare trust?' (2020) PCB 295.

15 [1951] Ch 521, CA.

16 [1944] All ER 548, CA, [1945] 1 All ER 667, HL.

17 [1958] Ch 1.

18 Inserted from April 2006 by the Small Business, Enterprise and Employment Act 2015 (SBEEA 2015).

ASSOCIATES OF A BENEFICIARY OF THE TRUST

28.22 The trust provision in IA 1986, s 435 is wide. A trustee of a trust is an associate of B if the beneficiaries of the trust include an *associate* of B. The term 'beneficiary' is not defined.

28.23 The association extends beyond a direct beneficiary to include a person in whose favour a power may be exercised under the trust: ie where 'the terms of the trust confer a power that may be exercised for the benefit of, that other person …'.

28.24 The extension beyond a beneficiary to catch a person where the 'terms of the trust confer a power that may be exercised for the benefit of that other person' is presumably designed to deal with the issue of when a person is a beneficiary. An object of a discretionary trust may not be a full beneficiary for some purposes, but is presumably within this category. If the trust includes a power to include a wide class (eg a general power) this seems to mean that the trustee is associated with all the potential members of that class? Even if perhaps if other consents needed or conditions need to be fulfilled (the wording is 'may' be exercised).

JOINT HOLDERS OF PROPERTY

28.25 Jointly holding property as joint tenants or tenants in common, seems to be enough to make each of the trustees associated with each of the beneficiaries.

28.26 In *Re Calder, Salter v Wetton*[19] Briggs J dealt with an appeal from the County Court in a claim for reversal of a transaction at an undervalue (under IA 1986, s 339) involving an individual bankrupt, Captain Calder, who had transferred a property to Mrs Salter. Before the transfer Captain Calder and Mrs Salter were trustees for sale of the property (for themselves in equal shares and HHJ Belcher had decided in the County Court that this meant that Mrs Salter was therefore a person associated with Captain Calder within s 435(5), so that the presumption of insolvency applied under s 341(2). This part of HHJ Belcher's decision was not the subject to the appeal to the High Court and was not commented on further by Briggs J.

28.27 Merely being joint trustees of a trust does not seem to be enough to make the trustees associated with each other, unless one of them is also a beneficiary (or person in whose favour a power may be exercised[20]). So if A and B are both trustees of a trust, but neither is a beneficiary (or person in whose favour a power

19 [2011] EWHC 3192 (Ch), [2012] BPIR 63 (Briggs J). See [2].

20 It seems unlikely that the existence of an indemnity in favour of a trustee out of the assets of the trust (in relation to liabilities properly incurred) is enough to make the trustee a beneficiary of the trust or a person in whose favour a power may be exercised.

may be exercised), they will not (by reason of this trustee position) be associated with each other. They are not, just by virtue of being trustees, treated as being in partnership with each other[21] and so the partnership provision in s 435(3) does not apply.

28.28 But if one trustee (say A) is also a beneficiary (or an associate of a beneficiary), this means that the other (B) will be associated with A under s 435(5). This then means that A will be associated with B as well (under s 435(1)).

SOLICITORS AND CLIENTS?

28.29 A solicitor is, by reason of acting for a client, a fiduciary in relation to the client, but he or she is not necessarily a trustee of a trust in the client's favour. But if the solicitor receives property on behalf of the client, or opens a client account with funds received from the client, then it seems difficult to say that the solicitor is not a trustee of that property (or the funds in the client account) with the client as the beneficiary.

28.30 This is probably a bare trust. Thus *Jackson & Powell on Professional Liability* states[22] that it is clear that money received by a solicitor is held on trust, citing eg, *Twinsectra Ltd v Yardley*[23] and *Bristol & West Building Society v May, May & Merrimans.*[24]

28.31 The same position will usually apply for many agents.[25]

28.32 It may be that the solicitor is associated with the client only in his or her 'capacity as trustee' of the relevant trust and not for other purposes. The limits of this are difficult – see 28.33 below.

ASSOCIATION ONLY FOR LIMITED PURPOSES?

28.33 If a person is associated with another by virtue of the relevant test, then there is nothing express in most of s 435 to say that they are not associated for all purposes (not just for (say) a transaction at an undervalue involving the trust

21 Trustees are not 'persons carrying on a business in common with a view of profit' within Partnership Act 1890, s 1(1).

22 In relation to money received by a solicitor, see Powell, Stewart and Jackson, *Jackson & Powell on Professional Liability* (8th edn, Sweet & Maxwell, 2017) at 11-04 stating that such trust will be subject to the Solicitors' Accounts Rules 2011.

23 [2002] UKHL 12; [2002] 2 AC 164 at [12] per Lord Hoffmann.

24 [1996] 2 All ER 801 (Chadwick J) at [819] that the Solicitors Accounts Rules were terms of the implied trust.

25 Watts and Reynolds, *Bowstead & Reynolds on Agency* (22nd edn, Sweet & Maxwell, 2021) at 6-041.

or its property). However, the trust provision in s 435(5) does refer to a person acting in their 'capacity as a trustee of a trust'.

28.34 It may therefore be arguable that an association as a trustee does not make the trustee an associate of the beneficiary for other purposes. See further Chapter 33 below.

EXCLUSION OF BANKRUPTCY TRUSTS

28.35 A trust arising in bankruptcy (under IA 1986, second Group of Parts) is excluded from the trust provision – s 435(5)(a) – see Chapter 30 below.

29

Pension scheme as a trust – s 435(5)(b)

29.1 As discussed in Chapter 28 above, the Insolvency Act 1986 (IA 1986), s 435(5)[1] provides for a trustee of a trust to be an associate of another person if the beneficiaries of the trust include that other person (or an associate of that other person).

29.2 But for an exclusion, s 435(5) would practically always mean that a pension trustee would be an associate of the employer company:

(a) if the trust includes the company (or an associate of the company) as a beneficiary. This will be quite likely, for example if the company has rights under the trust (eg to surplus on a winding-up) or

(b) if associates of the company (for example employees or directors of the company[2]) are members of the trust.

But s 435(5) has an exclusion. It is expressly stated not to apply to a trustee of a pension scheme.

29.3 The term 'pension scheme' is not defined in IA 1986 for the purposes of s 435.

29.4 There is now a definition of 'pension scheme' for the purposes of the moratorium provisions in IA 1986, Part 1A,[3] but this is stated only to apply for that Part and so is not expressed to apply for s 435.

29.5 The term 'occupational pension scheme' is also used in IA 1986 in relation to super-priority for adopted employment contracts in administration (IA 1986, Sch B1, para 99), but is undefined.

1 See ch 28 above.
2 Employees: IA 1986, s 435(4). Directors: IA 1986, s 435(9) and (4).
3 See new IA 1986, s A54(1), added by the Corporate Insolvency and Governance Act 2020 (CIGA 2020) (with effect from 26 June 2020).

MEANING OF PENSION SCHEME

29.6 In *Granada Group Ltd v Law Debenture Pension Trust Corporation plc*[4] at first instance Andrews J considered the meaning of the term 'pension scheme' as used in the Companies Act 1985 (CA 1985). She noted that there is no definition in CA 1985 of the term 'pension scheme' as used in s 346(3)(b), but considered it 'to be assumed that Parliament intended that expression to be interpreted consistently with other legislation'. She went on to look at the meaning of the term 'pension scheme' in the Social Security Pensions Act 1975 and the later the Pension Schemes Act 1993 (PSA 1993).

29.7 Andrews J held that there was no justification for taking a restrictive view of the term 'pension scheme' and hence the exemption. She held:

> 'I am not persuaded that there is any justification for applying any special or restricted interpretation to the words "pension scheme" in s 346(3)(b). It was Parliament's intention that such schemes, however structured, should not be caught by s 320, and there is no distinction drawn in the 1985 Act between pension schemes of any particular size.'

29.8 Andrews J was supported in this view by the decision on IA 1986, s 435(5) of Hazel Williamson QC in *Re Thirty-Eight Building*. In *Granada*, Andrews J held:

> '[83] In *Re Thirty-Eight Building Ltd* [1999] 1 BCLC 416 the issue was whether a retirement benefit scheme administered by an independent trustee for the benefit of the sole director and his family (who were also trustees of the scheme) was caught by the prohibition against preferences, or fell within the exception in s 435(5). The liquidator's counsel ran similar arguments to those put forward by Mr Furness in the present case, namely (i) that regard should be paid to the substance of the transaction, rather than to its form, where the latter involves the interposition of a trustee into what would otherwise be a transaction to the benefit of a 'connected person', and (ii) that the exception for trustees of a pension scheme should be given a limited construction. (In that case, unlike the present, it was contended that the expression should be understood as meaning pension schemes for the benefit of all the company's employees, rather than pension schemes just for the benefit of the director and his family.)
>
> [84] The judge, Hazel Williamson QC, rejected both those arguments. She said (at 423):
>
>> "In my judgment, there is no basis on which this exception, applying to a trustee in his capacity as trustee of a 'pension scheme' can be taken at anything less than its face value. As such it applies even to a 'small' pension scheme, whose beneficiaries are limited to persons who are 'connected with the company' such as in the present case …
>>
>> … Parliament has not seen fit to make any distinction between pension schemes of different size or application."'

4 *Granada Group Ltd v Law Debenture Pension Trust Corporation plc* [2015] EWHC 1499 (Ch), [2015] 2 BCLC 604 (Andrews J) at [86] to [89].

29.9 Generally, whether a public sector pension scheme[5] (usually established by statute) is probably not a trust. In relation to a funded scheme, the administrators have been considered to be 'quasi-trustees' for investment purposes,[6] but the point has not been analysed in depth in the caselaw.[7] In any event, even if a trust, a public sector pension scheme is likely to fall within the exclusion in s 435(5)(b) as being a 'pension scheme'.

29.10 Some statutory pension schemes are clearly still trusts – for example the National Employment Savings Trust (NEST) established under the Pensions Act 2008 – PA 2008, s 67(2).

ISSUES

29.11 If the trustee is not otherwise associated with the employer, where the trustee is acting in its capacity as a trustee of a pension scheme, it will be exempted by the 'pension scheme' exclusion in s 435(5)(b) from being treated as associated with the employer under the trustee provision in IA 1986, s 435(5).

29.12 The issue gets more complex if the trustee (or one of a group of trustees) is otherwise associated with the employer company. Even where the relevant scheme or trust qualifies as being a pension scheme, the question can arise as to whether a trustee of an occupational pension scheme still counts as associated with an employer (usually a company) for this purpose.

29.13 The issue can turn on the four points below:

(a) Whether the trustee is connected with or an associate of the company in any event (ie ignoring the effect of s 435(5));

(b) If the trustee is otherwise associated with the company in any event (ie ignoring the effect of s435(5), does the exclusion of a 'pension scheme' in s 435(5)(b) apply to exclude it?

(c) Are all of a group of trustees otherwise associated (ie save by reason of being the trustee of the relevant trust)? If not all are associated and the transaction involves all of the trustees acting as a group, it would seem that the trustees as a body are not associated – *Re Thirty-Eight Building Ltd (No 1)*;[8]

(d) If the trustee is not otherwise associated, does it matter if the beneficiaries of the pension trust are associated?

5 PSA 1993, s 1 and the Public Service Pensions Act 2013.

6 *R (Palestine Solidarity Campaign Ltd) v Secretary of State* [2020] UKSC 16, [2020] 4 All ER 347, [2020] 1 WLR 1774 per Lord Wilson at [31].

7 Newman 'Topical issues in public sector pensions' (2021) June Nugee Lecture, discussing *Martin v City of Edinburgh DC* 1988 SLT 329, [1989] Pens LR 9 (Lord Murray), *Bain, Petitioner* 2002 SLT 1112 and *Palestine Solidarity* [2020] UKSC 16.

8 [1999] 1 BCLC 416; [1999] OPLR 319 (Hazel Williamson QC).

LIMB (A): TRUSTEE COMPANY OTHERWISE AN ASSOCIATE?

29.14 Looking at whether a trustee company is an associate otherwise (ie 29.13(a) above), subject to the discussion below about the effect of the exclusion in s 435(5), a trustee company within often be an associate of the employer company if it is an in-house trustee company. One of the other grounds in s 435, outside s 435(5), may well apply. An example would be if:

(a) the shares in the trustee company are held by the employer company (or under common control of an entity that controls the company and the trustee company) so that IA 1986, s 435(10)[9] applies; or

(b) one of the directors of the trustee company is also a director of the employer company.

29.15 If the trustee company is (for example) in the same group of companies as the employer company[10] (eg is a wholly-owned subsidiary of the employer company or its parent), then the trustee company will be an associate of the employer company by virtue of the common control through the shareholdings. The impact of the grant of security over some or all of the shareholdings (eg in favour of a third party lender) or any of the companies entering a formal insolvency process (eg administration) can be complex.[11]

ISSUE (1): TRUSTEE COMPANY AN ASSOCIATE OF A DIRECTOR (OR SHADOW DIRECTOR)

29.16 A trustee company will be connected with the employer company if it is an associate of a director (or shadow director) of the employer company – s 249 (see Chapter 23 above).

29.17 In practice, directors of the employer company are most likely to be individuals.[12] In this case, the trustee company will be associated with an

9 See Parts 7 to 10 above.

10 It is quite common for the shares in a sole purpose trustee company to be held by the employer company (or another group company). The other model is for the shares to be held by the trustee company directors (or for the trustee company to be a company limited by guarantee). See Pollard, *The Law of Pension Trusts* (OUP, 2013) at 4.31.

11 See ch 38 and Part 10 below.

12 Some jurisdictions (eg Australia and Singapore) provide that only natural persons (ie individuals) may be directors. Currently in the UK the statutory requirement is that at least one director must be a natural person – CA 2006, s 155(1). A change to this position in the UK (but subject to exceptions) is envisaged. The Small Business, Enterprise and Employment Act 2015 will (when s 87 it comes into force at some future date) amend CA 2006 to provide that a person may not (subject to exceptions) be appointed a director of a company unless the person is a natural person (CA 2006, s 156A, as inserted by the Small Business, Enterprise and Employment Act 2015 (SBEEA 2015), s 87). But these amendments are not, at the time of writing, yet in force.

individual (who is also a director of the employer company) if (for example) the individual is also a director of the trustee company.[13]

29.18 It would not be enough to make the trustee company associated with the employer company if one (or more) of the trustee company directors was not a director of the employer company, but was an employee of the employer company, nor if they were a director or employee of another group company (eg the parent company of the whole group). The connected status in relation to the employer company only applies under s 249 if the individual with whom the trustee company is associated is also a director (or shadow director) of the employer company.

29.19 It is likely to be much more difficult in practice to work out if a person is a shadow director[14] of the employer company. If a person is a shadow director of the employer company, then if the trustee company is an associate of that person (eg that person is also a director of the trustee company), then the trustee company will be connected with the employer company. It is also conceivable that a company could be found to be a shadow director of the employer company.

ISSUE (2): TRUSTEE COMPANY OTHERWISE AN ASSOCIATE, BUT IS IT EXCLUDED UNDER S 435(5)?

29.20 It could be argued that the exclusion of pension trustees from s 435(5) is wide enough not just to cover the specific trust provision in s 435(5), but also generally to mean that a pension trustee is not associated with the employer company under any of the other provisions in s 435.

29.21 But it is unlikely that such an expanded argument would succeed. The point was argued in *Re Thirty-Eight Building Ltd*,[15] but not decided.

29.22 A similar (but not identical) provision in CA 2005, s 254, was applied in relation to a member of a charitable company in *Children's Investment Fund (UK) v Attorney General*.[16] Vos C (as he then was) held that it did not matter that the relevant transfer was to a charitable company that would hold the proceeds on a charitable trust that would not benefit the member of the company.

13 IA 1986, s 435(9) treating directors in the same way as employees and so associated with the company of which they are directors under s 435(4).

14 Presumably as defined in IA 1986, s 251. See ch 21 above.

15 [1999] 1 BCLC 416, [1999] OPLR 319 (Hazel Williamson QC). See also 29.13 above. The judge commented at p 423h:

> 'I should make it clear that my decision is not intended to be of wider application than the facts of this case. In particular, I make no decision as to whether the exception in s 435(5)(b) would still apply in the absence of the fifth respondent as a trustee of the scheme, ie if the trustees had been only the first four respondents, who are all 'persons connected with the Company', and the beneficiaries had also been the very same connected persons.'

16 [2017] EWHC 1379 (Ch), [2018] Ch 371 (Vos C) at [96] and [97].

ISSUE (3): GROUP OF TRUSTEES

29.23 On the point in 29.13(c) above, in relation to a group of trustees, it seems that usually at least it is only if all trustees in a group are associated that the pension scheme will be associated.

29.24 In *Re Thirty-Eight Building Ltd (No 1)*[17] Hazel Williamson QC held that a pension scheme with five trustees was not connected with the company, even though four of the five were associates. Accordingly, the shorter (six-month) period under IA 1986, s 239 to challenge payments to the scheme as a preference applied.

29.25 Four of the five trustees were associated with the company (two of them owned the company and the other two were their children) but the fifth was not (it was an independent trustee, presumably as then required by the Inland Revenue as part of its approval process for a small self-administered scheme).

29.26 Hazel Williamson QC held that the fact that one of the trustees was not connected meant that the trustees as a body were not connected, even though the first four trustees were the only beneficiaries under the scheme. This was in the context of IA 1986, s 435(5)(b), which excludes pension trustees from the general provision in s 435(5) that trustees are deemed to be associated with a company if a beneficiary under the trust is the company or a person associated with the company.

29.27 Hazel Williamson QC held:

> 'It follows, in my judgment, that in the present situation, the relevant "creditor" for the purpose of s 239(4) is the five respondents collectively, and that creditor is not rendered an "associate" of the first respondent by virtue of s 435(5) of the Act owing to the exception in sub-s (b).'

The deputy judge expressly reserved the position on the interpretation of s 435(5)(b) in a case where all the trustees are connected to the company.

29.28 In a later judgment *Re Thirty-Eight Building Ltd (No 2)*[18] the deputy judge, refused to review or vary her earlier decision. She held that it was immaterial that the trustees could act by a majority (ie not unanimously) or that the company could remove the independent trustee.

29.29 There may be a contrast to be drawn between the decision in *Re Thirty-Eight Building Ltd* and the decision of Neuberger J in *Re Torvale Group Ltd.*[19]

17 [1999] 1 BCLC 416; [1999] OPLR 319 (Hazel Williamson QC). Decided on 30 November 1998, before the judgment in *Torvale Group* (below).

18 [2000] 1 BCLC 201 (Hazel Williamson QC).

19 [1999] 2 BCLC 605 (Neuberger J). Judgment given in July 1999. *Re Thirty-Eight Building* is not cited.

He held that a transaction involving five trustees was invalid under CA 1985, s 322A(2)[20] for infringing a provision in the articles of association even though only one of the five trustees was a director. Neuberger J validated the transaction (acting under CA 1985, s 322A) in the circumstances of the case.

OTHERWISE UNCONNECTED PENSION TRUSTEE (BUT BENEFICIARIES INCLUDE ASSOCIATES)

29.30 On the point in 29.13(d) above, in relation to a pension trustee who is otherwise unconnected, an analogous situation arose in *Granada Group Ltd v The Law Debenture Pension Trust Corporation PLC.*[21] The case involved the definition of 'connected' in CA 1985 (and now in CA 2006), but the relevant provision is similar to that in IA 1986, s 435.

29.31 *Granada Group* involved the grant of security by a company to a trustee[22] of an otherwise unfunded occupational pension scheme (where directors of the company were among the beneficiaries of the scheme and the trust). The Court of Appeal held that the grant of security was not a transaction needing shareholder approval under CA 1985, s 320.[23]

29.32 The primary issue in the case was whether the directors had received a relevant non-cash asset by reason of the assets being charged to the trustee (it was held that the directors' interest under the trust was not a sufficient interest in the underlying assets charged to the trustee).

29.33 One further question was whether the trustee was itself connected with the directors by reason of being a trustee of a trust including the directors as beneficiaries (CA 1985, s 346(2)(c)) or whether it was 'acting in its capacity a trustee under a pension scheme'[24] and so excluded from being connected under s 346(2)(c) by reason of CA 1985, s 346(3)(b).[25] The two CA 1985 provisions (and now those in CA 2006), when combined, have very similar wording to that in IA 1986, s 435(5).

29.34 Lewison LJ (Christopher Clark and Hamblen LJJ agreeing) held that the exclusion applied, dismissing the argument that the exclusion did not apply

20 Now CA 2006, s 41.
21 *Granada Group Ltd v Law Debenture Pension Trust Corporation plc* [2016] EWCA Civ 1289, [2017] 2 BCLC 1. Upholding [2015] EWHC 1499 (Ch), [2015] 2 BCLC 604 (Andrews J).
22 The trustee was presumably not otherwise connected with or an associate of the company. The point does not arise one way or the other in the judgments.
23 Now CA 2006, s 190.
24 Lewison LJ at [44].
25 Now CA 2006, s 252(2)(c).

where the trustee was only acting as security agent. The Court of Appeal agreed with Andrews J at first instance,[26] including where she held:

> '[88] It is clear that the security element is an integral part of an arrangement designed to ensure that the relevant benefits are paid to the members of the pension scheme in accordance with the employer's obligations under the Special Terms. In taking that security, with a view to being able to enforce it in future, and in becoming the trustee of Granada's promise to maintain the value of the security (and if necessary to top it up) under rule 6, the Trustee is undoubtedly acting as a trustee of a pension scheme and performing the duties of a trustee. It is not acting as a security agent, or an agent of any kind. Indeed the trustee-beneficiary relationship between the Trustee and the Directors was the very foundation for Granada's primary argument that the Directors themselves had an interest in the charge over the gilts.
>
> [89] It does not matter that before this Scheme was put in place, there was an unsecured supplementary pension scheme in otherwise identical terms. That scheme was expressly revoked and replaced by a new, secured scheme, as is clear from the Special Terms. I see no justification for Mr Furness' argument that the Trustee has no role in the Scheme because its function is to hold, and if necessary enforce, the security for the employer's obligations to pay the retirement or death benefits to the Directors or the contingent beneficiaries. The security arrangement would not have come into being but for the (fresh) contractual arrangement to pay retirement and death benefits to the members of the scheme. It cannot be regarded as something entirely independent; these arrangements are all part and parcel of a composite Scheme. The Trustees are acting as trustees of a pension scheme; it is one of their key duties to take steps, in appropriate circumstances, to enforce Granada's obligations to pay the benefits and those steps are not limited to realising the security.'

29.35 In *Children's Investment Fund (UK) v Attorney General*[27] it was argued at first instance that the decision in *Granada Group* applied by analogy, but Vos C preferred other arguments.

26 *Granada Group Ltd v Law Debenture Pension Trust Corporation plc* [2015] EWHC 1499 (Ch), [2015] 2 BCLC 604 (Andrews J) at [86] to [89]. Approved by the CA, [2016] EWCA Civ 1289 at [46].

27 [2017] EWHC 1379 (Ch), [2018] Ch 371 (Vos C) at [95] to [97]. Point not discussed on appeal.

30

Other trusts: Employee Share Schemes and Charities

TRUST ARISING UNDER THE SECOND GROUP OF PARTS

30.1 A 'trust arising under any of the second Group of Parts' is outside the Insolvency Act 1986 (IA 1986), s 435 trust extension. Section 435(5)(a) excludes 'a trust arising under any of the second Group of Parts or the Bankruptcy (Scotland) Act 2016'.

30.2 The second group of parts is indicated by the headings in IA 1986 to cover Parts 7A to 11, dealing with individual insolvency. This exclusion will therefore apply to a trustee in bankruptcy.

This also applies to bankruptcy in Scotland, but not seemingly a bankruptcy or equivalent in other jurisdictions.

30.3 The exclusion in s 435(5)(a) does not therefore cover any trust that can arise under the terms of a CVA (made under IA 1986, Part 1). The terms of the CVA may envisage that the assets and sums received by the supervisor are held on trust exclusively for the benefit of the CVA participants – *Re NT Gallagher & Son Ltd*[1] and *Re Leisure Study Group Ltd.*[2]

30.4 Similarly the trust that can arise under a liquidation (under *Ayerst*[3]) is not excluded by s 435(5)(a).

1 [2002] EWCA Civ 4904, [2002] 3 All ER 474 per Peter Gibson LJ at [54].
2 [1994] BCLC 65 (Harman J). Funds in the hands of a supervisor were held on trust for the company's unsecured creditors and so were not caught by a floating charge.
3 *Ayerst (Inspector of Taxes) v C&K (Construction) Ltd* [1976] AC 167, HL. Discussed in ch 53 below.

EMPLOYEES' SHARE SCHEME -- S 435(5)(B)

30.5 The term 'employees' share scheme' is defined in IA 1986, s 436:[4]

> 'employees' share scheme' means a scheme for encouraging or facilitating the holding of shares in or debentures of a company by or for the benefit of—
>
> (a) the bona fide employees or former employees of—
>
> (i) the company,
>
> (ii) any subsidiary of the company, or
>
> (iii) the company's holding company or any subsidiary of the company's holding company, or
>
> (b) the spouses, civil partners, surviving spouses, surviving civil partners, or minor children or step-children of such employees or former employees;

30.6 This definition is the same as in the Companies Act 2006.[5]

CHARITY TRUSTEES

30.7 There is no express exclusion in s 435(5) for a trustee of a charity. Note the terms 'charity trustees' and 'trusts' are given an expanded definition in Charities Act 2011, ss 177 and 353(1).

30.8 This means that if (for example) A was a director of company Z (ZCo) and A (or an associate of A) was a beneficiary under a charitable trust, with trustee T, then:

(a) T would be associated with A – under s 435(5); and

(b) By reason of T's association with A, T would also be connected with Z Co (s 249);

(c) But T would not (by reason of that link alone) be associated with ZCo, nor would ZCo be associated with T; and

(d) T would be connected with ZCo, but ZCo would not be connected with T.

4 This definition used to cross refer to the definition in the Companies Act 1985, but the definition in IA 1986, s 436 is now free standing following the changes made by the Companies Act 2006 (Consequential Amendments, Transitional Provisions and Savings Order 2009 (SI 2009/1941) from 1 October 2009.

5 CA 2006, s 1166 (formerly CA 1985, s 743).

30.9 A similar (but not identical) provision in CA 2005, s 254 was applied in relation to a member of a charitable company in *Children's Investment Fund (UK) v Attorney General.*[6] Vos C held:

> 'It matters not that the payment might not be within section 252(2)(c) [the equivalent of s 435(5)] because it is made to a company that will hold the money on trust for beneficiaries other than the director personally.'

6 [2017] EWHC 1379 (Ch), [2018] Ch 371 (Vos C) at [96] and [97].

31

Partners – s 435(3)

31.1 A person is an associate of any person with whom he, she or it[1] is in partnership – Insolvency Act 1986 (IA 1986), s 435(3).[2] A person is also an associate of the husband or wife or a relative (each as defined at Chapter 27 above) of any individual with whom he is in partnership.

> (3) A person is an associate of any person with whom he is in partnership, and of the husband or wife or civil partner or a relative of any individual with whom he is in partnership; and a Scottish firm is an associate of any person who is a member of the firm.

31.2 This association does *not* extend to relatives of the partner's spouse or spouses (or former spouses etc) of a relative or spouse of the partner.

31.3 Partnership for this purpose probably has the same meaning as in the Partnership Act 1890 (although this is not a term defined in the Interpretation Act 1978).

1 Strictly, s 435(3) refers to a 'person', usually taken as including a corporation (Interpretation Act 1978), but goes on to refer to someone 'with whom he is in partnership', using the term 'he' only. This does not seem enough to rebut the presumption that 'person' in s 435(3) refers to a corporation as well as an individual. But see Briggs and Tribe *Muir Hunter on Personal Insolvency* (Sweet & Maxwell, Looseleaf, service to March 2021) at 3-3091 noting that the point might be contended.
It is noticeable that the new formulation of s 435 for Scottish bankruptcies in the Bankruptcy (Scotland) Act 2016, s 229(5) avoids any doubt on this point by using letter designations:

> 'A person (in this subsection referred to as 'C') is an associate of any person (in this subsection referred to as 'D') with whom C is in partnership and of any person who is an associate of D'.

2 For example, in *Re Scientific Investment Pension Plan, Clark v Hicks* [1992] OPLR 185, [1992] PLR 213 (Mervyn Davies J), it was noted that a solicitor would be allowed to continue to act as an independent trustee on insolvency if he was a sole practitioner and he (or perhaps his employees) provided services to the scheme, but not if he was in partnership – because he would then be associated with his other partners. The independent trustee requirement was under Social Security Pensions Act 1975, s 57C, now PA 1995, s 22 – see ch 61 in Pollard *Corporate Insolvency: Employment and Pension Rights* (7th edn, Bloomsbury Professional, 2021).

31.4 Former partners do not continue to be associated (contrast former spouses – see s 435(8)). But persons remain partners for this purpose even though their partnership has ceased carrying on business, while they are winding up the partnership's affairs – *Goel v Pick.*[3]

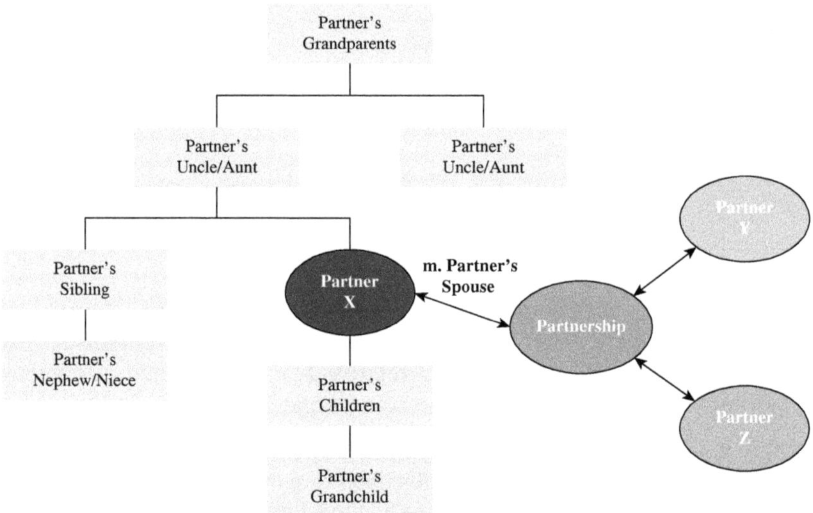

31.5 Partners Y and Z will be associates of Partner X. Partners Y and Z will also be associates of Partner X's spouse and all of Partner X's 'relatives' as shown in the diagram. Partners Y and Z will *not* be associates of the relatives of Partner X's spouse or the spouses of Partner X's 'relatives'.

31.6 This is an extension compared to the position of a company director. A director is not (without more) treated as associated with his or her fellow directors (or their spouses/relatives).

31.7 A Scottish firm[4] is an associate of any person who is a member of it – s 435(3).

31.8 The partnership provision in s 435(3) just refers to a person being a partner of another. Unlike the trustee provision in s 435(5), it does not refer to a person 'in his capacity' as a partner. The partnership provision for persons connected with a director in Companies Act 2006, s 252(2)(d) also refers to 'a person acting in the capacity as a partner'. It is not clear if the omission of this 'capacity' wording in s 435(3) has any impact (see Chapter 33 below).

3 [2006] EWHC 833 (Ch), [2007] 1 All ER 982 (Sir Francis Ferris) at [28] to [30] referring to Partnership Act 1890, s 39.

4 A Scottish firm, unlike an English partnership, is deemed to have a separate personality from its partners – Partnership Act 1890, s 4(2). An LLP under the Limited Liability Partnerships Act 2000 is a corporate body with legal personality separate from its members – s 1(2).

32

Limited liability partnerships (LLPs) – s 435(3A)

32.1 Partnership does not seem for the purpose of the Insolvency Act 1986, s 435(3) to include members of a LLP established under the Limited Liability Partnerships Act 2000. Instead the Limited Liability Partnerships Regulations 2001[1] provide for modified provisions in IA 1986 to apply to LLPs (see reg 5). These include modifications to IA 1986, ss 249 and 435.

32.2 The modifications (under reg 5) are in Sch 3 to the 2001 Regulations.

The modifications to s 249 are:

> 'For the existing words substitute
>
> "For the purposes of any provision in this Group of Parts, a person is connected with a company (including a limited liability partnership) if—
>
> (a) he is a director or shadow director of a company or an associate of such a director or shadow director (including a member or a shadow member of a limited liability partnership or an associate of such a member or shadow member); or
>
> he is an associate of the company or of the limited liability partnership."'

32.3 The modifications to s 435 are:

> 'Insert a new subsection (3A) as follows—
>
> "(3A)
>
> A member of a limited liability partnership is an associate of that limited liability partnership and of every other member of that limited liability partnership and of the husband or wife or civil partner or relative of every other member of that limited liability partnership.".

1 SI 2001/1090.

For subsection (11) there shall be substituted

"(11) In this section "company" includes any body corporate (whether incorporated in Great Britain or elsewhere); and references to directors and other officers of a company and to voting power at any general meeting of a company have effect with any necessary modifications.""

32.4 Broadly the effect of the modifications is to treat an LLP in the same way as a company, with the members being treated as directors; and to treat the members in the same way as partners.

32.5 Shadow directors are treated as including 'shadow members', defined (in reg 2) in identical terms to that used for a shadow director (save referring to a member instead of a director) ie a person in accordance with whose directions or instructions the members of the LLP are accustomed to act (but so that a person is not deemed a shadow member by reason only that the members of the LLP act on advice given by him in a professional capacity).

32.6 The new s 435(3A) under the 2001 Regulations provides that a member of an LLP is an associate of:

(a) that LLP;

(b) every other member of that LLP; and

(c) the spouse or relative of every other member of that LLP.

This is an extension compared to the position of a company director. A director is not (without more) treated as associated with his or her fellow directors (or their spouses/relatives).

33

Is the capacity of association or connection relevant?

33.1 For trustees, the Insolvency Act 1986 (IA 1986), s 435(5) refers to a trustee 'in his capacity as trustee'. This may mean that a trustee is only associated with a beneficiary where that association is somehow connected with the trust, but the effect of this is unclear. Conversely, the partnership provision in s 435(3) just refers to a person being a partner of another. Unlike the trustee provision in s 435(5), it does not refer to a person 'in his capacity' as a partner. The partnership provision for persons connected with a director in Companies Act 2006, s 252(2)(d) also refers to 'a person acting in the capacity as a partner'.

It is not clear if the inclusion (or omission) of this 'capacity' wording in s 435(3) has any impact.

33.2 It may be possible to argue that the effect of finding a person connected or associated with another for one reason (eg they are related or a director of an otherwise separate company) does not mean that they are associated (or connected) in another capacity. However, such a restrictive interpretation seem difficult to find (save in relation to trustees). Any restriction may need to be found in the underlying provision that uses the concept of association or connection.

33.3 In relation to pensions moral hazard (see Chapter 14 above), the association (or connection) is stated in some of the cases to be just a gateway condition for the relevant statutory power to apply.

For example, an agent holding property for a client could be held to be a bare trustee of that property and so associated with its client with a consequence that a CN or FSD could be made against the agent, even though the agent's involvement with the client (and the relevant pension scheme) had nothing to do with agency or the property held on trust. A reasonableness condition would usually apply under the CN and FSD provisions in addition and it would seem that this should involve looking at all the circumstances and not limited to those that caused the association or connection.

33.4 Existing caselaw on s 435 has not directly addressed this. But it seems likely that the courts would hold that the literal wording of the statute is likely only to have the relevant connection as a gateway condition and in many cases not to look at the capacity in which the association arises.

33.5 Arguably this gateway approach is supported by the cases where the courts are unwilling to take a purposive approach when determining whether or not a person falls within the definitions – see *Re Thirty-Eight Building Limited*[1] and *Box Clever.*[2]

33.6 Similarly, in *Darty Holdings*[3] Miles J rejected an argument that the association provisions should not apply against a background of the sale transaction where the connection would be severed. He held (at [92] to [97]) that the court needed to construe the words actually used in the statute, that there 'is nothing in s 435 to suggest that it should be read restrictively to exclude cases where the association was intended to come to an end shortly after the relevant transaction' and there was not a 'workable criterion for determining which cases would fall within s 435 for the purpose of ss 239–240 and those that would not.'

33.7 In relation to a similar (but not identical) provision in the Companies Act 2006, s 254, a similar wide approach was applied in relation to a transfer envisaged to be made to a company connected with a member of a charitable company. In *Children's Investment Fund (UK) v Attorney General*[4] at first instance Vos C held that it did not matter that the relevant transfer was to a new charitable company that would hold the proceeds on a charitable trust that would not benefit the member of the first company.

33.8 Conversely, there may however be an analogy with *Wilson v Masters International Ltd Re Oxford Pharmaceuticals Ltd*[5] a case on preferences under IA 1986, s 239. Mark Cawson QC held (at [70]) that the preference of a creditor must arise in their capacity as a creditor and not in some other capacity.

33.9 On the facts, Mark Cawson QC held (at [72] and [73]) that the payments to the parent company (which it on-paid to the bank to reduce its indebtedness to the bank) did not (on the facts) have the effect of being a sufficient benefit to Dr Masters (as a guarantor of the obligations to the bank). This was because the bank was, and remained fully covered by the other relevant security (cross guarantees and charges over book debts) and so Dr Masters was in no different position as against the bank had no payments been made.

1 [1999] 1 BCLC 416 (Hazel Williamson QC, sitting as a deputy High Court judge).

2 *Granada UK Rental & Retail Ltd v The Pensions Regulator* [2019] EWCA Civ 1032, [2020] ICR 747 at [126]: 'an elaborate provision'. See 9.9 above.

3 *Darty Holdings SAS v Carton-Kelly* [2021] EWHC 1018 (Ch) (Miles J) at [109]. See ch 41 below.

4 [2017] EWHC 1379 (Ch), [2018] Ch 371 (Vos C) at [96] and [97].

5 [2009] EWHC 1753 (Ch), [2009] 2 BCLC 485 (Mark Cawson QC, sitting as a judge of the High Court).

33.10 In a slightly different context, it has been held that the duties of shadow director only relate to matters where they have given instructions. In *Standish v The Royal Bank of Scotland Plc*[6] Trower J held:

> '[55] It is therefore quite clear that section 170 of the 2006 Act cannot be read as imposing the full range of fiduciary duties owed by a de jure director on somebody merely because they have acquired the status of a shadow director. Put another way, because the status of shadow directorship can be acquired through the giving of instructions that are limited to only some part of a company's activities or affairs, there can be commensurable limitations on the nature and extent of the duties that they will thereby owe.
>
> [56] It also follows that the extent of any fiduciary duty owed by a person who is in the position of being a shadow director will reflect the extent and nature of the instructions that he gives. Those acts of instruction are the basis of the relationship between him and the company (and its de jure directors). Fiduciary duties flow from relationships and it necessarily follows that when shadow directorship (and nothing else) is relied on as the source of the fiduciary duty, it is only those acts of instruction which can form the foundation for any fiduciary duties that he may owe.
>
> [57] Thus, where any instructions are pervasive and all-encompassing, extending over the full range of the directors' decision-making, it is possible that the shadow director may owe fiduciary duties across the entire range of the company's activities. In other instances, the extent and nature of the instructions may be more restricted, being limited to particular aspects of the company's business or affairs. It seems to me that it follows that, where there is no relationship between the instruction and the act or omission of which complaint is made, it would be wrong in principle for any fiduciary duty to be owed. There is no principled basis on which a person whose shadow directorship arises out of unrelated matters ought thereby to be treated as having committed a breach of duty.'

6 [2019] EWHC 3116 (Ch), [2020] 1 BCLC 826 at [55].

34

Associate – companies

34.1 As discussed above, references to companies in the Insolvency Act 1986 (IA 1986), s 435 include overseas companies and catch any body corporate – s 435(11). On limited liability partnerships (LLPs) see Chapter 32 above.

34.2 A company is an associate of another company:

(a) if one company controls the other company; or

(b) if the same person has 'control' of both; or

(c) if a person (A) has control of one and persons who are associates of A, or A together with persons who are his associates, have control of the other; or

(d) if a group of two or more persons has control of each company, and the groups either consist of the same persons or could be regarded as consisting of the same persons by treating (in one or more cases) a member of either group as replaced by a person of whom he is an associate.

(IA 1986, ss 435(6) and (7)).

34.3 A company can also be an associate of another company if one of the other limbs in s 435 applies, for example if:

(a) the first company is in partnership with the second – s 435(3); or

(b) the first company is the trustee of a trust (other than an excluded trust) of which the second is a beneficiary (s 435(5), discussed at Chapter 28 above).

There is no reason in principle why a company cannot be a partner of another[1] or a trustee.[2]

1 *Ashbury Railway Carriage and Iron Co Ltd v Riche* (1875) LR 7 HL 653, *Pinkey v Sandpiper Drilling Ltd* [1989] ICR 389, EAT; *Newstead v Frost* [1980] 1 WLR 135; *Hogar Estates Ltd in Trust v Shebron Holdings Ltd* (1979) 25 OR (2d) 543; *Re European Society Arbitration Acts* (1878) 8 Ch D 679 at [704], CA. Cited on this in Blackett-Ord and Haren *Partnership Law* (6th edn, Bloomsbury Professional, 2020) at 3.2.

2 For a company being sole trustee of a trust, see *Attorney-General v Landerfield* (1744) 9 Mod. 286 and *Attorney-General v St John's Hospital Bedford* (1865) 2 DJ&S 621, 635 cited in *In re Thompson's Settlement Trusts* [1905] 1 Ch 229 (Swinfen Eady J).

There was an issue with a company being a trustee jointly with others before 1899. This was because it was impossible for a company to be a joint tenant with a natural person as the company could not die – *Law Guarantee and Trust Society Ltd v Bank of England.*[3] This issue was cured by the Bodies Corporate (Joint Tenancy) Act 1899.[4]

34.4 Similarly, if one company is a beneficiary under a trust where the other is trustee – s 435(5). A formal trustee/beneficiary relationships between companies set out in a formal written declaration of trust may be easier to spot than an informal trustee/beneficiary relationship (eg a resulting trust or constructive trust, or a bare trust as part of a transaction – eg a trust receipt in a shipping transaction.

34.5 From the above it follows that, looking at a group of companies (ie a parent and its subsidiaries):

(a) all companies in a *wholly owned* group of companies will be associates of each other and hence connected with each other; and

(b) all companies in a *non-wholly-owned group* will usually be associated with each other where the relevant group shareholding is *one-third* or more of the voting power;

(c) companies will be associated if under common 'control' of an individual or associated persons.

EXAMPLES OF ASSOCIATED COMPANIES

34.6 The chart below looks at a group of companies:

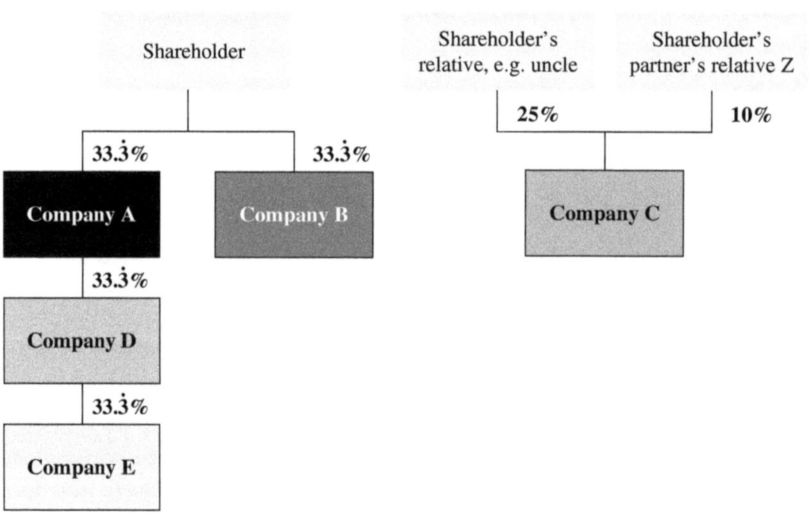

3 (1890) 24 QBD 406 (Mathew J) at 411.

4 *In re Thompson's Settlement Trusts* [1905] 1 Ch 229 (Swinfen Eady J) at 232. Discussed in *Jasmine Trustees Ltd v Wells & Hind* [2007] EWHC 38 (Ch) , [2008] Ch 194 (Mann J) at [12].

Companies A, B, C, D and E are all 'associates' of each other and hence connected with each other under IA 1986, s 249(b):

(a) *Company A*: a shareholder (X) owns one third of the voting stock of each of companies A and B. Therefore X has 'control' of both company A and company B. As the same person has 'control' of both companies, company A and company B are associates[5] – IA 1986, s 435(7).

(b) *Company D*: X owns one third of the voting stock of company A, which in turn owns one third of the voting stock of company D. X has control of company A and company A has control of company D. Therefore, X has control of company D – IA 1986, s 435(10)(b).

Because X has 'control' of each of company D, company A and company B, all three companies are associates of each other. Company C would also be an associate of A, B and D (see below).

(c) *Company E*: Company A owns one third of the voting stock of company D, which in turn owns one third of the voting stock of company E. Company A has control of company D and company D has control of company E. Therefore, company A has control of company E.

(d) X has control of one-third of the votes in company A and so s 435(10)(b) applies in that X 'controls the exercise of one-third or more of the voting power at any general meeting of … another company [that is, company A] which has control of' company E. So X controls company E and is associated with company E.

(e) *Company A*: company D and company E are associates of each other. Companies A and B and company D are associates of X (see below). Company A and company D both have control of company E. Therefore, as company A and company D are associates of X and X also has control of company B, company B and company E are associates.

(f) *Company C*: no one individual has control of the company. However, as Y and Z together hold over one third of the voting power together they together they have control of the company. As they are both 'associates' of X, company C is an associate of companies A and B and subsidiaries D and E because X has control of these companies. However, as Y and Z are not associates of each other, they are probably not themselves associates of company C (see discussion of s 435(10) in Part 7 below).

5 For an example of this, see *Clements (liquidator of HHO Licensing Ltd) v Henry Hadaway Organisation Ltd* [2007] EWHC 2953 (Ch), [2008] 1 BCLC 22 (Peter Leaver QC).

PART 7

CONTROL

35

'Control' as defined in s 435(10)

35.1 The definition of 'control' for the purposes of s 435 is contained in the Insolvency Act 1986 (IA 1986), s 435(10):

> **435.** (10) For the purposes of this section a person is to be taken as having control of a company if—
>
> (a) the directors of the company or of another company which has control of it (or any of them) are accustomed to act in accordance with his directions or instructions, or
>
> (b) he is entitled to exercise, or control the exercise of, one third or more of the voting power at any general meeting of the company or of another company which has control of it;
>
> and where two or more persons together satisfy either of the above conditions, they are to be taken as having control of the company.

There are two limbs to the control test in s 435(10). Limb (b), looking at voting power, is examined in Part 8 below. Limb (a), looking at 'domination' of the directors, is looked at in Part 9 below.

35.2 The definition in s 435(10) is incorporated by reference in some other legislation – eg the Pensions Act 2004 (PA 2004), s 38(7)(b) (relevant factor for a CN including whether a person had control of the employer) and a relinquishing control is a notifiable event under the regulations made under PA 2004, s 69[1] (see Chapter 16 above).

1 The Pensions Regulator (Notifiable Events) Regulations 2005 (SI 2005/900), reg 2(2)(f). The term 'controlling company' is construed accordingly – reg 1(2).

USES OF THE CONTROL TEST IN S 435(10)

35.3 Control can only apply to a company. The concept of control under s 435 does not apply to an individual. An individual can control a company, but a person cannot control an individual.

35.4 Control, as defined in s 435(10), is important in a variety of places:

(a) A person (individual/company) controlling an employer company will be an associate of the employer.

(b) The chain principle (see 2.8 above) applies to control:

- if A controls B; and B controls C; and C controls D; then
- A controls C and D (and is associated with both C and D) and so on.

(c) Control is not limited to shareholding.

(d) Control is one of the factors to be considered by TPR when looking at reasonableness for a CN – PA 2004, s 37(7)(b).

(e) A decision to relinquish control is a notifiable event to the Pensions Regulator – PA 2004, s 69 and Notification Regulations 2005,[2] reg 2(2). But this notification obligation does not apply if the scheme is funded to the PPF level and there has been no materially significant failure by the employer to pay contributions in last 12 months.

DERIVED FROM THE COMPANIES ACT 1967?

35.5 The test for control in s 435(10) looks very similar to the test formerly found in the Companies Act 1967 (CA 1967) dealing with declaration by directors of their interests in shares of the company. CA 1967, s 28(3) stated:

> '(3) A person shall be deemed to be interested in shares or debentures if a body corporate is interested in them and:
>
> (a) that body corporate or its directors are accustomed to act in accordance with his directions or instructions; or
>
> (b) he is entitled to exercise or control the exercise of one third or more of the voting power at any general meeting of that body corporate.'

The provision in CA 1967 dealing with declarations of interests in shares by directors was followed in later Companies Acts, ending up with ss 324–326 and 328 and 329 of CA 1985, but this requirement was repealed by the Companies Act 2006 (CA 2006).

35.6 CA 2006, s 255 does include a definition of a director 'controlling' a body corporate' for the purposes of Part 1 of CA 2006. This includes similar

2 The Pensions Regulator (Notifiable Event) Regulations 2005 (SI 2005/900).

wording on the exercise of voting power limb. CA 2006, s 255(2)(a)(ii) refers to a person who 'is entitled to exercise or control the exercise of any part of the voting power at any general meeting …'.

35.7 Conversely para 5 of Sch 1 to CA 2006 (dealing with connected persons) uses slightly different wording, referring to 'voting power at general meetings' (ie leaving out the word 'any').

PART 8

CONTROL THROUGH VOTING POWER – S 435(10)(B)

36

Voting power – *Unidare* and *Box Clever* cases

36.1 Limb (b) of the Insolvency Act 1986 (IA 1986), s 435(10) provides for 'control' to apply using a test relating to 'voting power':

> '435(10) For the purposes of this section a person is to be taken as having control of a company if—
>
> …
>
> he is *entitled to exercise*, or *control the exercise of*, one third or more of the *voting power* at any general meeting of the company or of another company which has control of it;
>
> *and where two or more persons together satisfy either of the above conditions, they are to be taken as having control of the company*.' (emphasis added)

Two main cases consider this voting power limb in s 435(10)(b): *Unidare v Cohen*[1] and, more recently the Court of Appeal in *Box Clever*.[2]

36.2 The 2005 case of *Re Kilnoore Ltd (in liquidation), Unidare plc v Cohen*,[3] involved a shareholder holding shares on a bare trust for a third party purchaser. The parties intended the shares to be transferred – they just had not completed all the necessary steps at the time.

36.3 In *Unidare*, Lewison J held that the use of the phrase '*voting power*' in s 435, rather than '*voting rights*' as used for the definition of 'subsidiary' in ss 736 and 736A, Companies Act 1985,[4] was significant. This gave him 'some encouragement to look to the economic reality of the case'. He noted:

> 'A registered shareholder who holds his shares on a bare trust under which he is required to cast his vote in accordance with the directions of the beneficial owner might be said to have voting rights, but I do not consider that in any real sense he can be said to have voting power'.

1 [2005] EWHC 1410 (Ch), [2006] Ch 489, [2005] 3 All ER 730 (Lewison J).
2 *Granada UK Rental & Retail Ltd v The Pensions Regulator* [2019] EWCA Civ 1032, [2020] ICR 747, [2019] Pens LR 20.
3 [2005] EWHC 1410 (Ch), [2006] Ch 489, [2005] 3 All ER 730 (Lewison J).
4 See now Companies Act 2006 (CA 2006), s 1159.

36.4 However, in 2019 in *Box Clever* the Court of Appeal disagreed on this point with Lewison J's judgment in *Unidare.* It held that this approach did not give sufficient weight to the terms of s 435(10), in particular the Court of Appeal considered that the registered holder of the shares remained entitled to exercise the relevant voting power, despite any voting agreement with a third party.

36.5 The Court of Appeal held that the use of the term 'voting power' did not take matters further. There seemed to be no difference between voting power and voting rights:

> '[128] Lewison J attached some significance to the reference to "voting power" in s.435(10)(b) IA 1986. The word "power" gave him "some encouragement to look to the economic reality of the case" (see [58]). In our view, however, the use of the word "power" takes matters no further. "[V]oting power" is apt to refer simply to the sum of the voting rights attached to the issued shares. It may be that the draftsman could have substituted "voting rights", but nothing can be inferred from his choice. It is notable that "voting rights" and "voting power" were used interchangeably in the *Bibby* case, especially in Lord Simonds' speech.'

36.6 The Court of Appeal went on to hold that the registered holder (in a mortgage situation) remained 'entitled to exercise' the relevant voting power:

> '129. In all the circumstances, we respectfully take a different view from Lewison J. As we see it, a person registered as the holder of shares carrying a third or more of the total votes attaching to the relevant company's issued shares, and so as between himself and the company "entitled to exercise … one third or more of the voting power", is also to be considered to be so entitled within the meaning of s.435(10)(b) IA 1986 and, hence, an associate of the company.
>
> 130. In the present case, it would doubtless have been the Administrative Receivers rather than THSP's directors who would have decided how the company's shares in TUK should be voted had there been a general meeting on 31 December 2009. That, however, is neither here nor there. The Administrative Receivers would have been voting in THSP's name and on its behalf. It was THSP that was "entitled to exercise" the voting power and it is, accordingly, to be taken as having had control of TUK and so an associate of it. That the Administrative Receivers were also, presumably, associates of TUK is immaterial.'

36.7 The *Box Clever* approach seems to mandate regarding the 'voting power' test as applying to look at both the registered holder ('entitled to exercise') and any contractual party ('entitled to … control the exercise') as having the voting power of the relevant shares.

36.8 This could mean that both have 'control' at the same time. This is of course possible anyway given the one-third requirement. Even without a voting agreement, three shareholders each holding one third of the voting shares would each be treated as having control.

36.9 Obviously, as between the company and the registered shareholder, it is the registered shareholder that exercises the relevant voting rights. Generally trusts and other interests are not reflected on the share register (see CA 2006, s 126, Art 45 in CA 2006 Model Articles[5] and reg 5 in 1985 Table A[6]). This was mentioned by Lewison J in *Unidare* at [37].

VOTING POWER – *BOX CLEVER*

36.10 Registered shareholders will be treated as having voting power and so can be 'associated' with company even if they are holding the relevant shares on trust or as security. The Court of Appeal in *Box Clever* changed the position from that following *Unidare*.

36.11 The Court of Appeal in the *Box Clever* case, *Granada UK Rental & Retail Ltd v The Pensions Regulator*[7] considered when a registered shareholder (eg a custodian or nominee), or person holding power over voting (eg a lender with security over shares) will, if the relevant shares represent one-third or more of the voting rights at any general meeting of the company, be taken as having 'control' of the underlying company (for the purposes of the Insolvency Act definition).

36.12 The Court of Appeal overturned *Unidare* where Lewison J had held that a registered shareholder holding the shares on trust for a third party (with the third party having power to direct the shareholder how to vote) did not 'control' the relevant shares and so was not 'associated' with the company.

36.13 This was a major shift in what was previously thought to be the position. It means that registered shareholders (such as nominees and custodians) will fall within the 'control' definition in s 435(10)(b) even though they do not exercise the relevant voting rights attaching to the shares (save at the direction of a third party). Any person who itself 'controls' the registered shareholder will then also be treated as controlling the company. For example a bank which owns more than one-third of the shares in the custodian or security agent will be an 'associate' of the underlying company.

36.14 In the *Box Clever* case,[8] the Court was looking at whether holding companies remained in 'control' for s 435 purposes of an employer subsidiary where a debenture had been granted over the relevant shares (including a fixed mortgage) and the underlying company had entered administrative receivership.

5 Schedule 3 to the Companies (Model Articles) Regulations 2008 (SI 2008/3229).

6 Schedule to the Companies (Tables A to F) Regulations 1985 (SI 1985/805).

7 [2019] EWCA Civ 1032, [2020] ICR 747, [2019] Pens LR 20. Leave to appeal to the Supreme Court was refused in February 2020. Discussed in Wilkins, 'Granada Rental v The Pensions Regulator: the Court of Appeal considers the power to issue financial support directions' (2021) 18(1) International Corporate Rescue, 70.

8 *Granada UK Rental & Retail Ltd v The Pensions Regulator* [2019] EWCA Civ 1032, [2020] ICR 747, [2019] Pens LR 20.

36.15 The Court of Appeal held that the original chargor did retain control for s 435 purposes (the debenture dealt expressly with voting issues and it was held that this applied to leave control with the chargor even where some of the shares were registered in the name of the security agent). The Court of Appeal extended the ambit of control in s 435(10), overruling the previous main authority on this point, *Unidare*.

36.16 The Court of Appeal held that there is a two-limb test in s 435(10)(b). A person is taken as being able to exercise voting power in shares if that person is 'entitled to exercise, or control the exercise of, one third or more of the voting power at any general meeting'. The Court of Appeal held that this meant there are two limbs. A person will have control if he, she or it is either:

(a) 'entitled to exercise … voting power'; or

(b) 'entitled to … control the exercise of … voting power'.

36.17 The Court of Appeal held that the first limb applies to registered holder of shares, but the second limb can apply to a person with a voting arrangement with registered shareholder.

36.18 It seems inevitable from this that two persons can each be treated as holding the voting power in one set of shares.

36.19 So in the *Box Clever* case, the targets were held to have retained control (on the relevant date) of the employers by virtue of the shares in the employers, even where the shares had been registered in the name of the security agent. Under the debenture, the parent companies retained the ability to direct the security agent on how to vote the shares.

36.20 The Court of Appeal did not expressly deal with the position of the security agent (it was not one of the targets of an FSD by the Pensions Regulator), but the effect of the Court of Appeal judgment is clearly that the security agent will be treated as having control under s 435(10)(b) by reason of being the registered owner of the shares. This will apply despite the terms of the debenture giving the parent company chargor the ability to direct how the shares are voted (at least until a notice was given).

36.21 The Court of Appeal noted that 'control' in s 435 does not necessarily need actual control in the sense of a need for a majority of votes,

> 'it would seem that a person could be deemed to have control in the context of IA 1986 if, say, he held just 35% of the shares in a company which in turn held 35% in a company holding 35% in another company with a 35% holding in a yet further company. Plainly, Parliament did not wish s.435(10) (and thus s.435(7)) to bite only on people or entities who control a company in practical terms. It was evidently Parliament's intention that s.435(7), and the term 'associate' more generally, should have a wide meaning for the purposes of, for example, the preference and transaction at an undervalue provisions (see e.g. ss.239(6), 240(1)(a) and 249(b) IA 1986).' [126]

36.22 The Court of Appeal ultimately upheld the decision of the Determination Panel of the Regulator to issue FSDs. ITV/Granada was refused leave to appeal to the Supreme Court in February 2020 and the FSDs were subsequently issued.

36.23 In *Darty Holdings*,[9] at first instance,[10] Deputy ICC Judge Agnello QC considered *Unidare* and *Box Clever*, holding that the Court of Appeal decision on this point, even if technically obiter, should be followed:

> '[48] Mr Strong invited me to consider that the passages above are in reality obiter because effectively, the decision relating to the administrative receivers being entitled to exercise the vote did not arise in *Unidare* (referred to in the Court of Appeal as *Kilnoore*). Moreover, he submitted that this part of the judgment was also obiter by reason of the decision in relation to the other three employer companies in relation to the terms of the debenture. In my judgment, the Court of Appeal gave a clear and reasoned judgment which included consideration of the decision in *Unidare*. In so far as it took a different view from that taken by Mr Justice Lewison in *Unidare*, this was in relation to those who hold as bare trustees. As I have already set out above, KHL is not a bare trustee and does not argue before me that it is in the same exceptional and extreme case of a bare trustee. What the decision in Box Clever does, is conclude that even a bare trustee is caught under section 435(10)(b). In my judgment as I have already set out above, Mr Strong's reliance upon *Unidare* fails because KHL's position was not one of a bare trustee and the passages of Mr Justice Lewison relating to those in KHL's position, having contractual or fiduciary restraints apply. However, the Court of Appeal in *Box Clever* makes it clear that the provision is actually wider than Mr Justice Lewison considered because even bare trusteeships are caught as being entitled to exercise a voting power. In those circumstances, I cannot see how KHL is able to assert that it is not connected pursuant to section 435(10) (b). Regardless as to whether the passages I have set out above can be said to be obiter, Mr Strong's argument fails both in relation to his reliance on *Unidare* and any "last gasp" in his argument fails under *Box Clever*. I am not prepared to ignore the passages I have set out above from *Box Clever* but even if I were so minded, as I have made clear above, the argument based on *Unidare* fails in any event.'

CHILDREN'S INVESTMENT

36.24 In *Children's Investment Fund (UK) v Attorney General*[11] Vos C held that an individual, Miss Cooper who was the only member of a charitable company, BWP, which was limited by guarantee, was connected with BWP for the purpose of CA 2006, s 254(2)(b), (which, save for the relevant percentage, has very similar wording to IA 1986, s 435(10)(a) on the voting power point).

9 *Darty Holdings SAS v Carton-Kelly* [2021] EWHC 1018 (Ch) (Miles J) at [109]. See ch 41 below.

10 *Re CGL Realisations Ltd* [2020] EWHC 1707 (Ch) (Deputy ICC Judge Agnello QC).

11 [2017] EWHC 1379 (Ch), [2018] Ch 371 at [98].

36.25 Vos C held that this was not affected by the fact that the charitable company would apply any payment to it (the 'Grant') for charitable purposes and not for the benefit of the member. He held:

> '[98] … the relevant subsection, section 254(2)(b), provides that a director is connected with a body corporate if, but only if, she and the persons connected with her are "entitled to exercise or control the exercise of more than 20% of the voting power at any general meeting of that body".
>
> [99] As it seems to me, the answer to this latter question is simple. It is unaffected by Ms Cooper's somewhat convoluted arguments that she cannot properly be regarded as exercising the members' voting power of BWP because of its exclusively charitable objects, the controls in section 201 of the Charities Act 2011, or the ringfencing of the uses to which the Grant can be put. The fact is that Ms Cooper is the only member of BWP, which is a company limited by guarantee without a share capital. She is, therefore, entitled to exercise or control the exercise of 100% of the voting power in BWP at any general meeting of BWP. It, therefore, seems to me that the Grant will be a payment for loss of office to Ms Cooper within the proper meanings of subsections 215(1)(c), 215(3)(a), 252(2)(b) and 254(2)(b). It will, therefore, require the approval of a resolution passed by the members of CIFF [the transferor charitable company], subject to the following issues that the court must determine.'

This point was not discussed in the subsequent appeals to the Court of Appeal and the Supreme Court.

37

Voting power – Nominees and custodians

37.1 If a company (A Co) 'controls' a company (Z Co) and A Co is itself controlled (eg wholly owned) by B Co, the Insolvency Act 1986 (IA 1986), s 435(10) applies so that B Co is treated as 'controlling' Z Co as well (and so is 'associated' with Z Co). Other members of B Co's group would also be treated as associated with Z Co.

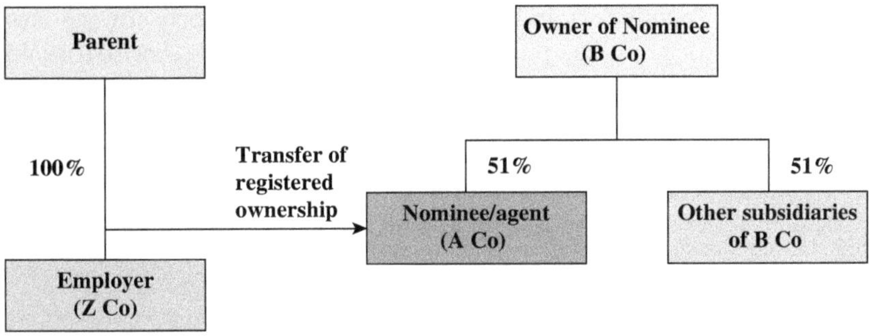

A Co 's 435 controls' Z Co by reason of its registered holding of 100% of the shares in Z Co.

This means that B Co also 's 435 controls' Z Co and any other companies 's 435 controlled' by B Co (eg its other subsidiaries) are each 's 435 associated' with Z Co.

CUSTODIANS AND SECURITY HOLDERS?

37.2 What happens where interests in shares (say in a wholly-owned employer subsidiary) are held by parties other than the parent company? For example:

- where a custodian or nominee is the registered shareholder of the shares in the employer subsidiary (but on trust for the parent); or

- where a lender takes a fixed mortgage or charge over shares in the employer subsidiary (sometimes with the shares then being registered in the name of the lender or a security agent so the mortgage is a legal security, as opposed to equitable).

37.3 If the custodian or nominee is the registered shareholder of the shares in the employer subsidiary, the decision of the Court of Appeal in *Box Clever*[1] means that the custodian will be considered to have 'control' of the employer subsidiary within s 435. This means that the custodian (and members of the same group of companies as the custodian) will also be 'associated' with the employer subsidiary.

37.4 The tax and company law rules in such circumstances are much clearer. Generally bare trust or security claims are ignored (at least prior to an enforcement event) leaving the original owner still treated as owning the shares or the voting power – eg for group accounting purposes.

For example, in the definition of subsidiary under the Companies Act 2006 (CA 2006), Sch 6, paras 5 and 6 (nominees or fiduciaries) and para 7 (security) or for the purposes of working out who has 'significant control' – CA 2006, Sch 1B, para 19 (nominees) and para 23 (security). Similarly for the issue of 'control' as used for group tax purposes – eg Corporation Tax Act 2010, s 451(3) (right or powers exercisable at someone else's direction to be attributed to that person), also used in Income Tax Act 2007, s 994(1).

37.5 The Insolvency Act definition of 'control' in s 435(10) is not so sophisticated. It does not expressly deal with trust or security rights.

IMPLICATIONS FOR CUSTODIANS

37.6 In practice for custodians or trustees who end up being registered shareholders in a company (and hold shares carrying over one-third of the votes), they will satisfy the control test in s 435(10). This means that they (and any entity that in turn 'controls' them or is under common 'control' etc) will be associated with the underlying company and so potentially at risk of the relevant insolvency and pensions issues noted above.

37.7 In theory this could even be the case for a listed company, if the relevant custodian ends up holding shares with more than one-third of the votes.

1 *Granada UK Rental & Retail Ltd v The Pensions Regulator* [2019] EWCA Civ 1032. See ch 36 above.

37.8 In practice it may be unlikely that a pure nominee or trustee would satisfy the other tests for an FSD order (eg that the Pensions Regulator considers it reasonable to issue an order), but

- a controlling entity of the custodian or security agent (eg a bank) could, depending on what has happened, have had significant involvement with the underlying company (by virtue of the relevant lending arrangements and security) and so be potentially within the Pension Regulator's sights as a target, if 'associate' status can be shown (lenders are probably not as such usually associates, unless they step over a shadow director line);
- these further conditions for FSDs do not apply in all cases (eg the limits on employer-related investment do not seem to depend on knowledge by the trustee or fund manager of the association).

37.9 The lack of a coherent exclusion for trust holdings in s 435 could raise issues for pension trustees with significant shareholdings in a company.

(a) If a pension trustee company is a subsidiary of the employer and holds shares (as an investment under the pension trust) in another company which give the pension trustee company control of that other company, then this will mean that the shares in the other company are likely to count as employer-related investment.

(b) This is because the trustee company controls the investment company and the employer 'controls' the trustee company, so that the employer 'controls the investment company. So the shares in the investment company potentially count as employer-related investment,

(c) The trustee company would need to check that the relevant employer-related investment limits in Pensions Act 1995, s 40 are not infringed (see Chapter 15 above).

38

Share mortgages

38.1 A person ('security holder') (eg a bank or security trustee) holding the benefit of a mortgage or charge over all the issued shares[1] in a company could become 'connected with' or an 'associate of' the company solely by virtue of having that charge.[2] This is because the security holder could be held to have 'control' over the voting power in the company conferred by the shares.[3]

38.2 It may be a feature of a security package that the security holder will have a mortgage or charge over shares of the borrower (and other companies in the group). This could be:

- a legal mortgage (ie with the shares transferred into (and registered in) the name of the security holder or its nominee); or
- an equitable mortgage or charge (where the shares remain registered in the name of the parent, but a security document has been signed and blank transfers and/or a power of attorney given to the security holder).

38.3 Some comfort was, before *Box Clever*, available from Lewison J's judgment in *Unidare*[4] (that the use of the phrase '*voting power*' in the Insolvency Act 1986 (IA 1986), s 435, rather than '*voting rights*' in the Companies Act 1985 (CA 1985), ss 736 and 736A was significant.

EQUITABLE MORTGAGE

38.4 Where the security is equitable (rather than legal), the security holder (mortgagee) will not be the registered holder of the securities – these will remain held in the name of the mortgagor/current owner.

1 Control of one-third or more of the voting power is all that is needed. But in many cases the charged shares will be of a wholly-owned subsidiary, so will all be charged.
2 See also Griffiths and Clark, 'Not so clever? The potential dangers of taking security over shares' (2012) 6 JIBFL 351.
3 It is noticeable that both SIP 13 and SIP 16 exclude from the connected or related party provisions in those SIPs a secured lender who controls one-third or more of the shares in the insolvent company 'as part of the secured lender's normal business activities'.
4 [2005] EWHC 1410 (Ch) (Lewison J) at [58].

If, in addition, the terms of the charge make it clear that the mortgagor (parent) can exercise the voting rights attached to the shares unless and until (say) an event of default occurs or is declared, it seems likely that, until such an event of default does occur, the mortgagor (parent) retains the voting rights and voting power and so remains associated with the subsidiary, but the mortgagee (security holder) does not. This would mean that the mortgagor (parent) remains in control of the underlying company/subsidiary (and so 'connected with' or an 'associate of' that company), but that the mortgagee (security holder) does not.

38.5 This is on the basis that there is no current 'entitlement' in the mortgagee (security holder) before the occurrence of an event of default. Section 435(10) uses the present tense, ie the person '*is* entitled to exercise, or control the exercise of … the voting power'.

38.6 Once an event of default is declared or has taken effect, the security document may provide that the mortgagee (security holder) becomes entitled to exercise, or control the exercise of, one third or more of the voting power at any general meeting. On such exercise, the mortgagee will fall within the net of association.

38.7 Formal loan documentation will often involve a cascading timeline:

- occurrence of an event of default;
- borrower obligation to tell Lenders;
- lender ability to declare acceleration (eg loan becomes immediately due and payable/ obligation to make further advances ends).

38.8 Security holders will often want to ensure that the voting powers are not *automatically* triggered on the simple occurrence of an event of default under the finance documentation. An event of default could be a simple factual event (eg default in some other agreement). If the occurrence of such an event brought about automatic change (rather than giving the lenders the right to take action) there could be unintended consequences (for example in the context of the moral hazard pensions legislation).

Such an approach would be consistent with the approach in the financial services legislation. FSMA 2000, s 422[5] defines 'control' by reference to voting power and expressly includes voting power of shares held by a person (H) by way of collateral, but 'provided that H controls the voting power and declares an intention to exercise it' – s 422(5)(a)(iii). The implication seems to be that if H has not made the relevant declaration then H is not treated as having the relevant voting power.

5 See 5.25 above. The relevant legislation is set out in Appendix C to this book.

LEGAL MORTGAGE

38.9 The same analysis can be applied to a legal mortgage (where the security holder or its nominee will become registered holder of the shares) if there is provision in the mortgage document dealing with exercise of voting rights and powers by the mortgagor (parent).

38.10 Here the security holder will be the person registered as the holder of the shares and so the one prima facie entitled to exercise the voting and other rights attached to the shares (articles of association generally envisage that companies can ignore any other interests in shares – see eg reg 5 of 1985 Table A[6]) .

38.11 But the legal mortgagee/security holder, although the registered holder of shares, will often contractually agree in the lending documents not to be entitled to exercise, or control the exercise of, the voting rights or powers. Following *Unidare*, but before *Box Clever*, it would only be on an event of acceleration that the mortgagee will become entitled to or control the exercise the voting power of the shares.

ABILITY TO DECLARE AN EVENT OF DEFAULT/ACCELERATION?

38.12 The position is more difficult if the mortgagee/security holder becomes entitled to declare an acceleration and so (under the terms of the mortgage document) to trigger control of the exercise of voting power by the mortgage/ security holder to the exclusion of the mortgagor/borrower. It could be argued that this power to declare an acceleration could mean that, even before it has been declared, the mortgagee/security holder is 'entitled to … control the exercise of … the voting power'.[7]

38.13 Antony Zacaroli did so in the footnote to former para H5-03 in the looseleaf book '*Insolvency*',[8] commenting that the taking of blank transfers may be said to give control, but that taking a charge over shares in a holding company would not give control over shares in a subsidiary.

38.14 This may well be too cautious (it is difficult to see why, if the security holder has control over the parent, it does not have control of the subsidiary). It would be clearer if the security document expressly provided for voting rights to remain with the chargor/borrower (rather than passing to the security holder) until an actual acceleration (or trigger of power to exercise voting power) had been declared by the security holder.

6 See also CA 1985, s 360 and CA 2006, s 126.
7 See Segal, Totty and Moss, *Insolvency* (Sweet & Maxwell) at page H5/3.
8 See Segal, Totty and Moss, *Insolvency* (Sweet & Maxwell).

BOX CLEVER

38.15 In June 2020 in the *Box Clever* case,[9] the Court of Appeal upheld the decision of the Upper Tribunal, including its treatment of share mortgages over the employers on whether the target ITV companies remained associated with the employers.

38.16 The security granted by the Box Clever companies to the banks included provision for the shares in the five employer companies (all subsidiaries of Box Clever Technology Limited, the holding company) to be mortgaged to the security agent (JP Morgan). In 2005, the shares in three of the employers were transferred to JP Morgan so that it became the registered holder of the shares.

38.17 The DP noted that the evidence about ownership and voting powers was not full but held that the security agent held the shares as mortgagee, so that the beneficial ownership remained with the relevant Box Clever companies.

38.18 The Court of Appeal interpreted the voting provisions in the bank security document as meaning that the Box Clever companies retained a right to vote the shares (or direct the security agent how to vote the shares) even though a 'Declared Default' had occurred in September 2003 (when the administrative receivers were appointed). The Court of Appeal decided at that this meant that the Box Clever holding companies retained 'control' of the employers and so the ITV companies (as 50% shareholders in Box Clever Technology Limited) remained associated with the employers.

38.19 The Court of Appeal held that the ability of the security agent to serve notice removing the Box Clever companies power to exercise votes did not mean that control had passed away from the Box Clever holding company to the security agent (at least before such a notice was given).

IMPLICATIONS FOR SHARE MORTGAGES

38.20 If a parent (or large shareholder) grants a mortgage over shares, one issue for the lender will be whether to agree to leave the shares registered in the name of the charger (ie an equitable security) or whether to arrange for the registered owner to become the lender (or a nominee or agent for the lender (a legal mortgage). The two approaches can result in different priorities. In either case, the relevant security document will usually deal with whether the charger can continue to exercise the voting rights attaching to the shares (whether retained in the name of the chargor or registered in the name of the lender).

38.21 The Court of Appeal decision in *Box Clever* means that a significant impact of taking a legal mortgage over all the shares in a company is that the

9 *Granada UK Rental & Retail Ltd v The Pensions Regulator* [2019] EWCA Civ 1032, [2020] ICR 747, [2019] Pens LR 20.

lender/nominee will become registered holder of the shares and so an associate of the company, even if the chargor retains the power to direct how the shares are voted (at least up to an event or default or notice from the lender) – see 36.16 above.

38.22 This issue will not apply if the chargor retains the registered shareholding and is less likely to apply (as in some of the cases in *Box Clever*) if the chargor expressly keeps the relevant power to vote the shares (at least until a voting notice was served).

38.23 There was perhaps previously an analogy with the decision of the Court of Appeal in *Kapoor v National Westminster Bank*[10] to the effect that the assignee of a debt became the relevant creditor with voting rights when looking at whether or not a majority had been obtained in an individual voluntary arrangement (IVA).

38.24 Chargors will also generally want to seek to ensure that there are no circumstances which might suggest that the security holder could be viewed as a shadow director of the company.

38.25 It is possible that a power to exercise voting rights but subject to a condition could be enough to give control even before the relevant condition has been met. This is because the power could be exercised at a future general meeting (and s 435(10)(b) refers to 'any' general meeting). This seems an odd result and the better view is that it would not apply. But see the discussion of the decision in *Qualter Hall*[11] in Chapter 39 below.

10 [2011] EWCA Civ 1083, [2012] 1 All ER 1201, CA. Discussed by PG Turner 'May the assignee of part of a debt vote at a creditors' meeting?' [2012] *CLJ* 270.

11 *Qualter, Hall & Co. Ltd v Board of Trade* [1962] Ch 273, CA.

39

What is voting power 'at any general meeting'?

39.1 The voting power limb of the 'control' test in the Insolvency Act 1986 (IA 1986), s 435(10)(b) refers to a person having the right to exercise more than one third of the voting power 'at any general meeting of' the relevant company.

CONTRAST WITH CA 2006

39.2 Similar 'at any general meeting' wording is used in the Companies Act 2006 (CA 2006) ss 254 and 255[1] dealing (for the purposes of Part 1 of the 2006 Act) with when a director is connected with a body corporate and when a director controls a body corporate.

39.3 But contrast the slightly different wording in CA 2006, s 988(3)(b)[2] dealing with associates in the context of Chapter 3 of Part 28 of the 2006 Act (Takeovers). The definition is very similar here, but refers to one-third or more of the voting power 'at general meetings of the body'. This seems clearer in referring to hypothetical meetings, rather than one specific meeting. It also cross refers to CA 2006, s 823(2) and (3) dealing with when a person is treated as entitled to exercise or control the exercise of voting power.[3] There is no equivalent provision in IA 1986, s 435(10).

1 Deriving from CA 1985, s 346.

2 See also the Petroleum Act 1998, s 30(8) and (9) dealing with 'control' for the purposes of persons who may be given notices requiring them to submit abandonment programmes in relation to offshore installations. This is similarly worded to CA 2006, s 988(3)(b) and refers at s 30(8)(b) to 'such rights as would entitle it to exercise one half or more of the votes exercisable in general meetings of the company'. The Legal Services Act 2007 in Sch 13 refers to a percentage of voting rights or voting power without specifying which general meetings are used.

3 Broadly providing that:

(a) a person (Z) is entitled to exercise voting power in Company A if Z controls one third or more of the voting power in another body corporate (Company B) and Company B is entitled to exercise the voting power in Company A; and

(b) an entitlement arises if the person has a right or obligation (whether or not conditional) which would make him so entitled.

39.4 CA 2006, Sch 1 deals with interests in shares or debentures. Para 5 deals with bodies corporate and refers to 'more than half of the voting power at general meetings of another body corporate'. This is expanded in para 5(2).

39.5 See also CA 2006, Sch 1A dealing with references to people with significant control over a company for the purposes of the PSC register provisions in CA 2006, s 790A to 790V.[4] Para 14 deals with voting rights 'at general meetings of the entity on all or substantially all matters'. Para 19 excludes nominees and paras 20 to 23 deal with rights held by persons who control their exercise and rights only exercisable in certain circumstances.

EFFECT OF GENERAL MEETING LIMB IN S 435(10)

39.6 The wording in s 435(10)(b) raises the issue of whether this test covers either:

- any particular general meeting; or
- all current and future general meetings.

39.7 By way of example, would the test be satisfied if, at a particular general meeting, a relevant person was able to control over one third of the votes at that meeting (eg because class rights were involved or some of the other shareholders did not attend)?

It seems better that the test should mean that the relevant control has to be at *all* general meetings – not a particular one – and look at who could potentially vote (and not just who actually votes)?

39.8 The most likely meaning is that s 435(10) is meant to cover generic or hypothetical general meetings, not just a particular one at which (say) an individual shareholder does not appear. This has some support from the comment by Lewison J in *Unidare*[5] that:

> 'In my judgment the general meeting of which the subsection speaks is a hypothetical general meeting ….'

But no reasoning for this was given.

4 Inserted from April 2006 by the Small Business, Enterprise and Employment Act 2015 (SBEEA 2015).

5 [2005] EWHC 1410 (Ch) (Lewison J) at [34].

Example:

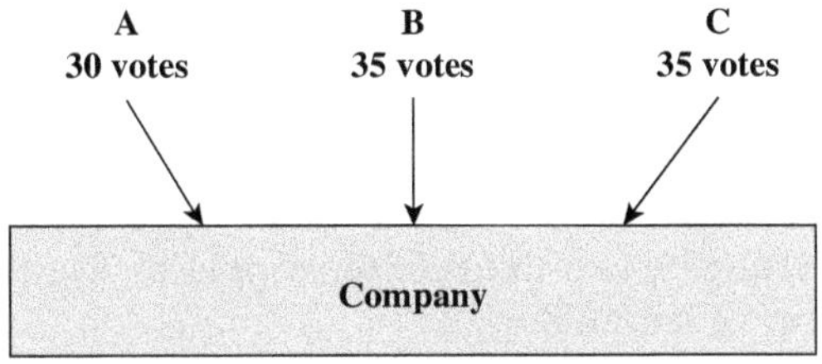

39.9 Say that:

- a company has 100 voting shares and three shareholders, A, B and C.
- A holds 30 out of the 100 voting shares.
- the other two shareholders, B and C, each hold 35 voting shares.

If a general meeting is called at which only A and B attend (and C does not, nor appoints a proxy). This means that:

(a) A has 30 out of 75 votes at that meeting.

(b) This is 40% of the votes at that meeting, even though A only holds 30% of the voting shares in the entire company.

39.10 The better view is that A does not, even for the time of the meeting, have 'control' of the company within s 435(10)(b). A does not control over one third of the votes at 'any' general meeting.

39.11 But what if:

- C gave A her proxy (with unlimited discretion as to how to vote) for the meeting?[6]
- Or if A and C have a voting agreement that allows A to vote C's shares on some matters only? Eg on removal of A's nominee as a director – see eg the voting agreement in *Bushell v Faith.*[7]

39.12 Such majority provisions clearly cause difficulties. Examples of the difficulties (in other statutory contexts[8]) are:

- *Knowles v Zoological Society of London:*[9] The constitution provided that new by-laws could be made 'if a majority of fellows entitled to vote' should

6 Contrast the express exclusion of proxies in para 4(3), Sch 1, CA 2006.

7 [1970] AC 1099, HL.

8 Noting the danger of applying cases on the meaning of words in other statutes – see Woolf J in *Walters v Babergh District Council* [1983] 82 LGR 235 mentioned in ch 4 above.

9 [1959] 1 WLR 823, CA.

vote in their favour. There were over 7,000 fellows in the Society. A meeting was held at which 3,034 fellows voted in person or by proxy. The Court of Appeal held on the facts that the word 'majority' meant the majority of those present and voting; and

- *Alexander v Burne:*[10] a resolution required a two-thirds majority of unitholders. The New South Wales Court of Appeal held that this could be passed at a meeting by two-thirds of those present, even if not two thirds of the total number of unitholders.
- Contrast the Queensland decision in *Peters v Kerle*[11] dealing with the meaning of the expression 'two-thirds majority of the voting members'. Fryberg J held that that phrase referred to 'two-thirds majority of the whole of the members who were entitled to vote'.

RESTRICTED VOTING RIGHTS?

39.13 Similar issues can arise in determining what the position is if voting rights are restricted for some reason[12] or held by another person under a proxy or contract.

39.14 For example, the discussion in the Takeover Code on 'voting rights'.

(a) In the Takeover Code at C7 defines 'control':

'Control' means an interest, or interests, in shares carrying in aggregate 30% or more of the voting rights (as defined below) of a company, irrespective of whether such interest or interests give de facto control.

(b) Voting rights of a company means all the voting rights attributable to its share capital which are currently exercisable at a general meeting.

(c) Except for treasury shares, any shares which are subject to:

(a) a restriction on the exercise of voting rights:

(i) in an undertaking or agreement by or between a shareholder and the company or a third party; or

(ii) arising by law or regulation; or

(b) a suspension of voting rights implemented by means of the company's articles of association or otherwise, will normally be regarded as having voting rights which are currently exercisable at a general meeting.

10 [2015] NSWCA 377.

11 [1997] QSC 68, (Fryberg J).

12 For example by statute – CA 2006, ss 793 and 794. Or under the articles of association – eg *Eclairs Group Ltd v JKX Oil & Gas plc* [2015] UKSC 71, [2016] 3 All ER 641.

QUALTER HALL V BOARD OF TRADE (1962)

39.15 In 1962 in *Qualter, Hall & Co. Ltd v Board of Trade*[13] the Court of Appeal considered the Companies Act 1948 dealing with the definition of an 'exempt private company' (which was exempt from filing audited accounts).

39.16 At first instance Cross J held that the company was not an exempt private company as the exemption in CA 1948, Sch 7, para 7 applicable for banks and finance companies did not apply on the facts. This decision was upheld by the Court of Appeal but for different reasons.

39.17 Cross J (and the Court of Appeal) also looked at the proviso to Sch 7, para 7 stated:

> 'Provided that this exception shall not apply if the banking or finance company has the right … to exercise or control the exercise of one-fifth or more of the total voting power at any general meeting of the relevant company.'

Finance companies held preference and 'A' shares, but these only had votes if the dividends were six months in arrear or at 'meetings proposing reduction of capital or winding up or a sale of the company's undertaking or the variation or abrogation of the rights attached to the shares and kindred matters'. Neither of these conditions currently applied.

At first instance Cross J held that the proviso did not apply so that the finance companies did not hold the relevant voting power. This meant that if para 7 had applied, the holding of the shares by the finance company would not have meant that the company would not be an exempt private company.

39.18 On appeal, Harman LJ (Donovan LJ and Pennycuik J agreeing) disagreed with the decision of Cross J on the question of 'at any general meeting' in the proviso.

This was strictly obiter as the Court of Appeal (and Cross J) had already decided that para 7 did not apply. Harman LJ considered ('as a matter of first impression') that:

> 'the words must be taken to mean what they say, namely, 'is there any general meeting at which the finance companies have the right to vote?'

He considered that 'if the other meaning were intended, the words would be "at general meetings."'

39.19 In *Qualter*, Harman LJ held (at p 289):

> 'The defendant argued both below and here a further and independent point depending on the proviso to paragraph 7, which, so far as relevant, is in these

13 [1962] Ch 273, CA.

> terms: "Provided that this exception shall not apply if the banking or finance company has the right … to exercise or control the exercise of one-fifth or more of the total voting power at any general meeting of the relevant company." The question here was merely the meaning of the words "any general meeting." As a result of the arrangement made, the finance companies held shares which in certain events gave them the control of one-fifth or more of the total voting power. Article 72 of the Articles of Association adopted by the plaintiff company as part of the scheme gives every member one vote for every share, but by a proviso confines the voting powers of preference shareholders and "A" ordinary shareholders (these being the classes held by the finance companies) as regards preference shares to occasions when dividends are six months in arrear and as regards both classes to meetings proposing reduction of capital or winding up or a sale of the company's undertaking or the variation or abrogation of the rights attached to the shares and kindred matters. The question is whether "any general meeting" means every general meeting or whether it includes those meetings only at which these classes of shareholders are entitled to vote. The judge favoured the former meaning, partly because the proviso was an exception to a privilege granted by the paragraph, and partly because in his opinion directors of the finance companies, if asked whether they were entitled to vote at any general meeting, would reply: "No, as things now are."
>
> This is a matter of first impression and for myself I prefer the second interpretation. I feel that the words must be taken to mean what they say, namely, "is there any general meeting at which the finance companies have the right to vote?" In my judgment if the other meaning were intended, the words would be "at general meetings." One of the basic conditions laid down is that no corporation is to be a member of an exempt private company. By this exception corporations are allowed to become members and it seems to me natural to confine that privilege to cases where the corporate bodies can in no circumstances obtain such a voting interest as might enable them to control the company.'

39.20 Donovan LJ agreed with Harman LJ:

> 'With regard to the alternative argument advanced by the respondents based on the proviso to paragraph 7 (1) and the words "any general meeting," I agree with the conclusion reached by my brother Harman, and have only this to add: Mr. Instone argued that the proviso applied only where a body corporate had a right to a constant proportion of the total voting power, and that this was not such a case. But the language of the proviso is not, in my judgment, directed to such a case alone, though prima facie it would cover it. I think it contemplates also the case where, looking at numbers of votes alone, the banking or finance company can exercise or control the exercise of more than one-fifth of them.'

39.21 It is perhaps relevant in the light of this decision that some of the CA 2006 provisions use the 'at general meetings' wording, rather than 'at any general meeting'. But CA 2006, ss 254 and 255 still refer to 'at any general meeting', although cross referring to CA 2006, Sch 1 (which uses the 'at general meetings wording' in relation to interests in shares (but not voting power) – see eg, s 255(2).

39.22 The comments of the Court of Appeal in *Qualter, Hall* are obiter and relate to a different statute. Given that the test in s 435 is relating to control (rather than a shareholding for qualifying as an exempt private company), the better view is that the Quilter Hall test does not apply and that the s 435(10)(b) provision only applies where the relevant condition for exercise of the voting power has actually been met.

VOTING AT ANY MEETING: *THE CHILDREN'S INVESTMENT FUND FOUNDATION*

39.23 The charitable status of a company does not affect the voting power tests in relation to that company.

The Children's Investment Fund Foundation (UK) v Attorney General[14] concerned an application for court approval of a transfer of charity assets from one charity to another, in connection with one of the directors of the first charity leaving office. It was accepted that, under the CA 2006 regime, this transfer needed the approval of the members of the first charity if the transfer was to a body corporate with which the director is connected. It was argued at first instance that the director was not connected with the second charity on the basis that its assets were held on charitable trusts. At first instance[15] Vos J (as he then was) held that this charitable status did not affect the position.

> '98. In these circumstances, one should move from a consideration of [Companies Act 2006] section 252(2)(b) to a consideration of section 254 as section 252(2)(b) specifically directs. In this case, the relevant sub-section, section 254(2)(b), provides that a director is connected with a body corporate if, but only if, she and the persons connected with her are 'entitled to exercise or control the exercise of more than 20% of the voting power at any general meeting of that body.
>
> 99. As it seems to me, the answer to this latter question is simple. It is unaffected by Ms Cooper's somewhat convoluted arguments that she cannot properly be regarded as exercising the members' voting power of BWP because of its exclusively charitable objects, the controls in section 201 of the Charities Act 2011, or the ring-fencing of the uses to which the Grant can be put. The fact is that Ms Cooper is the only member of BWP, which is a company limited by guarantee without a share capital. She is, therefore, entitled to exercise or control the exercise of 100% of the voting power in BWP at any general meeting of BWP. It, therefore, seems to me that the Grant will be a payment for loss of office to Ms Cooper within the proper meanings of sub-sections 215(1)(c), 215(3)(a), 252(2)(b) and 254(2)(b). It will, therefore, require the approval of a resolution passed by the members of CIFF, subject to the following issues that the court must determine.'

The point was not considered by the Court of Appeal or Supreme Court.

14 [2017] EWHC 1379 (Ch). On appeal [2018] EWCA Civ 1605, [2019] 1 All ER 845 and [2020] UKSC 33.

15 [2017] EWHC 1379 (Ch) per Vos J at [99].

40

Are groups of shareholders aggregated for control purposes?

AGGREGATION OF PEOPLE?

40.1 The wording at the end of the Insolvency Act 1986 (IA 1986), s 435(10) is difficult. It states:

> 'and where two or more persons together satisfy either of the above conditions, they are to be taken as having control of the company'.

There is as yet no reported case in England and Wales on this wording in s 435(10).

40.2 Taken literally this wording would allow aggregation of any small shareholdings to get over the one-third threshold. Thus it could be argued that since the shareholders in any company together control the exercise of more than one-third of the votes, they are to be treated as individually as having control. But this seems to be illogical and the wrong result.

40.3 Logically it seems that something more than this must be needed – some degree of association between the two or more persons whose shareholdings in the company are being aggregated – see for example the group references in s 435(6).

40.4 This is the view taken in *Goode on Consumer Credit Law and Practice*[1] looking at the very similar definition in the Consumer Credit Act 1974, s 189.[2]

1 Looseleaf, LexisNexis at [5.369]:

> '… in general each such person must be a "controller"; in his own right, and it is not permissible, for example, to take account of the aggregate of share-holdings held by more than one person each of which, individually, falls below the one third voting power referred to in para (b) (and see *Floor v Davis* [1980] AC 695, [1979] 2 All ER 677); but such aggregation is permissible once it established that two or more persons are "associates"; within the meaning of CCA 1974, s 184 …'.

2 See ch 5 above.

40.5 The loose-leaf book '*Insolvency*' previously seemed to take the contrary view, stating[3] in a footnote to a description of the control test in s 435(10)(a) that 'where there are two or more persons who together fulfil … [the test in s 435(10)(a)] then they are each associates of the company'.[4]

This is difficult to understand (given that s 435(10) deals with control, not directly with associate status), but indicated that a more several approach was favoured.

Moyola

40.6 The Northern Ireland decision in *Moyola*[5] indicates that, when looking at an individual and whether he or she is associated with a company, it is not enough that the company is controlled by the associates of the individual (eg his or her family members) if the individual him or herself has no shares in the company.

40.7 In the Northern Irish case *Agnew v Moyola Estates Ltd*[6] McBride J considered the provisions of Article 4 of the Insolvency (Northern Ireland) Order 1989,[7] which is identical to IA 1986, s 435. McBride J held that the company in this situation was not an associate of the bankrupt individual. It would be different if the bankrupt had held a shareholding in the company because then his interests could be aggregated with those of his family (associates) to give control of the company.

40.8 McBride J commented:

> '[25] The answer to the central question in dispute depends on the true construction to be placed upon art 4(7). Counsel were unable to find any direct authority on the construction of art 4(7) or a similar provision.
>
> [26] Article 4(7) sets out the circumstances in which a company is an associate of a bankrupt. The first limb of the definition states that a company is an associate of the bankrupt where the bankrupt has control of the company. A person has control, in accordance with art 4(10) when either the directors of the company act in accordance with his directions or instructions or he is entitled to exercise or controls the exercise of one third or more of the voting power at any general meeting of the company. Both parties agreed that the company was not an associate of Mr Dougan under the first limb of art 4(7) as he was not a director and the directors did not act in accordance with his directions or instructions and he did not have the requisite voting power.

3 Former chapter by Anthony Zacaroli on 'Associated and Connected Persons' in *Insolvency* (loose-leaf, Sweet & Maxwell).
4 Fn 2 on page H5/2.
5 *Agnew v Moyola Estates Ltd* [2016] NICh 19 (McBride J).
6 [2016] NICh 19 (McBride J).
7 SI 1989/2405 (N.I. 19).

[27] Under the second limb of art 4(7) a company is an associate of the bankrupt where the bankrupt and his associates together have control of the company. The parties agreed that this limb covers the scenario where the bankrupt has a minority shareholding in the company and when this interest is added to the interest of his associates, they collectively have the requisite control over the company. Counsel accepted that the use of the words 'and' and 'together' in art 4(7) supported this construction. Thus if Mr Dougan owned even one share in the company, the company would be an associate of his, as his associates, namely family members exercised the requisite control over the company.

[28] The dispute before the court therefore was whether the second limb of art 4(7) covered a scenario where the bankrupt was neither a director nor a shareholder in the company, but his associates exercised the necessary control over the company.

[29] On a literal construction of art 4(7) I find that it does not include this scenario. If the legislature had wanted to include in the definition of associate a person who was neither a director nor shareholder it could have done so simply by adding the words, 'or if his associates have control of it' at the end of art 4(7). Parliament did not do this.

[30] The mischief of the 1989 Order is to ensure that preferential transfers can be set aside. Such transfers are usually given to family and friends or to someone who effectively holds the property on trust for the bankrupt and the bankrupt is therefore in a position to have the property returned to him at some future date. To ensure this mischief was met Parliament included as associates, persons who had control over the company either individually as directors or shareholders and persons who held a minority interest which when added to the interests of their associates amounted to the requisite control of the company. It is 'control' of the company which enables individuals to give preferential transfers. A person without control over a company would not be in a position to ensure that property transferred would be returned to him at some future date.

[31] Individuals who are directors or shareholders, even of a minority interest have the ability to control decision making. As directors and shareholders they have legal rights for example to vote at company meetings, have access to company papers etc. Parliament included such individuals as associates because the mischief of the 1989 Order is to prevent transfers to friends and families or to a company which effectively holds a transfer on trust for the bankrupt as he can then use his control over the company to ensure the transferred property is returned to him after the bankruptcy ends. In contrast a person who is not a shareholder has no such legal rights. He cannot attend company meetings and cannot vote. He does not even have a right to see company papers. Such a person is not therefore able to exercise 'control' over the company. For this reason I find Parliament did not intend that such an individual should be included in the definition of associate. Whilst such an individual may seek to exercise influence over family members in a company this is not the same as having control over the company. Article 4(7) specifically refers to persons exercising 'control' rather than mere 'influence'.

[32] I have considered the provisions relating to preference when a company transfers assets to individuals. The wording of these provisions is markedly different and I therefore do not find them of assistance in the construction of art 4(7).'

Show Theatres

40.9 In *Show Theatres*,[8] the Singapore Court of Appeal commented on what seem to be identical statutory provisions to those in the UK in the context of a preference claim.

40.10 The insolvent company (Show Theatres) had repaid a loan to its two shareholders (both companies) before entering liquidation. The claim was by the liquidator looking to reclaim the repayment of the loan as a preference. The statutory reclaim period was two years for a connected or associated person, but only six months otherwise.[9] The repayment was made over six months, but under two years before the insolvency process started.

40.11 One shareholder, Show, held 75% of the shares; the other, Eng Wah, held 25%.[10] So Show was clearly associated with the insolvent company, but was Eng Wah?

40.12 The Court of Appeal held that Eng Wah was also associated (and so the loan needed to be repaid). This was because one of the directors of Eng Wah was also a director of the insolvent company. So the extended chain provision in the definition of 'connected' in the equivalent of s 239 applied.[11]

40.13 The Court of Appeal however went on to look at the control provisions in the equivalent of s 435(10)(b):

> '28 … If two companies, X and Y, both receive repayments from the insolvent company, and between them they exercised 1/3 or more of the voting power of the latter company, then by virtue of the proviso they are deemed to be associates of the latter. And if X and Y were to hold 100% of the voting power in the insolvent company the proviso should apply to the situation with even greater force. All the more so where it was clear that the two companies … had acted in concert in getting their loans repaid by the insolvent company. This would be wholly in line with the scheme to render void payments made in unfair preference.
>
> 29 Accordingly, this would be a further basis to hold that [the two shareholders] were companies "connected with" Show Theatres.'
>
> [underlining in the original judgment]

40.14 Strictly, this conclusion was obiter (the Singapore Court of Appeal had already held that the shareholders were connected under the common directorship provisions applying through the equivalent of s 239), but it gives an indication of

8 *Show Theatres Pte Ltd v Shaw Theatres Pte Ltd* [2002] SGCA 42; [2002] 4 SLR 145, Singapore CA.
9 The same rule applies under the UK Insolvency Act 1986 – see IA 1986, s 240(1).
10 *Show Theatres* at [4].
11 See 2.10 above.

the potential breadth of the aggregation wording. It is noticeable that the Court of Appeal pointed to the fact that the two shareholders were acting in concert and that both received repayments of their loan at the same time.

40.15 In a later Singapore case, *Encus International Pte Ltd v Tenacious Investment Pte Ltd*,[12] Judith Prakash J held that a group of 'Investors' together holding 88% of the shares were associated with the company. Unfortunately, the judgment gives no breakdown of the relationship between the investors.

Kellogg Brown and Root Holdings

40.16 Back in England and Wales, in *Kellogg Brown & Root Holdings (UK) Ltd v Revenue and Customs Comrs*,[13] a 2010 tax case (but construing similar wording), the Court of Appeal held that such aggregation wording was wide enough to catch a diverse group of shareholders (with no common purpose).

40.17 In *Kellogg Brown & Root Holdings* the Court of Appeal considered whether two companies remained connected for tax purposes after there had been a demerger of one out of the other.

(a) The original parent was listed on the New York stock exchange and had a large number of shareholders (over 16,400) with only one having over 5% of the shares (holding 5.95%).

(b) Following the demerger, the spun-off company had the same shareholders, but this would gradually change as shares were traded.

(c) There was a disposal between the two companies about a week after the demerger, and the tax issue was whether or not they were still connected for the purposes of the tax legislation.

40.18 The relevant definition of control was in the Income and Corporation Taxes Act 1988 (ICTA 1988), s416.[14] This included a control test based on whether a person was able to exercise or entitled to acquire direct or indirect control of the other company. Section 416(3) went on to provide:

> '(3) Where two or more persons together satisfy any of the conditions of subsection (2) above, they shall be taken to have control of the company.'

This looks very similar to the wording at the end of IA 1986, s 435(10).[15]

12 [2016] SGHC 50 (Judith Prakash J).
13 [2010] EWCA Civ 118, [2010] Bus LR 957, [2010] STC 925.
14 See now Corporation Tax Act 2010, s 450.
15 But note the dangers of reading across legislation – see Woolf J in *Walters v Babergh District Council* [1983] 82 LGR 235 mentioned at 4.4 above. In *Box Clever* [2019] EWCA Civ 1032 the Court of Appeal did not find the tax cases cited to be helpful as 'the statutory provisions and contexts are too different' – see [126].

40.19 In addition, Taxation of Chargeable Gains Act 1992 (TCGA 1992), s 268(5) is concerned with a group of two or more persons having control and looks the same as IA 1986, s 435(6).

40.20 In *Kellogg* the Court of Appeal unanimously held that the two companies were still connected. Lord Neuberger MR held:

> '[29] On behalf of HHL, Mr Gardiner attacks this conclusion on two grounds. First, he says that the reference in section 416(3) to "two or more persons *together*" (emphasis added) means that there has to be some sort of agreement or other arrangement between those persons before it can be said that they fall within its ambit. I do not accept that argument. First, such a construction does not accord with the natural meaning of section 416(3). Secondly, such a construction would conflict the purpose of Pt XI of the 1988 Act, as it would be only too easy for two or more individuals to avoid its provisions by establishing that, however close their personal relationship, they exercised any shareholder rights independently. Thirdly, for the same reason, the question whether a company was close could lead to a long enquiry whose outcome would be unpredictable. Fourthly, as Mr Baldry, for HMRC, argues, HHL's more limited meaning is difficult to reconcile with the fact that "control" in section 416(2) is defined as extending to a person "able to exercise" control. Fifthly, there is no difficulty giving section 416(3) this meaning, given that the limit to the number of persons who can control a close company is five.
>
> [30] HHL contends that the word "together" has no purpose if section 416(3) applies where 'the two or more persons' act independently. That may well be right, but the mere fact that a word is unnecessary under a particular interpretation is a very weak reason for rejecting that interpretation, if, as here, the word could be seen as performing an emphatic function. In any event, it could be said that, without the word, it would be unclear whether the subsection applied where one individual satisfied one of the three conditions in sub-s (2), and another individual satisfied another of those conditions.'

40.21 The Court of Appeal also looked at the concept of a 'group' (the tax legislation being similar to that in s 435(6)(b), IA 1986) and held that no degree of common purpose or connection was needed.

40.22 In *Kellogg*, the Court of Appeal held it was not necessary for the relevant group to have any other connection between each other (save for being shareholders).

(a) So if any group (even of unconnected persons) added together has 'control' of both Company A and Company B, then the two companies will be associated under tax rule.

(b) Even if (as in *Kellogg*) the result is that two companies which were subsidiaries of different quoted companies are associated.

(c) The potential for 'surprising and inconvenient' consequences was insufficient to depart from natural meaning.

(d) But 'considerable force' in the point that the use of 'person' in the 'associate' test could not be read as extending to 'persons' – the wording was equivalent to s 435(7):

> 'A company is an associate of another person if that person has control of it or if that person or persons who are his associates together have control of it.'

40.23 This decision was on the terms of a tax statute and in a tax context. Arguably different considerations may apply in relation to the Insolvency Act definition, which is different in some respects (for example s 435(10)(b) looks at control at a one-third voting level, but the tax provision looks instead at a majority).

40.24 HMRC won on:

(a) the meaning of the word 'group' in TCGA 1992, s 286(5)(b) – no need for any 'commonality which allows it to act as a group on the grounds of some common relation or purpose'; and

(b) the ambit of ICTA 1988, s 416(2) – the reference to 'indirect control', and any other expression in subsection (2), should be given its natural meaning in the context of that subsection, and should not be given a narrow meaning because of subsections (4) to (6).

40.25 *Kellogg* dealt with the tax definitions, not those under the Insolvency Act 1986, but the wording looks very similar in many (not all) areas.

(a) TCGA 1992, s 286(5), is concerned with a group of two or more persons having control and looks the same as s 435(6), IA 1986.

(b) ICTA 1988, s 416(3), provides 'Where two or more persons together satisfy any of the [definitions of control], they shall be taken to have control of the company.' Save for the cross reference, this is the same as the last two lines of IA 1986, s 435(10).

40.26 In *Kellogg* the Court of Appeal held that it is *not* necessary for the relevant group to have any other connection between each other (save for being shareholders). See the comments made at paras [42] and [45].

40.27 If *Kellogg* were to be followed in the s 435 context, the quick message is that if any group (even of unconnected persons) added together has 'control' of two companies (Company A and Company B), then the two companies will be associated.

Control for this purpose under IA 1986, s 435(1) is: (i) over one-third of the voting power at a general meeting; or (ii) directors who are accustomed to act under the person/group's direction. When looking at a group, individual persons can be replaced by their associates – s 435(6).

40.28 It may be that neither Company A or Company B is associated in this case with the group of shareholders (or perhaps only if the group acts together? – eg receives a dividend or loan repayment as in *Show*?).

SOME AGGREGATION SCENARIOS

40.29 Example 1

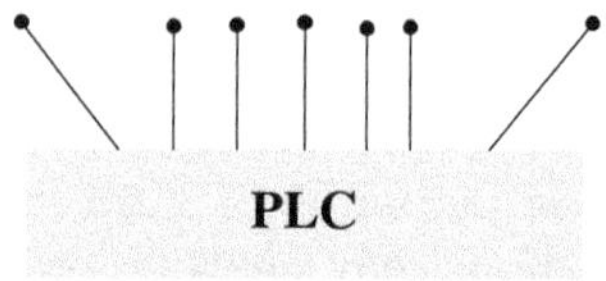

- Individual shareholders in PLC.
- No connection (save shareholding).
- Together have more than one third. But would be bizarre to say means that the group of three shareholders together have control.

40.30 Example 2

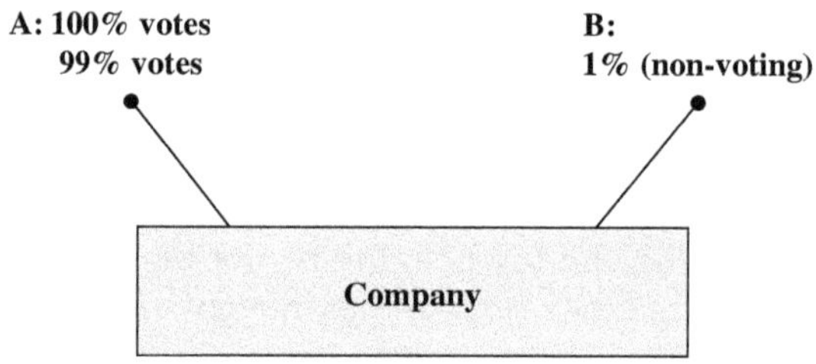

- A has 100% of voting shares and 99% of non-voting. B has 1% of non-voting. No connection with A.
- A has control of Company.
- B only has control if add to A. But no need to add B to A to get control.
- And B does not add anything to A's control at all. Use of word 'together' in s 435(10) means that B has to be needed for control to apply?

40.31 Same as example 2, but B has a connection with A. For example, B is associate of A (partners?) B and A have a shareholder agreement. *Show v Shaw* case in Singapore. (75/25 split, loans made in same proportion).

40.32 Same as example 2, but B has 1% of shares and they are voting shares too? Again, A already has control on its own (no need to add B). But A and B 'together' have more control?

40.33 It seems to be more logical that some other connection is needed. But the decision of the Court of Appeal in *Kellogg* would, if followed in relation to s 435 be against that. The decision in *Kellogg* is clearly one relating to another statute and so is not formally binding on later courts looking at s 435(10). Courts have commented on the danger of looking at similar words in different statutes – see Woolf J in *Walters v Babergh District Council*[16] discussed at 4.4 above.

40.34

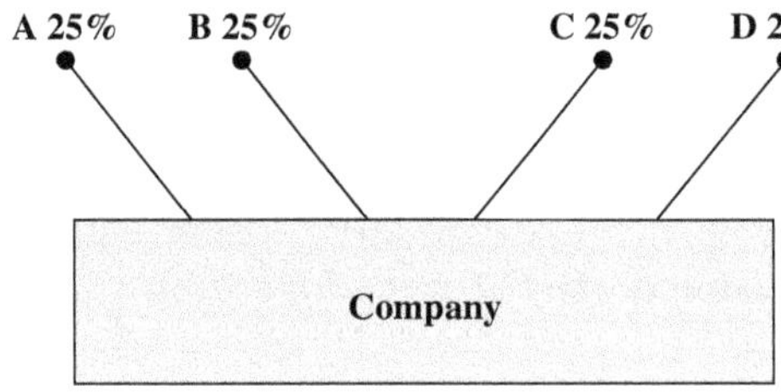

- A, B, C + D – no connection.
- Each has 25% of votes – so no control on own.
- But any two 'together' have 50%. So together have control? Only joint control?
- If A and B are associated, does the test in 435(6)(b) apply?

SOME FURTHER AGGREGATION SCENARIOS

40.35 An example looking across three companies.

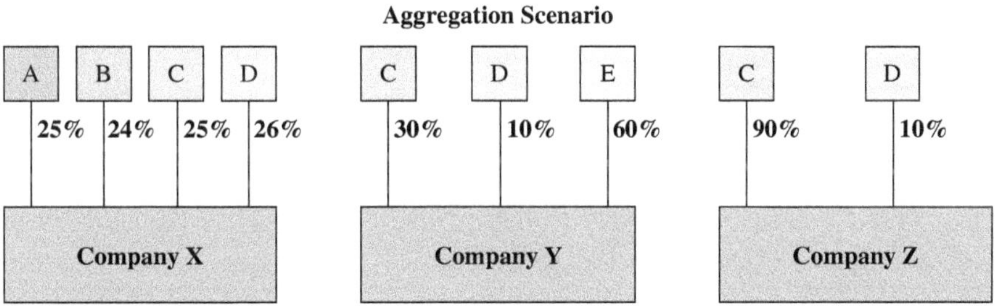

Assuming no other connection:

- Do C and D have control?
- Is D "associated" with Company X and Company Y?
- Is Company X with Company Y?
- Is Company Z "associated" with Company X?
- Does it make a difference if C and D are actually "together" or in "concert"?

16 [1983] 82 LGR 235.

TAX ANALYSIS

40.36 It is not clear that the tax cases will assist on analysis of s 435. As mentioned above (see 28.19 above) various tax cases were discussed by the Court of Appeal in *Box Clever* at [122] to [126], but the Court ultimately held that the three cases did not cast 'any real light' on how s 435 should be interpreted as the 'statutory provisions and contexts are too different' – at [126].

40.37 Tax commentary and guidance may perhaps be relevant here? For example:

- In a 2010 article in the Tax Journal[17] Preena Patani and John Watson discussed the decision of the CA in *Kellogg Brown & Root Holdings (UK) Ltd v R&CC*.

  The authors considered the facts of the case, and the finding of the Court of Appeal that 'group' in TCGA 1992, s 286(5)(b) should be given its ordinary meaning and includes a disparate group of shareholders which displays no common purpose. They consider that this approach involves simply asking oneself whether a collection of shareholders can be found which owns the majority of shares of each company. The authors looked at some of the potential implications of that approach, which they consider 'bizarre and impractical'.

- *Floor v Davis:*[18] Tax case on acting on concert:

  Taxpayer and two sons-in law acted in concert. Did they together 'control' the company for the purposes of capital gains tax (CGT) under FA 1965? The statute referred to a 'person' having control of a company. The House of Lords held (by a 3-2 majority) that the three acting in concert were a 'person' for that purpose.

- Should the test involve looking at a 'minimum controlling combination'? – See the HMRC Company Taxation Manual at CTM03730.[19] This includes a section on this 'minimum controlling combination':

> **Corporation Tax: small profits relief: control by the same person or persons CTA10/S 25(4)**
>
> More than one person (or group of persons) may have control of a company at the same time. For example, one person may have the greater part of the voting power, while another holds the greater part of the issued share capital and yet a third is entitled to the greater part of the assets in a winding-up. For the meaning of control see CTM60210 to CTM60230.

17 Patani and Watson, '*Kellogg: A rock pool*' (2010) 1045 Tax Journal.

18 [1980] AC 695, HL.

19 See www.gov.uk/hmrc-internal-manuals/company-taxation-manual/ctm03730 (accessed on 27 September 2021).

Whether or not two companies are under the control of the same person will appear after applying the control tests in CTA10/S 450[20] and S 451 to both companies. However, to determine whether two companies are under the control of the same persons it is necessary to look at which group or groups of persons control each company.

Two companies are only under the control of the same persons if:

- a group which controls one company is identical with a group which controls the other, and
- for each company, that group is a 'minimum controlling combination'.

A 'minimum controlling combination' means a group of persons which has control of the company but which would not have control of it if any one of the persons were excluded from the group.

For example, if three unconnected persons, A, B and C, each hold one third of the shares in a company, there are three minimum controlling combinations; A and B together, or B and C together, or A and C together. Control is held by any two together, so the addition of another person to the controlling combination is superfluous – A, B and C together do not form a control group for this purpose.

Example

Company CB

Shares

- Mr A – 50
- Mr B – 50
- Mr C – 50

Total issued shares = 150

Company AA

Shares

- Mr A – 50
- Mr B – 50
- Mr C – 50
- Mr D – 50

Total issued shares = 200

A, B, C and D are not associates.

Company CB is controlled by A and B together, or A and C together, or B and C together, that is by any two of them together.

20 CTA 2010, s 450 is derived from ICTA 1988, s 416, the section considered by the Court of Appeal in *Kellogg*.

Company AA is controlled by A, B and C together, or A, B and D together, or A, C and D together, or B, C and D together, that is by any three of them together.

As there is no group of persons controlling Company CB which is identical to a group of persons controlling Company AA, the two companies are not associated.

However, if A's and B's shares together entitled them to the greater part of the voting power in Company AA, then there would be an identical group controlling both companies, through applying the separate test in CTA10/S 450(3)(b) and so the two companies would then be associated.

GROUP OF PERSONS NEEDS TO BE ASSOCIATED?

40.38 It is more logical that, despite the decision of the Court of Appeal in the tax case, *Kellogg Brown & Root*,[21] something more than a group of unconnected persons must be needed under the s 435 tests – some degree of association between the two or more persons whose shareholdings in the company are being aggregated. Requiring some association would be inconsistent with the group references in s 435(6).

40.39 Such a need for an association or common purpose could arise based on one or more of the following:

(a) the word 'together' is used in the wording at the end of s 435(10) (stating 'where two or more persons *together* satisfy either of the above conditions') and this means a common purpose or association is required – this would be inconsistent with the Court of Appeal decision in *Kellogg Brown & Root*, but that case was on a different statute and in a different context;

(b) the wording at the end of s 435(10) ('they shall be taken to have control of the company') indicates that the relevant control applies to the group together (not individually). This seems to imply that the control only applies to group actions and not actions by an individual member of the group. The decision in *Show Theatres*[22] is to some extent consistent with this (in that it was seeking to clawback a dividend paid to both shareholders); and

(c) the aggregation wording at the end of s 435(10) is only meant to be a signpost into the other provisions of s 435 dealing with control, in particular ss 435(6) and (7) which each require a group to be comprised of associates. It is difficult to see why those sections include such an associate requirement if the aggregation wording in s 435(10) is already wider and does not include such a requirement.

21 [2010] EWCA Civ 118, [2010] Bus LR 957, [2010] STC 925, CA.
22 *Show Theatres Pte Ltd v Shaw Theatres Pte Ltd* [2002] SGCA 42, [2002] 4 SLR 145, Singapore CA. See 40.9 above.

41

Timing of control – eg on share sales?

41.1 The timing at which control (or association) is in place can be important.

- In insolvency recovery cases, the question can be whether the third party was associated at the time of the preference or undervalue etc.
- In pensions CN cases, the test is whether the third party was connected or associated with the employer at the time of the CN event or at any time after (and before the warning notice was issued) – PA 2004, s 38(3)(b)(i) and s 38(6)(b).
- In pensions FSD cases, the test is whether the third party was connected or associated with the employer at the relevant time (decided by the Pensions Regulator) fixed tor assessing whether the employer was a service company or under-resourced – PA 2004, s 43(5)(a) and (6).

41.2 For example in *Unidare*,[1] the issue was whether the charge granted by a company to its former parent was to an associated person. The former parent had agreed to sell the shares to an unconnected purchaser and this sale had been completed (eg the purchase price paid). But the former parent was still the registered shareholder. The transfer of shares to the Purchaser had not been registered in the books of the company.

Lewison J held that on these facts the former parent should be treated as holding the registered title on trust (and should exercise any voting rights at the direction of the purchaser) and that this meant that the former parent it no longer had 'control' of the company within the Insolvency Act 1986 (IA 1986), s 435(10).

41.3 But in *Box Clever*,[2] the Court of Appeal disagreed with Lewison J's judgment on this point in *Unidare*. The Court of Appeal held at [129] that a registered holder is to be considered to be entitled to exercise voting power and so has control under s 435(10)(b) – see Chapter 36 above.

1 *Re Kilnoore Ltd: Unidare plc v Cohen* [2005] EWHC 1410 (Ch), [2006] Ch 489 (Lewison J).
2 *Granada UK Rental & Retail Ltd v The Pensions Regulator* [2019] EWCA Civ 1032, [2020] ICR 747.

41.4 A similar timing point arose in *Darty Holdings SAS v Carton-Kelly*.[3] The payment was made to the former owner before the shares were transferred and this was enough to make the payment to a connected person.

41.5 The effect of these decisions is that on sales or companies (or share mortgages), the registered holder is still important for control purposes. It seems to be the consequence that in such a bare trust/custodian/mortgage case, both the roistered holder and the beneficiary are to be treated under s 435 as having the relevant voting power given by the shares.

41.6 Sellers on share transactions (and mortgagees on share mortgages) may be more concerned than otherwise that the registered holder of the shares is transferred.

DEATH OR DISSOLUTION

41.7 There may also in some cases be an issue as to whether or not a connection or association with an individual ceases on the death of that individual. This issue has been raised in relation to other legislation. In *Barker v Baxendale Walker*,[4] the Court of Appeal doubted that death of a participator in a remuneration trust meant that connected parties could thereafter benefit.

3 [2021] EWHC 1018 (Ch) (Miles J). Severance arguments were rejected by Miles J – see ch 33 above.

4 [2017] EWCA Civ 2056, per Asplin LJ at [47] and [152]–[157] and Henderdson LJ at [75], doubting Roth J at first instance [2016] EWHC 664 (Ch) at [152]–[157]. See *Bhaur v Equity First Trustees (Nevis) Ltd* [2021] EWHC 2581 (Ch) (Marcus Smith J) at [137].

PART 9

CONTROL THROUGH 'DOMINATION' OF DIRECTORS – S 435(10)(A)

42

Comparing s 435(10)(a) with the shadow director definition in s 251

42.1 The Insolvency Act 1986 (IA 1986), s 435(10)(a) states:

> '(10) A person is to be taken as having control of a company if:
>
> (a) the directors of the company, or another company which has control of it, (or any of them) are accustomed to act in accordance with his directions or instructions; …'

42.2 This provision only refers to directors, not 'shadow directors'. So 'dominating' or controlling shadow directors will not trigger control under this sub-section.

42.3 The definition in s 435(10)(a) has similarities with the definition of 'shadow director' used in IA 1986, s 251:[1]

s 435(10)(a), IA 1986 **Control**	**s 251, IA 1986** **Shadow director**
A person is to be taken as having *control* of a company if: (a) the directors of the company, or another company which has control of it, (or any of them) are accustomed to act in accordance with his directions or instructions;	'*shadow director*', in relation to a company, means a person in accordance with whose directions or instructions the directors of the company are accustomed to act but so that a person is not deemed a shadow director by reason only that the directors act – (a) on advice given by him in a professional capacity; (b) in accordance with instructions, a direction, guidance or advice given by that person in the exercise of a function conferred by or under an enactment (within the meaning given by section 1293 of the Companies Act 2006); or (c) in accordance with guidance or advice given by that person in that person's capacity as a Ministers of the Crown (within the meaning of the Ministers of the Crown Act 1975).[2]

1 A point made in *Unidare plc v Cohen* [2005] EWHC 1410 (Ch), [2006] Ch 489 (Lewison J) at [38] recording the argument of counsel. Also commented on in *Kirker (Liquidator of SMU Investments Ltd) v Holyoak Investments Inc* [2020] EWHC 875 (Ch) (ICC Judge Prentis) at [38].

2 Paras (b) and (c) were added to s 251 from 25 May 2015 by the Small Business, Enterprise and Employment Act 2015.

42.4 *Comparing s 435(10)(a) with the shadow director definition in s 251*

42.4 Both are sections in the same Act – the Insolvency Act 1986.

42.5 There are similarities. Both sections require that the relevant director(s):

- 'are accustomed to act';
- in 'accordance with' [his/whose] 'directions or instructions'.

But there are also two key contrasts:

- Is 'domination' of just one of the directors of a company enough to give control of a company or is a majority needed?
- There is no express exemption in s 435(10) for professional advisers/advice under an enactment or / directions from a minister of the crown.

42.6 This Part looks at three issues:

- What does 'accustomed to act' mean? – see Chapter 43.
- Could banks and advisors get control? – see Chapter 44.
- Is 'control' of a single director enough? – see Chapter 45.

43

What does 'accustomed to act' mean?

43.1 As already mentioned, there is very little reported caselaw on the meaning of the Insolvency Act 1986 (IA 1986), s 435(10) and none on s 435(10)(a). In practice the courts are likely to construe the following words in the two sections, s 435(10) and the shadow director definition in s 251, in the same way:

(a) '*are accustomed to act*';

(b) in '*accordance with*[1] [his/whose] '*directions or instructions*'.

43.2 It is highly likely that these phrases in s 435(10)(a) would be held in most cases to mean broadly the same as in the shadow director cases, so that:

(a) there is a need for habitual compliance – *Unidare*,[2] *Buzzle;*[3]

(b) a one-off direction is not enough – *Unidare;*[4]

(c) (perhaps) the domination need not cover all the company's activities – can just dominate one part of the company's activities – *AS Nominees;*[5] *Re Kaytech;*[6] *Deverel;l*[7] *Smithton;*[8] *McKillen;*[9]

(d) there must be a causal link between the instructions and the conduct of the board – *Buzzle.*[10]

These are discussed in more detail below.

1 See the *Billiton* case in HCA (mentioned below).
2 *Unidare plc v Cohen* [2005] EWHC 1410 (Ch), [2006] Ch 489 (Lewison J) at [36].
3 *Buzzle Operations Pty Ltd v Apple Computer Australia Pty Ltd* [2011] NSWCA 109, (2011) 250 FLR 242, (2011) 277 ALR 189, (2011) 81 NSWLR 47.
4 *Unidare plc v Cohen* [2005] EWHC 1410 (Ch), [2006] Ch 489 (Lewison J) at [36].
5 *Australian Securities Commission v AS Nominees Ltd* (1995) 133 ALR 1 (Finn J) at [52]–[53].
6 *Re Kaytech International plc* [1999] 2 BCLC 351 per Robert Walker LJ at [424].
7 *Secretary of State v Deverell* [2001] Ch 340, CA per Morritt LJ at [35].
8 *Smithton Ltd v Naggar* [2014] EWCA Civ 939, [2015] 2 BCLC 22 at [32]. Also citing *Re Mea Corp Ltd; Secretary of State v Aviss* [2006] EWHC 1846 (Ch), [2007] 1 BCLC 618.
9 *McKillen v Misland* [2012] EWHC 251 (Ch) (David Richards J).
10 *Buzzle Operations Pty Ltd v Apple Computer Australia Pty Ltd* [2011] NSWCA 109.

NEEDS TO BE HABITUAL

43.3 It seems right that one off advice or one-off following of advice by the directors is not enough. In the words of s 435(10)(a), the director (or group of directors) must be 'accustomed to act' in accordance with the directions or instructions – see, eg, the shadow director case, *Unidare.*[11]

43.4 It also seems logical to say that it is not enough that the person could as an abstract matter give advice or could give directions (eg under a contract) if no such directions are in fact given. The directors must actually 'be accustomed to act' in accordance with the directions or instructions – see eg, *Buzzle.*[12]

43.5 Section 435(10) does not expressly refer to advice. The Court of Appeal in *Deverell*[13] held, in relation to shadow directors, that advice is within 'directions or instructions' for shadow director purposes, but that was in the context of a section (IA 1986, s 251) with the express exclusion for professional advice – see the discussion at 44.2 below.

ONE-OFF DIRECTION

43.6 A one-off direction is not enough – *Unidare.*[14] The relevant directors would not then be 'accustomed' to act in the relevant way.

NOT ALL THE COMPANY'S ACTIVITIES?

43.7 For shadow director purposes, the domination need not cover all the company's activities – the person can just dominate one part of the company's activities – *AS Nominees;*[15] *Re Kaytech;*[16] *Deverell;*[17] *Smithton;*[18] *McKillen.*[19]

43.8 But it is less clear that this also applies to the 'control' definition in s 435(10). It seems easier to consider that a person could be a shadow director if having 'dominance' over part of a company's activities. But 'control' seems to imply more.

11 *Unidare plc v Cohen* [2005] EWHC 1410 (Ch), [2006] Ch 489 (Lewison J) at [36].
12 *Buzzle Operations Pty Ltd v Apple Computer Australia Pty Ltd* [2011] NSWCA 109, (2011) 250 FLR 242, (2011) 277 ALR 189, (2011) 81 NSWLR 47.
13 *Secretary of State v Deverell* [2001] Ch 340, CA per Morritt LJ at [35].
14 *Unidare plc v Cohen* [2005] EWHC 1410 (Ch), [2006] Ch 489 (Lewison J) at [36].
15 *Australian Securities Commission v AS Nominees Ltd* (1995) 133 ALR 1 (Finn J) at [52]–[53].
16 *Re Kaytech International plc* [1999] 2 BCLC 351 per Robert Walker LJ at [424].
17 *Secretary of State v Deverell* [2001] Ch 340, CA per Morritt LJ at [35].
18 *Smithton Ltd v Naggar* [2014] EWCA Civ 939, [2015] 1 WLR 189, [2015] 2 BCLC 22 at [32]. Also citing *Re Mea Corp Ltd; Secretary of State v Aviss* [2006] EWHC 1846 (Ch), [2007] 1 BCLC 618.
19 *McKillen v Misland* [2012] EWHC 251 (Ch) (David Richards J).

CAUSAL LINK

43.9 There must be a causal link between the instructions and the conduct of the board – *Buzzle.*[20]

43.10 The words 'accustomed to act in accordance with his directions or instructions' also appear in various other places in the Companies legislation – for example: Companies Act 2006, ss 823; 988; Sch 1, para 5.

20 *Buzzle Operations Pty Ltd v Apple Computer Australia Pty Ltd* [2011] NSWCA 109.

44

Can advisers have 'control'? Is the shadow director test for advisers different from the control test?

PERSON HAVING CONTROL CONTRASTED WITH SHADOW DIRECTORS

44.1 Part (a) of the 'control' definition in the Insolvency Act 1986 (IA 1986), s 435(10)(a) is obviously similar to the definition of a 'shadow director' in s 251.[1] But there are two key differences between the definitions:[2]

(a) professional advisers are expressly excluded from the definition of shadow director in s 251, but not from s 435(10)(a); and

(b) in order to be a shadow director there must be domination of a majority of the board of directors (domination of one director or a minority is not enough). But s 435(10)(a) is worded differently on this point and it may be argued that domination of just one director is enough – see Chapter 45 below.

ADVISER EXCLUSION

44.2 The definition of shadow director in IA 1986, s 251[3] now includes three exceptions at the end. The first of these was in the 1986 Act from its enactment:[4]

> 'a person is not deemed a shadow director by reason only that:
>
> (a) the directors act on advice given by him in a professional capacity'.

1 A point made in *Unidare plc v Cohen* [2005] EWHC 1410 (Ch), [2006] Ch 489 (Lewison J) at [38] recording the argument of counsel, Raquel Agnello.

2 As Antony Zacaroli used to point out in ch H5 in Segal, Totty and Moss, *Insolvency* (Looseleaf, Sweet & Maxwell). See former para H5-03. Repeated in the current commentary at F2-26.

3 The definition of 'shadow director' is the same in Company Directors Disqualification Act 1986 (CDDA 1986), s 22(5).

4 This professional adviser exception is also in the expanded category of persons who can be made the subject of a disqualification order under CDDA 1986, ss 8ZA(3) and 8ZD(4), as inserted by SBEEA 2015, s 105.

44.3 The exception in the shadow director definition in s 251 was expanded in May 2015.[5] The change was made by the Small Business, Enterprise and Employment Act 2015 (SBEEA 2015), s 90(1) with effect from 26 May 2015. The change was to include two further exceptions:

(b) in accordance with instructions, a direction, guidance or advice given by that person in the exercise of a function conferred by or under an enactment (within the meaning given by s 1293 of the Companies Act 2006);

(c) in accordance with guidance or advice given by that person in that person's capacity as a Minister of the Crown (within the meaning of the Ministers of the Crown Act 1975).

The definition of shadow director in Companies Act 2006 (CA 2006), s 251(1) and (2) is also the same, but the additional exception in CA 2006 s 251(3) is not found elsewhere. This states that:

> '(3) A body corporate is not to be regarded as a shadow director of any of its subsidiary companies for the purposes of—
>
> Chapter 2 (general duties of directors),
>
> Chapter 4 (transactions requiring members' approval), or
>
> Chapter 6 (contract with sole member who is also a director),
>
> by reason only that the directors of the subsidiary are accustomed to act in accordance with its directions or instructions.'

44.4 By way of contrast, s 435(10)(a) does not expressly include any of these three exceptions in s 251.[6] This leaves open the argument that professional advisers may be taken to have 'control' under s 435(10)(a) in some circumstances even though they only give advice. The question is whether advice is enough to amount to a 'direction or instruction'.

44.5 In an article in September 2016, '*Liability of directors, professional advisors and lenders under the moral hazard provisions*',[7] Raquel Agnello QC argued that the 'connected' and 'associated' tests in IA 1986 and used in the Pensions Act 2004 (PA 2004) are 'deliberately left wide' and so could easily extend to cover lenders and professionals if the directors 'are accustomed to act' on the lender's or professional's directions or instructions – which she argued could easily occur (eg if the directors in fact follow advice of professionals or the lender imposes limits on actions).

5 The change was made by SBEEA 2015, s 90(1) with effect from 26 May 2015. Identical changes were made to the definition in CDDA 1986. No change was made to IA 1986, s 435.
6 Nor do the two new exceptions apply (alongside the professional adviser exemption) in the expanded category of persons who can be made the subject of a disqualification order under CDDA 1986, s 8ZA, as inserted by SBEEA 2015, s 105.
7 (2016) 9 JIBFL 522.

44.6 She relied for this argument on the provision[8] which provides that 'control' is found where 'the directors of the company (or any of them) are accustomed to act on that person's instructions or directions'. She pointed out that this does not include the carve out (for those who provide advice in a professional capacity) applicable in the definition of 'shadow director' in IA 1986, s 251.

44.7 Raquel Agnello went on to argue that a lender who makes it clear that future financing can depend on the borrower/employer taking steps required by the lender could arguably be held to become associated with the employer.

44.8 This is an argument for a wide interpretation of the control provision in s 435(10)(a), seemingly wider than that for the shadow director test.

44.9 Raquel Agnello went on to argue that all TPR would need to show was that 'on the facts' that the directors had been 'accustomed to act' in accordance with the relevant directions or instructions and that this does not distinguish between a contractual obligation or a dominant position or even professional advice.

44.10 She then went on to argue that the legislation 'appears wide enough to cover professional advisers' despite an argument that directors should be making their own decisions and not delegating to advisers (although she notes that there is no case law on this issue).

44.11 Again this would be a wide interpretation of the control provisions in s 435(10)(a) and is discussed further below.

44.12 Raquel Agnello went on to point out that association or connection is not enough on its own to found CN liability. The target must also be a party to a relevant act or omission (or knowingly assist) and the reasonableness test must be satisfied. She noted the DP decision in *Carrington Wire*[9] where a third party was found to have assisted (she does not point out the width of this finding – it involved an omission, namely a failure by the director of the third party purchaser to tell something to the trustees before the purchase took place).

44.13 The case law discussing the shadow director definition would, if followed for s 435(10) purposes, support arguments favouring a wide approach that could mean that lenders or professional advisers potentially have 'control' within s 435, depending on the relevant facts. This could be in circumstances that may well not support a finding of them being a shadow director. There is no caselaw on this, but the better view is this would be the wrong interpretation.

8 Presumably this is s 435(10)(a), but this is not expressly stated in the article.
9 See ch 75 'TPR's Practice on Moral Hazard Powers' in Pollard *Corporate Insolvency: Pension Rights* (7th edn, Bloomsbury Professional, 2021).

Deverell (2001)

44.14 Although not expressly cited by Raquel Agnello in her article, the comments of the Court of Appeal in *Secretary of State v Deverell*[10] in some ways point to a wide ambit for the interpretation of the 'directions or instructions' element of the s 435(10)(a) test (especially given that there is no express professional adviser exception). *Deverell* was a case concerned disqualification of a person from acting as a director under the CDDA 1986. So it was not even a case on IA 1986, although CDDA 1986 includes an identical definition of shadow director as in IA 1986, s 251 and CDDA 1986 is part of the group of insolvency legislation enacted in 1986. For this reason, *Deverell* has been referred to in later cases[11] on shadow directors under IA 1986 without comment (although strictly it is strictly not a binding precedent on IA 1986 cases).

44.15 Deverell has also been referred to in in Australia, in *Buzzle*.[12] However, Young JA did note at [214] that the second of Morritt LJ's five propositions in *Deverell* (that the provision should not be strictly construed because the legislation is protective of the public) 'might not be so strong outside the field of disqualification of directors'.

44.16 Morritt LJ (with whom Potter LJ and Morison J agreed) held (in a key passage):

> '35. I propose to express my conclusions on these and other issues in a number of propositions.
>
> (1) The definition of a shadow director is to be construed in the normal way to give effect to the parliamentary intention ascertainable from the mischief to be dealt with and the words used. In particular, as the purpose of the Act is the protection of the public and as the definition is used in other legislative contexts it should not be strictly construed because it also has quasi-penal consequences in the context of the 1986 Act. I agree with the statement to that effect of Browne-Wilkinson V-C in *Re Lo-Line Electric Motors Ltd* [1988] 2 All ER 692 at 699, [1988] Ch 477 at 489.
>
> (2) The purpose of the legislation is to identify those, other than professional advisers, with real influence in the corporate affairs of the company. But it is not necessary that such influence should be exercised over the whole field of its corporate activities. I agree with the statements to that effect of Finn J in *Australian Securities Commission v AS Nominees Ltd* (1995) 133 ALR 1 at 52–53 and Robert Walker LJ in *Re Kaytech International plc* [1999] 2 BCLC 351 at 424.

10 [2001] Ch 340, CA per Morritt LJ at [35].

11 Eg: *Ultraframe (UK) Ltd v Fielding; Northstar Systems Ltd v Fielding* [2005] EWHC 1638 (Ch); [2005] All ER (D) 397 (Jul); [2007] WTLR 835 (Lewison J) at [1260], *Vivendi SA v Richards* [2013] EWHC 3006 (Ch), [2013] BCC 771 (Newey J) at [125], *Smithton Ltd v Naggar* [2014] EWCA Civ 939, [2015] 2 BCLC 22 at [32].

12 *Buzzle Operations Pty Ltd v Apple Computer Australia Pty Ltd* [2011] NSWCA 109 at [210] to [214].

(3) Whether any particular communication from the alleged shadow director, whether by words or conduct, is to be classified as a direction or instruction must be objectively ascertained by the court in the light of all the evidence. In that connection I do not accept that it is necessary to prove the understanding or expectation of either giver or receiver. In many, if not most, cases it will suffice to prove the communication and its consequence. Evidence of such understanding or expectation may be relevant but it cannot be conclusive. Certainly the label attached by either or both parties then or thereafter cannot be more than a factor in considering whether the communication came within the statutory description of direction or instruction.

(4) Non-professional advice may come within that statutory description. The proviso excepting advice given in a professional capacity appears to assume that advice generally is or may be included. Moreover the concepts of "direction" and "instruction" do not exclude the concept of "advice" for all three share the common feature of "guidance".

(5) It will, no doubt, be sufficient to show that in the face of "directions or instructions" from the alleged shadow director the properly appointed directors or some of them cast themselves in a subservient role or surrendered their respective discretions. But I do not consider that it is necessary to do so in all cases. Such a requirement would be to put a gloss on the statutory requirement that the board are "accustomed to act in accordance with" such directions or instructions. It appears to me that Judge Cooke, in looking for the additional ingredient of a subservient role or the surrender of discretion by the board, imposed a qualification beyond that justified by the statutory language.'

PROFESSIONAL ADVISERS

44.17 Given the absence of an express professional adviser exemption from the 'control' definition in s 435(10)(a), it seems that Morritt LJ's conclusions on shadow directors could be argued to be read across into s 435, so that:

(a) the comment at 44.16(4) above in relation to the shadow director provisions could mean that that it is argued that all advice (including professional advice) can be enough to be a 'direction or instruction'; and

(b) at 44.16(5) above indicates that it may not be required that the directors have retained their discretion (and have not been in a subservient role).

44.18 But the better view is that this expanded view should not apply to 'domination' issues under s 435(10). The better view is that the findings in *Deverell* are limited to 'shadow directors' and that it is not necessarily the case that the same analysis should apply to the 'control' definition in s 435(10)(a) (which after all is for a different purpose and differently worded).

44.19 As mentioned above, 'in law, context is everything'.[13] Indeed, the very existence of the professional adviser exclusion in the shadow director definition

13 Lord Steyn in *R v Secretary of State for the Home Dept, ex p Daly* [2001] UKHL 26 at [28]. See 4.3 above.

in s 251 was used by Morritt LJ to support his interpretation of the words 'directions or instructions' as used in s 251 to be wide enough (in that section) to cover advice (see 44.16(4) above). As a general matter, the use of the same words in a different statute and a different context do not have to follow the same meaning.[14]

44.20 Morritt LJ did state that the words 'directions or instructions' include advice anyway, stating:

> 'Moreover the concepts of "direction" and "instruction" do not exclude the concept of "advice" for all three share the common feature of "guidance"'.

This is however difficult to understand – it seems better to view a 'direction' or 'instruction' as implying a binding communication, with the recipient expected to follow it (and not exercise his or her own judgement[15]). But professional advice is something that the recipient can be expected to consider and then make up his or her own mind[16].

NON-PROFESSIONAL ADVISERS (EG LENDERS/SHAREHOLDERS/ PARENT COMPANIES)

44.21 Claims relating to being a shadow director (or having control within s 435(10)(a)) could also apply to others who get involved with the decisions being made by a company. Obvious examples include parent companies, significant shareholders or lenders. They may give advice to directors or point out consequences should they not follow the 'advice'. But usually it will be the case that the directors will retain the ultimate decision making power. In the same way as for professional advisers, it seems to be open for such third parties to argue that they are not shadow directors, nor controllers within s 435(10)(a).

Buzzle

44.22 Conversely in *Buzzle Operations v Apple Computer Australia*,[17] the New South Wales Court of Appeal held that a parent company had not become a shadow director, finding that shadow directorship requires habitual compliance and a causal link between the instructions and the conduct of the board.

14 See Lord Hoffmann in *Oxfordshire CC v Oxford City Council* [2006] UKHL 25 at [27], discussed at 4.10 above.

15 For a director this would now be a breach of the general duties owed under CA 2006, Ch 2, Part 1, in particular the duty to exercise independent judgement under CA 2006, s 173.

16 See eg: Robert Walker J in *Scott v National Trust* [1998] 2 All ER 705 at [717g], discussed below.

17 *Buzzle Operations Pty Ltd v Apple Computer Australia Pty Ltd* [2011] NSWCA 109; (2011) 250 FLR 242; (2011) 277 ALR 189; (2011) 81 NSWLR 47. Discussed by Jamieson and Hughes, 'The identification of shadow directors under English law: what guidance might Buzzle provide?' (2012) BJIFL, 364.
Buzzle has been cited and followed in Ireland in *Pyne v Van Deventer* [2012] IEHC 263 (Dunne J).

44.23 The relevant definition in Australia used to be the same as that in the UK, referring to 'directions or instructions' this was changed in 1999 to refer to 'instructions or wishes'. In *Buzzle*,[18] Young JA considered that this change did not seem to have been given any significance, but that 'If there is any significance, it is that "wishes" covers a wider field than "directions"'. This means that if anything the test in Australia should be easier to meet than in the UK, so that where (as in *Buzzle*) shadow directorship was not found, that should be the same result in England and Wales.

44.24 The headnote summarises the findings in *Buzzle*:

> 'Per Young JA (Hodgson and Whealy JJA agreeing) – a "shadow director" under (b)(ii) of the definition of director in s 9 of the Corporations Law is a person in accordance with whose instructions or wishes the directors of a company are accustomed to act. "In accordance" requires a causal connection between the instruction or wishes and the action. The instructions or wishes must be in relation to board activities and not just managerial decisions, the distinction being one of fact. However, they do not have to be in relation to every board activity, one must approach this subject with an eye to the ultimate question – who is effectively making board decisions? "Accustomed" means a pattern of compliance over a period of time.'

44.25 Young JA gave the main judgment, including a review of the UK authorities on 'shadow director'. In a passage that should have equal application in England and Wales, he held[19] that from the leading authorities[20] five principles emerge:

> 'However, it seems to me that various principles emerge from the leading authorities.
>
> First, not every person whose advice is in fact heeded as a general rule by the board is to be classed as a de facto or shadow director.
>
> Secondly, if a person has a genuine interest of his or her or its own in giving advice to the board, such as a bank or mortgagee, the mere fact that the board will tend to take that advice to preserve it from the mortgagee's wrath will not make the mortgagee, etc a shadow director.
>
> Thirdly, the vital factor is that the shadow director has the potentiality to control. The fact that he or she does not seek to control every facet of the company or the fact that from time to time the board disregards advice is of little moment.

18 At [187].

19 At [228] to [233].

20 Having cited in particular, *Re Hydrodam (Corby) Ltd* [1994] 2 BCLC 180, *Revenue and Customs Commissioners v Holland: In re Paycheck Services 3 Ltd* [2010] UKSC 51, [2010] 1 WLR 2793, [2011] 1 All ER 430, *Secretary of State for Trade and Industry v Deverell* [2001] Ch 340, *Ultraframe (UK) Ltd v Fielding* [2005] EWHC 1638 (Ch), [2005] All ER (D) 397 (Jul).

> Fourthly, Millett J's proposition that the evidence must show "something more" than just being in a position of control must be shown. The whole of the facts of the case must be shown to see whether that power to control was put into practice. The emphasis that one must judge on the whole of facts and circumstances is made many times over in the leading cases, see eg *Secretary of State for Trade and Industry v Tjolle* [1998] 1 BCLC 333, 343–4 and *Re Kaytech International plc* [1999] 2 BCLC 351, 423–4.
>
> Fifthly, although there are problems with cases where the board of the company splits into a majority and minority faction, so long as the influence controls the real decision makers, the person providing the influence may be a shadow director.'

BHP Billiton v Commissioner of Taxation

44.26 *Buzzle* was briefly discussed early in 2020 by the High Court of Australia in *BHP Billiton Limited v Commissioner of Taxation.*[21] The High Court considered that the meanings in *Buzzle* were concerned with the shadow director definition (and so whether the person owed duties to the company) in contrast to the question of whether an entity fell within a statutory association test. The High Court held (at [43]):

> '[43] Ltd's submission that, consistent with the decision in *Buzzle Operations Pty Ltd (In liq) v Apple Computer Australia Pty Ltd*[40], s 318(6)(b) requires that the "directions, instructions or wishes" constitute a "sufficient reason to act" should also be rejected. Buzzle was concerned with provisions in the Corporations Act 2001 (Cth) relating to shadow directors: provisions in a different statute, using different language and directed to a different purpose – to identify those persons who, because of their control of a company, owe duties to that company. The immediate purpose of Pt X of the 1936 Act is to identify entities whose income should be brought to tax because of their connection to other entities. Consistent with that broader purpose, s 318(6)(b) not only refers to what a company "might reasonably be expected" to do but extends the relevant influence to the company or its directors, not just the directors themselves. Indeed, at the time of the enactment of s 318(6)(b), the definition of "director" in the Corporations Law which captured shadow directors was in different terms: it was concerned with a person in accordance with whose "directions or instructions" the directors were accustomed to act, but did not extend to "wishes"[41]. It was not until 1999 that the definition of "director" deleted "directions" and substituted "wishes"[42].
>
> [40] (2011) 81 NSWLR 47.
>
> [41] Corporations Law, s 9 definition of "director", s 60(1)(b).
>
> [42] Corporate Law Economic Reform Program Act 1999 (Cth), Sch 3, item 109.'

21 [2020] HCA 5, 94 ALJR 326.

44.27 Similarly in *ASIC v King*,[22] the Australian High Court also noted the adviser exclusion in one limb of the definition of 'officer' in s 9 of the Corporations Act (Cth). This includes the definition:

> 'officer of a corporation means:
>
> (a) a director or secretary of the corporation; or
>
> (b) a person:
>
> (i) who makes, or participates in making, decisions that affect the whole, or a substantial part, of the business of the corporation; or
>
> (ii) who has the capacity to affect significantly the corporation's financial standing; or
>
> (iii) in accordance with whose instructions or wishes the directors of the corporation are accustomed to act (excluding advice given by the person in the proper performance of functions attaching to the person's professional capacity or their business relationship with the directors or the corporation); or
>
> (c) a receiver, or receiver and manager, of the property of the corporation; or
>
> (d) an administrator of the corporation; or
>
> (e) an administrator of a deed of company arrangement executed by the corporation; or
>
> (f) a liquidator of the corporation; or
>
> (g) a trustee or other person administering a compromise or arrangement made between the corporation and someone else.

44.28 In *ASIC v King*, the majority in the High Court briefly referred to *Buzzle*:

> '[40] Section 179(2) of the Act notes that s 9 defines both "director" and "officer" and states that "[o]fficer includes, as well as directors and secretaries, some other people who manage the corporation or its property (such as receivers and liquidators)". Section 179(2) confirms that the definition of "officer" in s 9 is intended to capture those managing the corporation or its property, as distinct from those who are able to affect the corporation by the exercise of rights as a counterparty to a transaction involving the corporation. Thus, para (b)(ii) "does not refer to a person who has [the relevant] capacity as a third party but is not involved in the management of the corporation's affairs"55.
>
> [41] It may happen, of course, that a person who has legal rights against a corporation as a counterparty to a particular transaction or particular transactions is able to inveigle himself or herself into the decision-making processes of the corporation by means of the mere threat of the exercise of those rights. In such a case, that person may fall within either or both of para (b)(i) or (ii) of the

22 *Australian Securities and Investments Commission v King* [2020] HCA 4, 94 ALJR 293.

definition. But that depends on the facts of the case as to the nature and extent of the counterparty's control of, or capacity to control, the corporation's decision-making qua management; it does not depend on the counterparty's legal rights.

[42] In addition, although advisors and consultants may give advice which, if implemented, can significantly affect the financial standing of the corporation, it does not follow that it is the advisor or consultant who, in that circumstance, has the capacity to affect significantly the financial standing of the corporation. That capacity in fact resides in the person to whom the advice is given, because it is that individual who determines whether or not the advice should be acted upon. The giving of that advice is of no consequence, unless the advisor or consultant is, in fact, involved in the management of the corporation and is thereby able to ensure that the advice will be implemented.

[43] It is convenient to note here the parenthetical exclusion in para (b)(iii) of the definition. The exclusion makes it clear that, where the directors of the corporation are accustomed to act in accordance with advice given by the person "in the proper performance of functions attaching to the person's professional capacity or their business relationship with the directors or the corporation", that person is not captured by para (b)(iii). The parenthetical exclusion in para (b)(iii) serves to ensure that where the only connection between a person and decision-making in the management of a corporation is that described in the exclusion, the person so described will not be saddled with the responsibilities of an officer of the corporation even though the directors, who are engaged in the management of the corporation, are accustomed to act in accordance with the person's instructions or wishes. That is because the professional or business relationship between the person and the directors differentiates the person from those who manage the corporation. The parenthetical exclusion is neither necessary nor appropriate in relation to para (b)(i) and (ii) because sub-paras (i)

55 *Buzzle Operations Pty Ltd (In liq) v Apple Computer Australia Pty Ltd* (2010) 238 FLR 384 at 412 [126]; compare *Buzzle Operations Pty Ltd (In liq) v Apple Computer Australia Pty Ltd* (2011) 81 NSWLR 47 at 70–71 [191]–[192].'

The minority (Nettle and Gordon JJ) agreed with the ultimate orders, but gave a gloss on the 'officer' meaning:

'[96] Moreover, we do not accept that bankers and other third parties could never fall within the reach of one or more of para (b)(i)-(iii) of the definition of "officer" in s 9 of the Corporations Act 2001 (Cth). Those questions did not arise directly in this litigation but, to give just one example, lenders managing the way in which a company attempts to work its way out of financial distress may present real issues about the application of these provisions 123.

[123] See, eg, *Hill v David Hill Electrical Discounts Pty Ltd (In liq)* (2001) 37 ACSR 617 at 620 [12]; *Emanuel Management Pty Ltd (In liq) v Foster's Brewing Group Ltd* (2003) 178 FLR 1 at 72–73 [263]–[264]; *Buzzle Operations Pty Ltd (In liq) v Apple Computer Australia Pty Ltd* (2011) 81 NSWLR 47 at 51 [9]–[10], 76–77 [227]–[232]; *Re Akron Roads Pty Ltd (ACN 004 769 895) (In liq) [No 3]* (2016) 348 ALR 704 at 746–747 [271].[123]

[186] An officer of a corporation includes a person who has engaged in certain conduct (para (b)(i)), who has a certain kind of capacity (para (b)(ii)), or who

> has (or had) a certain influence on the directors of the corporation (para (b)(iii)). The question was not whether Mr King held a named office in MFSIM. Taken together, the facts and circumstances described compelled the conclusion that Mr King was a person who had the capacity to significantly affect the financial standing of MFSIM.'

ADVICE?

44.29 Returning to whether advice could be enough to give 'control' within s 435(10)(a), it is clearly less easy for advice (compared to a 'direction' or 'instruction') to meet the causal link test. Particularly if the recipient directors comply with their usual duties (see CA 2006, s 173) to each exercise their own independent judgement and make up his or her own mind on the advice.[23]

44.30 The comments made by Young JA in *Buzzle* on the changes to the law in Australia can also be seen as shedding some light on 'advice'. Young JA put forward the theory that the relevant Australian definition was changed to refer to 'wishes' instead of 'directions' in order to clarify that the definition catches an informal expression of wishes that the giver expects to be carried out (rather than a formal directions). Young JA held (at [186]):

> 'My theory is that the definition of "officer" was introduced into the legislation to cure the problem that emerged in some of the cases such as *Commissioner for Corporate Affairs (Vic) v Bracht* [1989] VicRp 72; [1989] VR 821; (1988) 14 ACLR 728 where (in that case) a father in law, or in other cases a husband, makes his wishes known to a family member whom he correctly expects will carry them out rather than a person making a formal direction where a family relationship is absent.'

44.31 The term 'advice' is a wide term and in this context can be categorised in at least four ways:

1. Lender/parent with interest to protect – eg making it clear on what terms it will continue to lend. But directors still have to decide – eg *Buzzle*,[24] even if the only real alternative may be the withdrawal of banking facilities so that the company then needs to enter formal insolvency proceedings. This is still a decision for the directors.[25]
2. Professional advisers – eg solicitors give advice. Directors should decide whether or not to follow their advice.

23 Advisers advise and trustees decide: Robert Walker J in *Scott v National Trust* [1998] 2 All ER 705 at [717g].

24 [2011] NSWCA 109.

25 See also Millett J's comments (extra-judicially) to the same effect in 'Shadow Directorship – a real or imagined threat to banks' (1991) Insolvency Practitioner, 14.

3. Hidden direction – third party 'in the shadows' gives 'advice' but the directors are expected to follow it. This type of advice is mentioned by the New South Wales Court of Appeal in *Buzzle*.[26]

4. Third party involved in decisions (eg negotiates with third parties).

44.32 It seems that the comments made in the shadow director cases about advisors potentially becoming shadow directors are looking at the types of 'improper' advice within categories 3 and 4 above and not 'proper' advice within categories 1 and 2 – for example *Buzzle*.[27] Although the terms 'proper' and 'improper' do not appear in the relevant judgments.

NEEDS TO BE HABITUAL

44.33 It seems right that the s 435 test should be similar to the shadow director test in that one off advice or one-off following of advice by the directors is not enough. In the words of s 435(10)(a), the director (or group of directors) must be 'accustomed to act' in accordance with the directions or instructions – see eg *Buzzle*[28] referring to a need for 'habitual compliance over a period of time'. There must be 'a pattern of behaviour' – Millett J in *Re Hydrodan (Corby) Ltd*.[29]

44.34 It also seems logical to say that it is not enough that the person *could give* advice or *could give* directions (eg under a contract) if no such directions are in fact given. The directors must actually 'be accustomed to act' in accordance with the directions or instructions – ie the power to control must be put into practice – see eg *Buzzle*.[30]

26 [2011] NSWCA 109.
27 [2011] NSWCA 109.
28 [2011] NSWCA 109 at [198], approving the first instance judge's finding that there needs to be 'habitual compliance over a period of time', citing *Ultraframe (UK) Ltd v Fielding* [2005] EWHC 1638 (Ch) at [1273] to [1278].
29 [1994] BCC 161 (Millett J) at [163].
30 [2011] NSWCA 109 at [232].

45

Is 'domination' of a single director enough?

45.1 The definition of shadow director in the Insolvency Act 1986 (IA 1986) s 251 refers to 'a person in accordance with whose directions or instructions the directors of the company are accustomed to act'. But conversely the 'domination' limb in s 435(10)(a) requires that:

> 'the directors of the company or of another company which has control of it *(or any of them)* are accustomed to act in accordance with his directions or instructions'.[1] (emphasis added)

45.2 Caselaw in relation to shadow directors looks clear that:

(a) 'Domination' of just one director is not enough – *Unidare*; *Sinai Securities;*[2] *Ultraframe.*[3]

(b) 'Domination' of a majority of the board is enough – *Ultraframe,*[4] *Buzzle,*[5] *McKillen.*[6]

(c) The test is seeking to see if who the real decision makers are – *Buzzle*[7] (this looks to be similar to the test used in the considering if there has been an improper purpose[8]).

1 Contrast also the controlling interest definition in the Companies Act 2006 (CA 2006), s 823 stating that a person is taken to be interested in shares if a body corporate is interested in them and 'the body *or its directors* are accustomed to act in accordance with his directions'. The words in italics are clearer in not referring to a single director, but of course s 435(10) is drafted differently.

2 *Lord v Sinai Securities Ltd* [2004] EWHC 1764 (Ch), [2005] 1 BCLC 295 (Hart J) at [27] 'all the directors or at least a consistent majority'.

3 *Ultraframe (UK) Ltd v Fielding* [2005] EWHC 1638 (Ch), [2007] WTLR 835 (Lewison J) at [1270] to [1272].

4 *Ultraframe (UK) Ltd v Fielding* [2005] EWHC 1638 (Ch), [2007] WTLR 835 (Lewison J) at [1270] to [1272].

5 [2011] NSWCA 109 at [238].

6 *McKillen v Misland* [2012] EWHC 2343 (Ch) (David Richards J) at [594].

7 [2011] NSWCA 109 at [233].

8 See eg: *Eclairs Group Ltd v JFX Oil & Gas plc* [2015] UKSC 71 per Lord Sumption at [22] and *Roadchef (Employee Benefits Trustees) Ltd v Hill* [2014] EWHC 109 (Ch) (Proudman J)

Is the s 435(10) test different? It refers to: 'the directors of the company, or another company which has control of it, (or any of them)'. Does the phrase 'or any of them' in this context apply to (i) the directors or (ii) the companies? There is no reported caselaw on this.

45.3 There was some discussion of the position in relation to shadow directors by the Company Law Review in 2000 – see Appendix B to this book. The Review asked whether domination of just one director should be enough to make a person a shadow director. Objections were received to this and no change was proposed (or made) to the relevant law.

45.4 Another insolvency statute has now expressly provided for a potential liability where there is a similar form of domination of a single director. The Company Directors Disqualification Act 1986 (CDDA 1986) was (from October 2015) amended[9] to extend it beyond directors and shadow directors. A court can now disqualify those who (broadly) 'dominate' a single director who is then disqualified (the 'main transgressor'). The new provision, in CDDA 1986, s 8ZA, extends the court's ability to make a disqualification order to cover a person ('P') who has 'exercised the requisite amount of control' over the main transgressor.

45.5 This is defined to require any of the relevant conduct leading to the disqualification of the main transgressor being 'the result of the main transgressor acting in accordance with P's directions or instructions'.[10] But there is an express exclusion where the requisite amount of influence over the main transgressor applies 'by reason only that the main transgressor acts on advice given by P in a professional capacity'.[11]

45.6 This is obviously different statutory wording compared to s 435(10), but it could be considered relevant that where Parliament wishes such individual director domination to have a consequence that the wording of the statute is fairly clear (unlike s 435(10)).

45.7 The words 'or any of them' in s 435(10(a) do not appear in the definition of shadow director in IA 1986, s 251 and are difficult here. Anthony Zacaroli[12]

at [129]. Discussed in Pollard, 'Exercising powers: Proper purposes rather than best interests: Fiduciaries and Eclairs' (2016) 30 TLI 71, 113 and Pollard, '*Pensions, Contracts and Trusts: Legal Issues on Decision Making*' (Bloomsbury Professional, 2020) at ch 58 (Multiple decision makers).
Also *BTI 2014 LLC v Sequana SA* [2016] EWHC 1686 (Ch), [2017] Bus LR 82 (Rose J) at [494] looking at the statutory purpose test under IA 1986, s 423(3), for challenging a transaction defrauding creditors. Upheld on appeal, *BTI 2014 LLC v Sequana SA* [2019] EWCA Civ 112, [2019] 2 All ER 784, but this point not considered. An appeal to the Supreme Court was heard in May 2021.

9 By the Small Business, Enterprise and Employment Act 2015 (SBEEA 2015), s 105.

10 CDDA 1986, s 8ZA(2).

11 CDDA 1986, s 8ZA(3).

12 This used to appear in the chapter by Zacaroli at ch H5 Segal, Totty and Moss, *Insolvency* (Looseleaf Sweet & Maxwell). See former para H5-03. Repeated in the current commentary at F2-26.

previously took the view that they render s 435(10)(a) 'far wider' than s 251 and that a person will control a company if just one director is accustomed to act in accordance with his instructions or directions. So there could be significant scope for a 'nominee' director giving rise to control (even if the majority of directors are not 'controlled' and so the controller is not a shadow director[13]).

45.8 This seems to be an odd result. If right, then the 'controller' would potentially not have control of the board (or a majority), but only of one director. A single director is not himself (or herself) treated as having control of the company.[14] There seems to be no logic in an interpretation that results in one person who gives directions to one director being treated as having control of the company.

45.9 This would be odd for a variety of reasons:

(a) The 'dominator' would not be a shadow director but would have s 435(10) control?

(b) A single director does not as such have control of the company – but his or her 'dominator' does?

(c) The use of the word 'are' later in s 435(10)(a) indicates plural directors?

(d) The definition would be expected to be looking for 'real influence' in the company's affairs? – eg the shadow director cases: *MC Bacon*,[15] *Deverell* and *Buzzle*.

(e) It seems possible to construe the words 'any of them' in s 435(10(a) to refer to the companies (not the directors).

45.10 The position may differ if the individual director is the main decision maker or driving force on the board (and the other directors tend to follow his or her lead). See eg, *Buzzle*. There is an analogy here with the position where questions of improper purpose arise in relation to a decision by a board.[16] In this area the courts look for the purpose of a majority of the directors (eg *Eclairs*[17]) or of the 'real driver' of the decision (eg *Roadchef*[18]).

13 Citing *Smithton Ltd v Naggar* [2014] EWCA Civ 939, [2015] 1 WLR 189, [2015] 2 BCLC 22 per Arden LJ at [89], *Re Unisoft Group Ltd (No 3)* [1994] 1 BCLC 609, 620 (Harman J), *Lord v Sinai Securities Ltd* [2004] EWHC 1764 (Ch) at [27]; [2005] 1 BCLC 295, 303 (Hart J) and *Ultraframe (UK) Ltd v Fielding* [2005] EWHC 1638 (Ch); [2005] All ER (D) 397 (Jul); [2007] WTLR 835 (Lewison J) at [1270].

14 A director is not, as such, treated as associated with his or her fellow directors under s 435 and so they do not as such have control as a group under s 435(6) (absent some other association – eg if they were all related).

15 *Re MC Bacon Ltd (No 2)* [1991] Ch 127 (Millett J).

16 See Pollard, *Pensions, Contracts and Trusts: Legal Issues on Decision Making* (Bloomsbury Professional, 2020) at ch 58 (Multiple decision makers).

17 *Eclairs Group Ltd v JKX Oil & Gas plc* [2013] EWHC 2631 (Ch), [2014] 1 BCLC 202 (Mann J) at [214], citing the Australian case, *Bell Group Ltd v Westpac Banking Corp (No 9)* [2008] WASC 239 at [4454]. Mann J's judgment was overturned by the Court of Appeal, but subsequently upheld by the Supreme Court [2015] UKSC 71 This point did not feature in the appeals.

18 *Roadchef (Employee Benefits Trustees) Ltd v Hill* [2014] EWHC 109 (Ch), [2015] WTLR 333 (Proudman J) at [129] and [130].

EXAMPLE OF ILLOGICALITIES OF AN EXPANDED 'CONTROL' TEST BASED ON A SINGLE DIRECTOR

45.11 Basing control through the domination limb in s 435(10)(a) to any one director would give rise to odd results. To look at a simple example:

- Mr A is a director of Company Z and one of many on its board. He is not the driving force or main decision maker on the board;
- Ms B gives directions or instructions to A in accordance with which he is accustomed to act, but not the other board members (so Ms B is not a shadow director of Company Z);
- Company Z is not an employer in a pension scheme, but wholly owns Company Y which is such an employer in relation to an occupational pension scheme;
- Neither A nor B are directors (or shadow directors) of Company Y;
- Neither A nor B have any other connection or association with Company Z or Company Y or the pension scheme.

45.12 So, a question for TPR's moral hazard powers in relation to the pension scheme is whether A or B is 'associated' or 'connected' with an employer, ie associated or connected with Company Y.

45.13 An association or connection with Company Z is not enough (on its own) as Company Z is not an employer (it is not enough for an association with Company Z to mean association with Company Y, even though Company Z wholly-owns and so 'controls' Company Y).

45.14 But someone who 'controls' Company Z will, by reason of that alone, be treated as controlling Company Y and so will be associated with Company Y.

45.15 So far as Mr A is concerned, as a director he is associated and connected to Company Z, but this is not on its own enough to make him associated with Company Y. So this means that (absent some other connection or association with Y) he is not within the net of potential targets for a moral hazard order in relation to the OPS.

45.16 Conversely if a wide interpretation of s 435(10)(a) is taken, it would mean that Ms B, although not a director or shadow director of Company Z is treated as having 'control' of Company Z by reason of her directions and instructions to A. So she would be treated by reason of that as also having control of Company Y and hence would be an associate of Company Y. So a contribution notice (CN) could potentially be issued against her (if the other required conditions for a CN are met).

45.17 This would be an illogical result. A director (A) of the parent company is not an associate of the subsidiary, but someone (B) who gives directions to

A (which A habitually follows) would 'control' the parent and so be an associate of the subsidiary.

45.18 It can be argued that it is inappropriate to give such a wide (and illogical) interpretation to the control test in s 435(10)(a). The question is whether this is sufficiently illogical to support a court taking a narrower view of the definition, even if it was more clearly expressed.[19]

INTERPRETING 'ANY OF THEM'

45.19 A better interpretation is to construe the words 'or any of them' in s 435(10(a) as applying not to 'the directors of the company', but to control of the directors of any of: (i) 'the company'; or (ii) 'another company which has control of it'. So, the s 435(10)(a) limb would require the directors of the relevant company to be accustomed to act in accordance with instructions or directions – ie the relevant board (or majority) and not just one single director. This would be similar to the position for shadow directors.

45.20 Such a narrower interpretation (requiring wider influence) is consistent with the wording of s 435(10)(a). To recap, it states,

> 'the directors of the company or of another company which has control of it (or any of them) are accustomed to act in accordance with his directions or instructions'.

45.21 The use of the word 'are' in the second half of the section looks to be a reference back to 'the directors' of the relevant company and therefore to be reinforcing the use of the plural.

45.22 This view (that more than one director is needed) is more consistent with the Court of Appeal decision in *Secretary of State for Trade and Industry v Deverell*[20] in relation to the statutory definition of shadow director that the purpose of the legislation was to identify those, other than professional advisers, with real influence in the company's corporate affairs. (As against this, however, the second limb of the definition of 'control' in s 435(10)(b) only requires a one-third shareholding, not a majority.)

45.23 In *Re a Debtor (No 87 of 1993) (No 2)*[21] Rimer J viewed 'control' of just one director (although the points raised above were not discussed) as falling within s 435(10)(a). The case dealt with a challenge to an arrangement in a

19 Compare the interpretation of a different provision of the Insolvency Act 1986 (adopted employment contracts) by the House of Lords in *Paramount Airways: Powdrill v Watson* [1995] 2 AC 394 per Lord Browne-Wilkinson at 447H referring to anomalous results.

20 [2000] 2 All ER 365, CA.

21 [1996] 1 BCLC 63 (Rimer J).

bankruptcy and one issue was whether a creditor, Stylemoney Limited, was an associate of the debtor under s 435. Rimer J held that it was, apparently on the basis that the debtor gave instructions to his wife who was one of the directors.

45.24 But Rimer J did not discuss whether s 435(10)(a) only requires 'control' of one director. The earlier part of the judgment shows that he seems to have been ready to conclude that the debtor was a de facto director anyway, based on the debtor's involvement in the company. Furthermore Rimer J suspected that the debtor's remuneration from Stylemoney had deliberately been left uncertain with a view to avoiding the risk that Stylemoney might become an associate by reason of being the debtor's employer. So Rimer J's conclusions look to have turned on the particular facts of this case.

45.25 In the shadow director case, *Ultraframe*,[22] Lewison J (as he then was) noted the difficulty with the language in the shadow director definition in s 251, but held that it was appropriate to construe that provision as requiring domination of a majority of the board, on the basis that this meant the definition caught a person who 'in reality controlled the activities of the company'. Such a person is to be 'subject to the same statutory liabilities and disabilities as a person who is a *de jure* director'. Applying the same analogy to the s 435(10)(a) test, it would be inappropriate to consider a dominator of just one director as having 'control', when that director did not have control.

SHADOW DIRECTORS AND CONTROLLERS – TIMING ISSUES

45.26 One potential issue in relation to the extension of the 'connected' and 'associated' provisions to catch shadow directors or controllers can be to work out the time period over which such shadow directors or controllers are in place (and so associated or connected). With express directors and employees, it will usually be clear over what period they have been in office in relation to a particular company. But for a shadow director or controller it may not be clear. It must be the case that a person who is a shadow director at one date (eg because he or she then gives a direction) can cease to hold that 'position' after a time. For example if instructions or directions were given (and habitually followed) five years ago, but not since, has the instructor now ceased to be a shadow director?

45.27 This point does not seem to have arisen much for discussion in the shadow director cases. But it could be relevant, depending on the facts. For example, in relation to an FSD claim based on insufficient resources, TPR must choose a date at which the insufficiently resourced test is carried out and

22 *Ultraframe (UK) Ltd v Fielding; Northstar Systems Ltd v Fielding* [2005] EWHC 1638 (Ch), [2005] All ER (D) 397 (Jul), [2007] WTLR 835 (Lewison J) at [1272]. The judgment in *Ultraframe* is rather long, being later described by Lewison LJ as 'for those with stamina and nothing better to do for a few days, the whole of the gargantuan judgment is reported at [2007] WTLR 835' – see *Granada Group Ltd v The Law Debenture Pension Trust Corporation Plc* [2016] EWCA Civ 1289, [2017] 2 BCLC 1, [2017] Pens LR 5 at [27].

the relevant target (say a company being claimed to be a shadow director of the employer) must be connected or associated with the employer on that date.[23] Is it enough if the target had been a shadow director by reason of actions which ended some time before the selected date?

45.28 It seems that a controller ceases to be a shadow director (or to have control) if the relevant practice ceases. Thus in Australia in *Commissioner of the Australian Federal Police v Courtenay Investments Ltd [No 4]*[24] Edelman J commented:

> '8.7.1 The meaning of "accustomed" in the Corporations Law.
>
> 271 Senior counsel for the defendant companies submitted that the notion of a custom was a present state informed by past practice. I accept this submission.
>
> 272 The Corporations Law did not define "accustomed". The word bears its ordinary meaning as a verb of being "in the habit of doing something" 164 or "to familiarise by custom or use".165 In *Buzzle Operations Pty Ltd (in liq) v Apple Computer Australia Pty Ltd*,166 Hodgson JA said of a similar statutory formula in relation to shadow directors that:
>
>> the statutory formula contemplates the directors being accustomed to act in accordance with the instructions or wishes of a person, in the sense of treating those instructions or wishes as themselves being a sufficient reason so to act, rather than making their own decisions in which those instructions or wishes are merely take into account as one factor, external to the management of the company, bearing on what is in the best interests of the company.
>
> 273 Habits, customs, or usage come to an end when a practice is terminated. Hence, as Finn J said in *Australian Securities Commission v AS Nominees Ltd*, 167 the concept of "accustomed to act" requires that "*as and when* directors are directed or instructed, they are accustomed to act" (emphasis added).
>
> 274 Apart from the continuing temporal notion inherent in a custom, it would not be consistent with the evident purpose of the relevant interest provisions of the Corporations Law to require a person to disclose an interest based on past practices or events that are no longer relevant at the time of disclosure.
>
>> 164 Oxford English Dictionary Online.
>>
>> 165 Macquarie Dictionary Online.
>>
>> 166 *Buzzle Operations Pty Ltd (in liq) v Apple Computer Australia Pty Ltd* [2011] NSWCA 109; (2011) 81 NSWLR 47, 51 [9].
>>
>> 167 *Australian Securities Commission v AS Nominees Ltd* (1995) 133 ALR 1, 52.'

23 See ch 75 'TPR: Moral Hazard Powers' in Pollard, *Corporate Insolvency: Employment and Pension Rights* (7th edn, Bloomsbury Professional, 2021).

24 [2015] WASC 101 (Edelman J).

46

Appointors of nominee directors or board representatives

46.1 This chapter looks at the issues in relation to 'connected' or 'associated' status where a person (here 'Investor') taking shares in an investee company (the 'Company') which is part of a group containing a UK defined benefit pension scheme. The Investor will want to consider if it has a risk of being treated as connected or associated with the Company (and perhaps with an employer in an occupational pension scheme) as a result.

46.2 There may be a particular concern because the Pensions Act 2004 (PA 2004) gives the UK Pensions Regulator powers, if relevant conditions are met, to make third parties liable to fund or contribute to a pension scheme. These are the 'moral hazard powers' – see Chapter 14 above.

46.3 This chapter looks at the risk of the Investor becoming connected with the Company if the Investor appoints one or more persons to the board of directors of the Company and has close dealings with them.

46.4 The Investor will become connected with the Company if any of the directors of the Company is associated with the Investor (eg is an employee or director of the Investor).

46.5 Take a typical situation:

- the Investor (and its associates) will after the investment have less than one-third of the voting rights at a general meeting of the Company;
- the Investor wants to be able to appoint one or more directors into the Company;
- the nominated person (the Individual) becoming a director may be an employee of the Investor or a director of the Investor;
- the Company (or one of its subsidiaries) is an employer (or former employer) in a UK defined benefit pension scheme.

Could there be a pensions issue for the Investor in these circumstances?

46.6 Broadly, TPR's moral hazard powers are not automatic just because a third party is associated or connected (contrast the Employee Retirement Income Security Act of 1974 (ERISA) rules in the US). Additional tests would need to be satisfied – in particular, that the Pensions Regulator considers it reasonable to make an order against the third party.

46.7 But the clearest 'safe haven' for an Investor is to try to ensure that it does not satisfy the connected or associated test. The issues on this are now discussed in the rest of this section.

ASSOCIATED OR CONNECTED?

46.8 The concern for pension purposes is whether the Investor (or a company in its group) ends up as being 'connected' or 'associated' with a company in the group which is an 'employer' (for statutory purposes) in relation to the Company pension scheme (an employer for this purpose generally means a company which employs active members of the pension scheme, but can also include former employers).

46.9 The test for being associated or connected is quite complex.

INVESTOR HAS ONE-THIRD VOTING CONTROL – IA 1986, S 435(10)(A)

46.10 The main way in which a third-party shareholding Investor would be associated would be if the Investor (and its associates) had control of a large enough number of votes (eg held voting shares in the Company or its parent) to be deemed to have 'control' of the Company.

46.11 The first limb of control is defined in the legislation as being entitled to exercise one third or more of the voting powers at any general meeting of the Company. Presumably the Investor can check whether or not this applies in any particular case.

46.12 Note that it is likely that the Investor would become entitled to exercise voting power if it controls the voting rights, even if it does not fully own the shares (eg if there is a charge over the shares in favour of the Investor or one of its associated entities) – the *Box Clever* case.

46.13 There may be issues if the Investor usually has less than one-third of the votes, but may be able to have more voting rights in some limited circumstances – see Chapter 39 above.

DIRECTOR 'ACCUSTOMED TO ACT' ON DIRECTIONS – IA 1986, S 435(10)(B)

46.14 The second limb of 'control' is if a director of the Company is accustomed to act in accordance with directions or instructions from the Investor.

46.15 This is similar to the 'shadow director' test for insolvency and corporate law – but it is unclear if this could apply if just one director so acts, or whether the whole board (or a majority) must so act.

46.16 Given that the Individual, as one of the directors of the Company:

- will have been nominated/appointed by the Investor; and
- may have an ongoing information/discussion role with the Investor (and can be seen for some purposes as representing the Investor to the Company),
- there may well be more risk of a claim that the Individual falls within this 'accustomed to act' limb of the control test.

46.17 The Investor should take care that the Individual acts and is seen to act independently. This will help to reduce any 'shadow director' risk as well.

NOMINATED DIRECTOR IS 'ASSOCIATED' WITH INVESTOR?

46.18 The connected/associated test includes a specific provision that a person (here the Investor) is deemed connected with a company (here the Company) if that person is associated with any director (or shadow director) of the Company.

46.19 If the Investor is 'associated' with any of the directors of the Company (including the nominated director), that will mean that the Investor is connected with the Company. This may well mean that the issue is whether or not the Investor is 'associated' with the nominated director?

46.20 The main grounds for a person being associated with the Investor are if the person is:

- a director (includes a de facto or shadow director) of the Investor. This will include if the Individual is a non-executive director of the Investor (or the Company); or
- an officer or employee of the Investor; or
- 'controls' (perhaps with associates) the Investor or is in partnership with it (or involved in trusts etc).

46.21 If the only connection of the Investor with the person is that he or she is a self-employed consultant (not an employee of the Investor) then this is not enough to make the Investor associated with the person.

COMPANY IS NOT A PENSION SCHEME EMPLOYER?

46.22 If the Investor is connected with the Company by this 'common director' route, the Investor will be connected with the relevant Company, but not (absent something else – eg deemed control of the Company) with the subsidiaries of the Company.

46.23 So if the actual employers in the group pension scheme are the subsidiaries and not the Company, the connection with the Company will not be a connection with an 'employer' and so will not (on its own) be enough to allow a moral hazard power order against the Investor.

46.24 The position will differ if the Company is still deemed to be an employer for statutory purposes eg in some circumstances if it used to be an employer under the pension scheme in the past.

OTHER POINTS TO NOTE

46.25 The Investor needs to consider its group structure. Interests of any associated person (eg other group companies) can also be relevant. Interests of associates (eg other Investor group companies) can be aggregated (eg for the voting control test). This may also apply to other third parties too.

46.26 The nominated person, as a director of the Company, will be associated with the Company and so in the same way as any director or employee (potentially) may be the subject of a pensions CN (although probably not an FSD) in relation to any occupational pension scheme of which the Company is (or potentially has been) an 'employer'. This may be a factor for the Individual in accepting appointment. The Investor should consider carefully the implications and extent of any comfort it may give to the Individual (eg an indemnity).

46.27 The connected/associated test applies to companies incorporated outside the UK as well as in the UK.

DIRECTOR IN HOLDING COMPANY – ASSOCIATED WITH SUBSIDIARIES?

46.28 What is the position if an investor (Investor) has a minority stake (less than one-third voting power) in a company (Holding Company) and perhaps appoints a director of the Holding Company? The other shareholders are not associated with the Investor but there may be a shareholder agreement. Is the Investor connected with or an associate of a subsidiary (Subsidiary) of the Holding Company?

46.29 Clearly the Holding Company is an associate of the Subsidiary because it controls the Subsidiary. It is much less clear whether the Investor would be considered to be connected or associated with the Subsidiary. The analysis is as follows:

(a) The Investor will be connected with the Holding Company if any of the directors of the Holding Company are associated with the Investor (eg officers, employees or directors of the Investor). This can be common. But merely because the Investor is connected with the Holding Company, does not mean that the Investor is associated with the Holding Company. So, if this is the only link, the Investor is not associated with companies controlled by the Holding Company and so is not connected or associated with the Subsidiary.

(b) If the Investor had control of the Holding Company, it would also have control of the Holding Company's subsidiaries (Insolvency Act 1986 (IA 1986), s 435(10)(b)) and so would be associated with those subsidiaries – s 435(7). But the Investor will often not have control of the Holding Company since control generally requires the Investor either becoming (in effect) a dominator or being entitled to exercise or control the exercise of one third or more of the voting power at any general meeting of the company – see Part 8 above.

(c) If the Investor were associated with the Holding Company (eg an individual who is also a director of the Holding Company), it seems unlikely that it would just by virtue of that association be treated as associated with the Subsidiary as well. Section 435(7) provides that a company is an associate of another person if 'that person and persons who are his associates together have control of it'. Given that the Holding Company has control of the Subsidiary, it does not seem appropriate to treat the Investor as 'together' with the Holding Company having control of the subsidiary. It seems more likely that these words are meant to catch the situation where the addition of the associates together is needed to show control – see chapter 40 above.

(d) It would seem wrong to apply a further 'chain principle': if A is associated with B and B controls C, this should not mean that A is associated with C by reason of s 435(7). Thus while the Investor is only connected with the Holding Company under s 249 (and not associated under s 435), it seems clear that s 435(7) will not apply.

(e) Depending on the facts, there may be an argument that the Investor's relationship with other investors could mean that the Investor is in fact controls with the Holding Company as well – see the Singapore cases cited in Chapter 40 above). The problem here is once again the wording at the end of s 435(10) and whether some degree of association is needed between the two or more persons whose shareholdings in the Holding Company are being aggregated with the Investor.

PART 10

CONTROL AFTER INSOLVENCY?

47

Is existing control lost if the company enters insolvency?

47.1 Does entry of a company into an insolvency process impact on its relationship with others in the group – eg do they cease to be associated? In other words, how is the association between members of the group affected where one of the companies involved enters a formal insolvency process – ie a liquidation, administration, administrative receivership (AR) or company voluntary arrangement (CVA)?[1] This chapter does not consider whether a Part 1A Moratorium has an impact on control.

47.2 For practically all purposes in a liquidation, administration or administrative receivership, real control of the business and affairs of the insolvent company will, on the appointment of the relevant insolvency practitioners, pass away from the board of directors (or shareholders) to the relevant insolvency practitioners.

47.3 Two formal insolvency processes are not considered further in this Part in relation to control:

- In a CVA the powers of the directors (and shareholders) will depend on the terms of the CVA, once approved (CVAs are considered further in Part 13 below).
- Liquidations which are member voluntary liquidations (MVLs) are, by definition solvent, so more powers remain with the directors and shareholders.

47.4 A less formal insolvency process is also not considered further: A fixed charge receivership, where a receiver (who is not an administrative receiver) is appointed under the terms of a mortgage or other security document (or under statute, in particular the Law of Property Act 1925). Such a fixed charge receiver takes charge of the relevant charged asset, but does not need to be a registered insolvency practitioner, under the Insolvency Act 1986 (IA 1986).

1 This Part is based on Pollard, 'Insolvency and control: the impact of corporate insolvency on 'control' under section 435(10) of the Insolvency Act 1986' (2019) 32(4) Insolvency Intelligence, 127.

47.5 Given that in a liquidation, administration or administrative receivership practical control has passed to the insolvency practitioners, does this mean that (say) a solvent parent company no longer has 'control' of the insolvent company under s 435(10)?

47.6 In such a group situation the actual practical control of the insolvent company will be with the insolvency practitioners, who will act independently and not at the control or direction of the parent. Looking at s 435(10), it seems that the effect of the formal insolvency will be that:

(a) for the purposes of s 435(10)(a) (what is called in this book the test of 'dominating' the directors[2]), the directors may no longer exercise any powers or responsibilities. Indeed in a liquidation (court or voluntary) the office holders may, by virtue of the appointment of the liquidators automatically cease to hold office. But they clearly do remain in post in receiverships and administrations (unless they resign or are removed). But in practice any control though 'domination' of directors is much less relevant, as the directors themselves no longer have any powers in relation to the company (save for minor residual powers) – see the discussion in Chapter 50 (Dominated Directors) below'.

(b) looking at s 435(10)(b) (control through voting power), this limb refers expressly to voting power at 'any' general meeting. But in practice general meetings of shareholders may no longer be held – they may theoretically be possible (and this hypothetical possibility may be argued to be enough – *Unidare plc v Cohen*[3]) but the practical power of such meetings has ceased.

47.7 So a more natural reading of the two limbs of the s 435 control test would seem to be that the parent has ceased to have control of the subsidiary. But is this the effect of s 435(10)? Ultimately this is a question of statutory interpretation, applying the tests in s 435(10) to what has happened.

47.8 The two limbs in the s 435(10) definition of 'control' are both to a degree technical tests that do not necessarily match 'actual' control. For example, before insolvency a voting shareholding of 40% in a two party joint venture company is enough to give 'control' within the shareholding limb in s 435(10)(b), even though it may not give practical control (which would usually rest with the 60% shareholder, subject to any shareholder agreement).

47.9 The existing caselaw is sparse, but the better view seems to me to be that the entry of a company into a formal insolvency process, with the appointment of insolvency practitioners, means that the parent/major shareholder:

(a) liquidation – no longer 'controls' the company within s 435(10); and

(b) administration – probably no longer controls; and

(c) administrative receivership – may still control – *Box Clever*.

2 Although note that the word 'dominating' does not appear in s 435.
3 *Re Kilnoore Ltd: Unidare plc v Cohen* [2005] EWHC 1410 (Ch), [2006] Ch 489 (Lewison J) at [34].

48

Insolvency and control: Existing caselaw

48.1 There is little reported case law on the effect of formal insolvency on the tests in the Insolvency Act 1986 (IA 1986), s 435, save for the decision the Court of Appeal in June 2019 in the *Box Clever* case, *Granada UK Rental & Retail Ltd v The Pensions Regulator*,[1] upholding the decision of the Upper Tribunal (UT) in 2018.[2]

48.2 *Box Clever* is discussed in more detail below. It dealt with a number of issues in relation to the Pensions Regulator's statutory powers, but for current purposes the material point is that it dealt with the position on administrative receivership (AR). This case is discussed further below, but broadly both the UT and the Court of Appeal held that the insolvent company (in AR) remained under the 'control' of its shareholders within s 435 and so the ultimate 50% joint venture partner was an 'associate' of the insolvent employer company at the relevant time and so could be made the subject of a financial support direction (FSD) order by the Pensions Regulator under the Pensions Act 2004.

48.3 Looking wider, the Insolvency Act definitions of 'connected' and 'associated' do not feature much in caselaw, whether in relation to insolvency or pensions. Until the *Box Clever/Granada* line of cases, the only reported case discussing in any detail the 'control' concept in s 435(10) was the decision of Lewison J in *Unidare plc v Cohen*.[3] In practice this may well be because in many cases the association test is clearly met and the timing for being associated arises prior to the relevant formal insolvency process starting (eg in relation to the statutory provisions under IA 1986 dealing with the avoidance of antecedent transactions).

1 *Granada UK Rental & Retail Ltd v The Pensions Regulator* [2019] EWCA Civ 1032, [2020] ICR 747, [2019] Pens LR 20 (Patten, Newey and Males LJJ).

2 [2018] UKUT 164 (TCC), [2018] All ER (D) 16 (Jun) (Rose J, HHJ Herrington and Ian Abrams).

3 *Re Kilnoore Ltd: Unidare plc v Cohen* [2005] EWHC 1410 (Ch), [2006] Ch 489 (Lewison J).

49

What is the effect if a company enters into an insolvency process?: example

49.1 Does entry of a company into an insolvency process impact on its relationship with others in the group – eg do they cease to be associated (or connected) within the Insolvency Act 1986 (IA 1986), s 435?

49.2 Take a (relatively) simple example, focusing mainly on the position of OpCo, the main trading company in a group:

- OpCo is a company, and the employer in relation to an occupational pension scheme, P Plan.
- B Co is the immediate parent of OpCo (holding all its shares) and A Co is the immediate parent of B Co (again holding all its shares).
- X is a director of OpCo and Y is a director of A Co.
- T Co is a trustee company, wholly owned by OpCo, and acts as the sole trustee of P Plan.

In diagrammatic form:

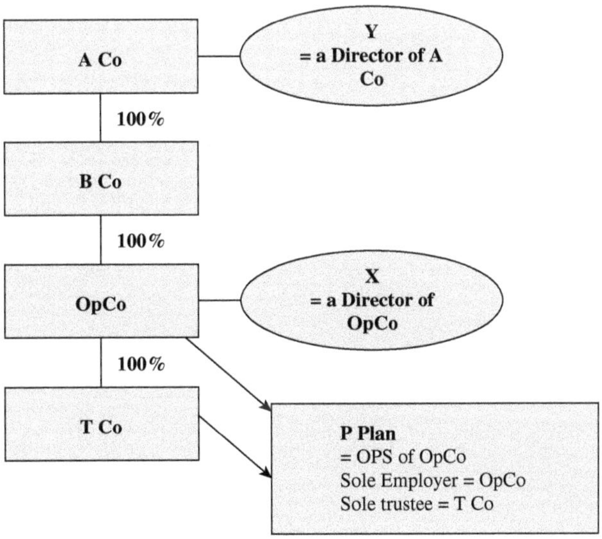

49.3 Before insolvency, these facts mean that for s 435 purposes:

- B Co controls OpCo by virtue of its 100% shareholding in OpCo – s 435(10)(b). A Co similarly controls B Co and so also controls OpCo. This means that both A Co and B Co are associated with OpCo – s 435(7).
- X is associated with OpCo by virtue of being a director of OpCo – s 435(4) and (9). Each of X and any companies associated with X (eg of which X is a director or employee) is also connected with OpCo – s 249.
- Y is not associated or connected with OpCo, unless some other association not stated above can be found (eg if Y were a shadow director of OpCo – s 249 – or was someone who had 'control' of A Co).
- T Co looks to be controlled by OpCo, by virtue of OpCo's shareholding in T Co. This seems to mean that T Co is associated with OpCo, despite the exclusions in some provisions in s 435 for pension scheme trustees – see s 435(5). This is also despite the directors of T Co including some member-nominated directors elected by the pension scheme members (under the member-nominated trustee and director provisions in the Pensions Act 2004 (PA 2004)) and an independent director (appointed under specific provisions in T Co articles of association). T Co may also be 'connected' with OpCo if any of T Co's directors (or employees) is also a director (or shadow director) of OpCo – IA 1986, s 249.

50

Insolvency and 'Dominated' Directors – s 435(10)(a)

50.1 In practice, in group situations it is more likely than 's 435 control' by a parent company would be shown through the voting power limb in the Insolvency Act 1986 (IA 1986), s 435(10)(b) than the 'dominated director' limb in s 435(10)(a). In practice the voting power limb is likely to be easier to show in a group context. In addition, there is a great similarity between the test in s 435(10)(a) and the general 'shadow director' test under s 251.[1] A large number of parent companies can be expected to be aware of the need to avoid becoming a shadow director (or a controller under s 435(10)(a)).

50.2 On the onset of formal insolvency over a company (and the appointment of IPs) the role of the directors usually ceases to be of importance altogether. Instead control of the business and assets of the company passes to the insolvency practitioners.

50.3 The general rule is that once a formal insolvency process starts, the directors cease to have any relevant powers in relation to the company.

- In a court winding-up order, all directors arguably cease to hold office automatically: *Measures Brothers Ltd v Measures*,[2] discussed below.
- In a voluntary winding-up (members' or creditors'), all powers of the directors cease: IA 1986, s 91(2) (MVL) and s 103 (CVL). There are some limited exceptions to this:
  - In an MVL, if the company in general meeting or the liquidator sanctions their continuance – IA 1986, s 91(2) – or if no liquidator is appointed by the company, in which case some limited powers remain – IA 1986, s 114.
  - In a CVL, if the liquidation committee (or if there is no such committee, the creditors) sanction their continuance – s 103.

1 See Part 9 above. Note that a person being a shadow director of a company does not make that person an associate of the company within s 435 (but it does make the person connected with the company within s 249).

2 [1910] 2 Ch 248, CA.

- There is no express provision in IA 1986 dealing with the powers of the directors in a court winding-up (it may perhaps have been assumed that they ceased to hold office automatically). In *Re Oriental Bank Corp ex p Guillemin*,[3] Chitty J applied the same position as for voluntary liquidations to a provisional liquidator. In practice it is generally taken that directors cease to have any powers.[4]

- In an administration, the directors remain in office, but cannot exercise any management powers without the administrator's consent – IA 1986, Sch B1, para 64(1). Management powers are defined to mean any power which could be exercised to interfere with the exercise of the administrator's powers – para 64(2)(a). Para 64 does not prevent directors from taking action to challenge the appointment of the administrator – *Stephen, Petitioner*[5] and *Closegate Hotel Development (Durham) Ltd v McLean*[6] The administrator may call meetings of the members (para 62) and can remove or appoint directors (para 61).

- In an administrative receivership, the directors remain in office, but generally where the receiver's powers extend to all the business assets and undertaking of the company, they are left with little to do. In *Moss Steamship Co Ltd v Whinney*[7] the Earl of Halsbury held that the appointment of a court receiver 'practically removes the conduct and guidance of the undertaking from the directors appointed by the company and places it in the hands of the manager and receiver'. Directors may have residual powers over any non-charged assets or trust assets or to challenge the receiver's appointment.[8]

3 (1884) 28 ChD 634 (Chitty J). Cited in Keay, *McPherson and Keay: The Law of Company Liquidation* (5th edn, Sweet & Maxwell, 2021) at 7-047, also citing *Re Mawcon* [1969] 1 WLR 78 (Pennycuick J) at [82] and *Re Union Accident Insurance Co Ltd* [1972] 1 WLR 640 (Plowman J).

4 For example, Keay, *McPherson and Keay: The Law of Company Liquidation* (5th edn, Sweet & Maxwell, 2021) at 7-047 and Anderson, *The Framework of Corporate Insolvency Law* (OUP, 2017) at 7.12, citing *Re Farrow's Bank Ltd* [1921] 2 Ch 164, CA per Lord Sterndale MR at [173].

5 [2011] CSOH 119, [2012] BCC 537 (Lord Glennie), following Plowman J in *Re Union Accident Insurance Co Ltd* [1972] 1 WLR 640 dealing with a challenge to provisional liquidators and Scottish cases on receivers: *Elwick Bay Shipping Co Ltd v Royal Bank of Scotland Limited* 1982 SLT 62 and *Toynar Limited v Whitbread Limited* 1988 SLT 433.

6 [2013] EWHC 3237 (Ch), [2014] Bus LR 405 (Richard Snowden QC), following the receivership cases: *Newhart Developments Ltd v Co-operative Commercial Bank Ltd* [1978] QB 814, CA and *Sutton v GE Capital* [2004] EWCA Civ 316, [2004] 2 BCLC 662.

7 [1912] AC 254, HL at [260]. To similar effect, Lord Loreburn LC at [257] and Lord Atkinson at [263] (holding that the appointment 'entirely superseded the company in the conduct of its business' and that the company's powers in relation to its business and assets 'are entirely in abeyance'). Cited by Henderson LJ in *Farnborough Airport v HMRC* [2019] EWCA Civ 118, [2019] 2 All ER 435 at [34] and by the UT in *Box Clever/Granada* [2018] UKUT 164 (TCC) at [178] and [179].

8 On residual powers to challenge the appointment of the receivers see *Newhart Developments Ltd v Co-operative Commercial Bank Ltd* [1978] QB 814, CA and *Sutton v GE Capital* [2004] EWCA Civ 316, [2004] 2 BCLC 662. On this and any residual powers to control any assets not the subject of the mortgage or charge (eg perhaps trust assets) – see Pollard,

An out of court administrative receivership follows similar principles – *Gomba Holdings UK Ltd v Homan.*[9]

50.4 This means that in practice the entry of the company into liquidation, administration or administrative receivership will mean that any control of the shareholder under the dominated director limb in the definition in s 435(10)(a) ceases to be applicable. This is for three reasons:

(a) In a court liquidation (but not a voluntary liquidation or an administration or administrative receivership) it may be that the directors automatically cease to hold office on the appointment of the liquidators. This seems to be the effect of some relatively old caselaw,[10] in particular the Court of Appeal in *Measures Brothers Ltd v Measures*,[11] where Buckley LJ commented:

> 'What has happened is that the plaintiffs did not by affirmative action on their part determine the employment either rightly or wrongly, but that by the operation of a winding-up order made on October 13, 1909, the office itself came to an end.'

This position is supported in some of the commentary,[12] but doubted in others.[13] In a recent book, Hamish Anderson has pointed out that some of the legislation seems to assume that directors remain in office (but not in power).[14]

Given that directors clearly remain in office in voluntary liquidations[15] and administrations,[16] there seems to be little reason for the courts to find that directors automatically cease to hold office in a court liquidation. The cases that indicate to the contrary are probably founded on the basis of an automatic termination because the business is now being run by the insolvency practitioners, instead of the board. A similar position can be seen

Corporate Insolvency: Employment and Pension Rights (7th edn, Bloomsbury Professional, 2021) at 55.35 to 55.45 and Robinson and Walton, *Kerr & Hunter on Receivers and Administrators* (21st edn, Sweet & Maxwell, 2020) at 21–22 to 21–29.

9 [1986] 1 WLR 1301 (Hoffmann J) at 1305E to G and 1307D. Cited by the UT in *Box Clever/Granada* [2018] UKUT 164 (TCC) at [180] and [181].

10 *The Madrid Bank Ltd v Bayley* (1866-67) LR 2 QB 37 (Blackburne J and Shee J) at [40]; *Re Ebsworth & Tidy's Contract* (1889) 42 ChD 23, CA at [43]; *Re Oriental Inland Steam Co* (1874) 9 Ch App 557 at [560]; *Fowler v Broad's Patent Night Light Co* [1893] 1 Ch 724; *Re Farrow's Bank* [1921] 2 Ch 164 at [173].

11 [1910] 2 Ch 248 (CA) per Buckley LJ (dissenting) at p 256.

12 See for example 33.89 in Mortimore, *Company directors: Duties, liabilities and remedies* (3rd edn, OUP, 2017) and Keay, *McPherson and Keay: The Law of Company Liquidation* (5th edn, Sweet & Maxwell, 2021) at 7-049, based on *Measures v Measures* (but commenting that the position is anomalous).

13 For example, Anderson *The Framework of Corporate Insolvency Law* (OUP, 2017) at 7.11 to 7.13.

14 At 7.13 in Anderson, *The Framework of Corporate Insolvency Law* (OUP, 2017) referring to IA 1986, s 133 (public examination of officers in a court liquidation).

15 See IA 1986, s 103 dealing with CVLs.

16 IA 1986, Sch B1, para 61 (an administrator may remove a director).

in relation to employees[17] in a court liquidation[18] or a court receivership,[19] but this seems to now be contrary to the usual position for employees at least before insolvency starts (repudiatory breach does not automatically end employment, but needs to be accepted by the employee[20]) .

In other processes, directors do not generally automatically cease to hold office just because an insolvency practitioner has been appointed. In the case of a liquidation or administrative receivership, there is nothing stopping them resigning. In the case of an administration, the administrator has power to appoint or remove directors (IA 1986, Sch B1, para 61).

(b) The parent has no reason to want to give (or continue to give) directions to the subsidiary's directors if they have no powers over the subsidiary's business or assets. Any pre-existing pre insolvency 'control' through the domination limb in s 435(10)(a) will in practice cease (as a factual matter).

(c) Given that the directors cease to have any real powers, any 'domination' of them ceases to give any meaningful control over the company in any real sense. Construing s 435(10)(a) in context (and taking account of the term being defined in the sub-section, ie 'control'), it is a better interpretation that the s 435(10)(a) limb ceases to apply on the appointment of insolvency practitioners.

50.5 Despite this, a parent company will remain 'connected'[21] with its subsidiary if one of the parent's associates (eg one of its directors or employees) is also a director (or shadow director) of the subsidiary. This is the effect (as mentioned above) of the limited chain in definition of 'connected' in IA 1986, s 249.

50.6 The definition in s 249 in effect allows one onward link if a person is associated with a director (or shadow director). IA 1986, s 249 states:

> '… a person is connected with a company if [that person] is a director or shadow director of the company or an associate of such a director or shadow director' (where 'associate' has the meaning given by s 435, IA 1986)'.

The effect of this is that if (say) A Co employs B, this means that A Co is associated with B (s 435(4)) and if B is a director (or shadow director) of C Co, then this means that A is connected with C Co (but conversely C Co is

17 See Pollard *Corporate Insolvency: Employment and Pension Rights* (7th edn, Bloomsbury Professional, 2021) at ch 12.

18 *Re General Rolling Stock* (1866) LR 1 Eq 346 and *Re Oriental Bank Corpn* (1886) 32 ChD 366. To similar effect, see also the Irish cases: *Donnelly v Gleeson* (1978), *Re Evanhenry Ltd* [1986] IEHC 33 and *Re Swedex* [2010] IEHC 237. And in Australia, similarly *McEvoy v Incat Tasmania Pty Ltd* [2003] FCA 810 (Finkelstein J) at [7].

19 But not in Australia – see *Sipad Holding DDPO v Popovic* [1995] FCA 1737 (Lehane J).

20 See *Geys v Societe Generale* [2012] UKSC 63, [2013] 1 AC 523. Not a case involving insolvency.

21 But not also an 'associate'.

not connected with A Co). But A Co is not 'associated' with C Co, or vice versa (absent some other reason).

50.7 Given the above, the rest of this Part focuses on the potential for 'control' (and hence 'association') to continue following a formal insolvency based on the 'voting power' limb in s 435(10)(b).

51

Insolvency and 'voting power in any general meeting' – s 435(10)(b)

51.1 If a parent company (or group company) was to remain associated through the control limb in the Insolvency Act 1986 (IA 1986), s 435(10)(b), it would need the parent to still be entitled to exercise (or control the exercise) of one-third or more of the 'voting power at any general meeting' of the company.

51.2 So answering this question requires a look at what actually happens in an insolvency process, whether of the parent or the employer company. This chapter goes on to look at the statutory trust over assets and beneficial ownership and whether general meetings can continue to be held.

WHAT IS A GENERAL MEETING OF THE COMPANY?

51.3 The term 'general meeting' used in the second (voting power) limb of s 435(10) is not further defined in s 435 or indeed the rest of the Insolvency Act 1986, save that s 435(11) (dealing with the extension of the provisions to other bodies corporate) provides that references to 'voting power at any general meeting of a company' have effect 'with any necessary modifications'. Nor is the term defined in the Interpretation Act 1978.

51.4 In practice, it seems right that it (and the other references to 'general meeting of the company' in IA 1986[1]) should be taken as a reference to a shareholder meeting under the companies legislation, in particular the Companies Act 2006. This is despite the term 'general meeting' not being included within the list of terms in IA 1986, s 436(2)[2] bearing the same meaning as in the Companies Acts. The term 'general meeting' is not defined in the Companies Act 2006, but in context is solely used in relation to a shareholder meeting.

51.5 IA 1986 was amended in 2017 by the Small Business, Enterprise and Employment Act (SBEEA 2015). In many areas this removed the previous

1 For example IA 1986, s 84 on MVLs: ss 91, 92, 93 and (before 2017) 94; on CVLs.

2 Added in 2009 – see the Companies Act 2006 (Consequential Amendments, Transitional Provisions and Savings) Order 2009 (SI 2009/1941), Sch 1, para 82.

requirements for the calling of meetings during the insolvency.[3] Instead for both members and creditors a 'qualifying decision procedure' is used (IA 1986, s 246ZE(11) and Insolvency Rules 2016,[4] Part 15), namely correspondence, electronic voting, virtual meeting, physical meeting and 'any other decision making procedure which enables all creditors who are entitled to participate in the making of the decision to participate equally'. A physical meeting cannot now be called unless the minimum number of creditors (or members) requests one – IA 1986, s 246ZE(2).

51.6 As an example, the previous requirements for a liquidator (in a CVL or court liquidation) to hold a final general meeting of the members and a general meeting of the creditors prior to dissolution (IA 1986, ss 106 and 146) have, since April 2017, been replaced under SBEEA 2015 by a requirement to send an account of the winding-up to members and creditors.

Meetings of creditors?

51.7 It seems unlikely that the references in s 435(10)(b) to a 'general meeting of the company' can also be construed to apply to a meeting of creditors, rather than members (shareholders or contributories). Various provisions in IA 1986 do refer to a general meeting of creditors. For example:

(a) s 101(2) dealing with appointments to a creditors' committee in a CVL;

(b) ss 106 and 146, dealing with a duty to summon a final meeting, which used as originally enacted (and before their replacement by SBEEA 2015) to use the term 'general meeting' for a meeting of creditors, referring to a 'final general meeting of the company's creditors'; and

(c) s 171(2) dealing with removal of a liquidator used (before its amendment by SBEEA 2015) to distinguish between different meetings in an MVL and a CVL. A liquidator in an MVL could be removed 'by a general meeting of the company' and in a CVL 'by a general meeting of the company's creditors'.

The distinction seems to be drawn between a 'general meeting of the company' (ie one involving members) and a 'general meeting of the creditors'. This strongly points towards a creditor meeting potentially being a general meeting, but would still not qualify as one 'of the company' for the control test within s 435(10)(b).

51.8 For example, rule 15.41 in the Insolvency Rules 2016 is headed 'Company meetings' and requires a 'company meeting' to be called and conducted in accordance with relevant law, including 'any applicable provision in or made

3 See Morgan 'Decision making in insolvency procedures: practical aspects of implementing the changes made by the Insolvency (England and Wales) Rules 2016' (2017) Insolvency Intelligence, 17.

4 Insolvency (England and Wales) Rules 2016 (SI 2016/1024).

under the Companies Act'. In addition, rule 15.39 in the Insolvency Rules 2016 expressly provides that in a decision procedure for contributories (ie including members), 'voting rights[5] are as at a general meeting of the company, subject to any provision of the articles affecting entitlement to vote, either generally or at a time when the company is in liquidation'.

It may be that strictly a later statutory instrument should not be used as a method of interpreting the underlying statute, but this usage does provide support for the view that the usual meaning of 'meeting of the company' is to refer only to a shareholder meeting.

Contributories?

51.9 The term 'contributories' is used in IA 1986. This means 'every person liable to contribute to the assets of the company in the event of it being wound-up' – IA 1986, s 79(1). Generally they will be members (and past members) in an unlimited company, company limited by guarantee (s 74(3)) or with shares that are not fully paid-up – s 74(2)(d). The term 'contributory' also includes a member in a limited company holding shares which are fully paid -up – *Re Angelsey Colliery Company.*[6]

5 IR 2016, rule 15.39 refers to 'voting rights' rather than 'voting power' (the term used in s 435(10)(b)). The use of the expression 'voting power' rather than 'voting rights' was considered significant by Lewison J (as he then was) in *Unidare Plc v Cohen* [2006] Ch 480, but the Court of Appeal in *Box Clever* [2019] EWCA Civ 1032 took a different view, holding, at [128]:

> '[128] Lewison J attached some significance to the reference to 'voting power' in s.435(10)(b) IA 1986. The word "power" gave him "some encouragement to look to the economic reality of the case" (see [58]). In our view, however, the use of the word "power" takes matters no further. "[V]oting power" is apt to refer simply to the sum of the voting rights attached to the issued shares. It may be that the draftsman could have substituted "voting rights", but nothing can be inferred from his choice. It is notable that "voting rights" and "voting power" were used interchangeably in the *Bibby* case, especially in Lord Simonds' speech.'

6 (1866) LR 1 Ch 555. Keay, *McPherson & Keay: The Law of Company Liquidation* (5th edn, Sweet & Maxwell, 2021) at 10-002 also cites *Re National Savings Bank Association* (1866) 1 Ch App 547; *Re Phoenix Oil & Transport Co* [1958] Ch 565; but contrasts *Re Aidall Ltd* [1933] Ch 323. In addition, *Re Hull & County Bank* (1886) 15 ChD 507 at 511, is also cited in *McPherson & Keay: The Law of Company Liquidation* at 7-060.

52

Insolvency: Are any shareholder general meetings actually held?

52.1 During an insolvency process (other than an MVL), by definition the company is insolvent and hence the economic interest of the shareholders in the company is likely to be zero or minimal.[1] The shareholders are unable to give binding directions to the insolvency practitioner (any direction role that remains will fall to the creditors). In these circumstances, it can be seen as less relevant to call and hold shareholder meetings. The cost and time involved would need to be balanced against the materiality of any views gained.

LIQUIDATIONS

52.2 Decisions of creditors or members can be sought in a liquidation, whether by the liquidator (Insolvency Act 1986 (IA 1986), s 168(2)) or as directed by the court (IA 1986, s 195(1)) or requisitioned by creditors or members (IA 1986, s 168(2)). These provisions used to refer to decisions in general meetings, but since the 2017 the amendments made by the Small Business, Enterprise and Employment Act (SBEEA 2015) now envisage use of a 'qualifying decision procedure' (IA 1986, s 246ZE(11) and Insolvency (England and Wales) Rules 2016 (IR 2016), Part 15).

52.3 As mentioned above, this means correspondence, electronic voting, virtual meeting, physical meeting and 'any other decision making procedure which enables all creditors who are entitled to participate in the making of the decision to participate equally'. A physical meeting cannot now be called unless the minimum number of creditors (or members) requests one – IA 1986, s 246ZE(2).

52.4 Views given under such a procedure (including by a meeting) are to be taken into account by the court (IA 1986, s 195) or by a liquidator, but are

1 Thus Keay, *McPherson and Keay: The Law of Company Liquidation* (5th edn, Sweet & Maxwell, 2021) at 8-001: '… where the company is insolvent the interests of the members or contributories as they are called upon liquidation occurring, naturally yield to those of the creditors … '.

not binding or directory – see eg in a court liquidation, IA 1986, s 168(4): 'the liquidator shall use his own discretion'.[2]

ADMINISTRATION

52.5 In an administration, creditors and, to a lesser extent, members, retain some role. But generally this is limited. The administrators must prepare and issue a statement of their proposals for achieving the purpose of the administration – IA 1986, Sch B1, para 49(1). These are then sent to the company's creditors and members – para 49(4). The proposals are then put to the creditors (but not the members) for approval – Sch B1, para 53. This could be at a meeting of creditors. Conversely, there is no requirement for members to approve the proposals.

52.6 If the administrator proposes a CVA and this proposal is agreed by the creditors, the relevant CVA will also require approval by the members (potentially in a meeting).

ADMINISTRATIVE RECEIVERSHIP

52.7 Unlike liquidation and administration, administrative receivership is a contractual enforcement process by a security holder under a floating charge. There is some statutory control now in IA 1986, but less direct effect on the internal operation of the relevant company. The requirements and procedures for general meetings of members will remain applicable under the companies legislation.

MEETINGS IN INSOLVENCY – IMPACT ON S 435(10)(B)

52.8 Ultimately then, in all three types of insolvency procedure there is still a potential for member general meetings to be called and held. But the changes made by SBEEA 2015 mean that in practice in liquidation and administration such physical meetings will become much less common (as contrasted to other forms of qualifying decision procedure).

52.9 The voting power limb of the definition of control in s 435(10)(b) was not changed by SBEEA 2015. In practice it seems better to consider that the limb

2 For example, Keay, *McPherson and Keay: The Law of Company Liquidation* (5th edn, Sweet & Maxwell, 2021) at 8-003 commenting that: 'The liquidator is not a mere servant of the creditors or contributories, and he or she is certainly not bound by any direction made by either group which conflicts with the proper execution of the duties of a liquidator' and citing:

> '*Re David Hamilton Ltd* [1928] NZLR 419 (creditors' resolution directing liquidator to pay in full a creditor's travelling expenses held not binding). Compare also *Re Allebart Pty Ltd* [1971] 1 NSWLR 24; and *Yeomans v Walker* (1986) 10 ACLR 753'.

only applies to a physical meeting of members (and not, say, another qualifying decision procedure, including a virtual meeting under IR 2016, rule 15.5).

52.10 This change in the approval process and the rules for meetings in an insolvency lends support to the view that the control limb based on 'voting power at any general meeting' falls away in a liquidation or administration. The relevant member meetings have ceased to have any control over the real decision maker (the insolvency practitioner) and in practice may well not be held in any event.

52.11 This is not dis-similar to the rules that shift the duties of directors to the company so that they must have regard to the interests of creditors when insolvency is imminent, ie 'when the directors know or should know that the company is or is likely to become insolvent': *BTI 2014 LLC v Sequana SA.*[3]

52.12 Lewison J in *Unidare Plc v Cohen*[4] considered that the reference in s 435(10) should be considered to be to a hypothetical general meeting (and not an actual general meeting). This element of the decision was not later over-ruled by the Court of Appeal in *Box Clever.*[5] Lewison J's comment supports an argument that the voting power limb in s 435(10)(b) remains applicable, even where an insolvency process has started, on the basis that shareholder meetings are still possible and so hypothetically could be held.

3 [2019] EWCA Civ 112 per David Richards LJ at [220], continuing: 'In this context, 'likely' means probable, not some lower test such as that adopted by Hoffmann J in construing the statutory test for the making of an administration order: see *Re Harris Simons Construction Ltd* [1989] 1 WLR 368.' An appeal to the Supreme Court in *Sequana* was heard in May 2021.

4 *Re Kilnoore Ltd: Unidare plc v Cohen* [2006] Ch 480 (Lewison J) at [34].

5 *Granada UK Rental & Retail Ltd v The Pensions Regulator* [2019] EWCA Civ 1032 at [127] to [129].

53

Statutory trust on a liquidation: *Ayerst*

53.1 On a liquidation (whether court or voluntary winding-up) starting, the powers of the directors cease (save perhaps for some limited purposes[1]) and the liquidator takes over the powers of managing the company and dealing with its assets.[2]

53.2 Lord Diplock summarised the position in *Ayerst v C&K (Construction)*[3] (citing the then applicable section numbers in the Companies Act 1948):

> 'Upon the making of a winding-up order:
>
> (1) The custody and control of all the property and choses in action of the company are transferred from those persons who were entitled under the memorandum and articles to manage its affairs on its behalf, to a liquidator charged with the statutory duty of dealing with the company's assets in accordance with the statutory scheme (section 243). Any disposition of the property of the company otherwise than by the liquidator is void (section 227).
>
> (2) The statutory duty of the liquidator is to collect the assets of the company and to apply them in discharge of its liabilities (section 257(1)). If there is any surplus he must distribute it among the members of the company in accordance with their respective rights under the memorandum and articles of association (section 265). In performing these duties in a compulsory winding up the liquidator acts as an officer of the court (section 273), and if the company is insolvent the rules applicable in the law of bankruptcy must be followed (section 317).

1 Save perhaps for limited residual powers to challenge the appointment of the liquidators? By analogy with the receivership case *Newhart Developments Ltd v Co-operative Commercial Bank Ltd* [1978] QB 814, CA.

2 Insolvency Act 1986 (IA 1986), Sch 4, paras 5, 7 and 13.

3 *Ayerst (Inspector of Taxes) v C&K (Construction) Ltd* [1976] AC 167, HL per Lord Diplock at p 176/7. Referring to a court or compulsory winding-up, but stating that the same position would apply to a voluntary winding-up.

(3) All powers of dealing with the company's assets, including the power to carry on its business so far as may be necessary for its beneficial winding up, are exercisable by the liquidator for the benefit of those persons only who are entitled to share in the proceeds of realisation of the assets under the statutory scheme. The company itself as a legal person, distinct from its members, can never be entitled to any part of the proceeds. Upon completion of the winding up, it is dissolved (section 274).'

BENEFICIAL OWNERSHIP

53.3 The consequence of this statutory trust is that the normal rule (for example for tax purposes) is that on a liquidation the 'beneficial ownership' of the assets of the company moves away from the company to be held on a form of statutory trust (controlled by the liquidator) – see *Ayerst*.[4]

53.4 This means that the effect of the entry into liquidation of a parent company (B Co in our example) is that the parent is no longer the beneficial owner of the shares in its subsidiary (in our example OpCo). This means that where the relevant legislation includes a requirement requiring one company to be the beneficial owner of the shares in the other, this test will no longer be met. It does not matter that the company in liquidation (here B Co) retains the legal ownership of its assets.[5]

53.5 Millett LJ summarised the position in *Mitchell v Carter*:[6]

> 'The making of a winding-up order divests the company of the beneficial ownership of its assets which cease to be applicable for its own benefit. They become instead subject to a statutory scheme for distribution among the creditors and members of the company. The responsibility for collecting the assets and implementing the statutory scheme is vested in the liquidator subject to the ultimate control of the court. The creditors do not themselves acquire a beneficial interest in any of the assets, but only have a right to have them administered in accordance with the statutory scheme. These principles were established in *Ayerst (Inspector of Taxes) v C & K (Construction) Ltd* [1976] AC 167. They apply to all the assets of the company, both in England and abroad, for the making of a winding-up order is regarded as having worldwide effect.'

4 [1976] AC 167, HL per Lord Diplock at [179], following *In re Albert Life Assurance Co, The Delhi Bank's case* (1871) 15 SJ 923 per Lord Cairns at [924] and James LJ and Mellish LJ in *In re Oriental Inland Steam Co* (1874) 9 Ch App. 557.
See the discussion in Davis, *Taxation in Corporate Insolvency and Rescue* (6th edn, Bloomsbury Professional, 2009) at 4.6 to 4.15.

5 *Ayerst v C&K (Construction) Ltd* [1976] AC 167, HL per Lord Diplock at [177].

6 [1997] 1 BCLC 673, CA at [686]. Cited in *Re HIH Casualty and General Insurance Ltd* [2005] EWHC 2125 (Ch), [2006] 2 All ER 671 (David Richards J) at [115] and *Fraser Turner Limited v Pricewaterhousecoopers LLP* [2018] EWHC 1743 (Ch) (Philip Marshall QC) at [68].

A similar statement (citing *Ayerst)* was made by Lord Hoffmann in *Buchler v Talbot*[7] itself cited by the Court of Appeal in *Stanford International Bank Ltd v HSBC Bank plc.*[8]

53.6 In Australia, a different view on beneficial ownership has been taken. In *Commissioner of Taxation v Linter Textiles Australia Ltd*[9] the High Court referred to *Ayerst* and the earlier cases it cited, but reached a different decision, holding:

> '55 By analogy with the general law, the circumscribing or suspension by reason of the appointment of the liquidator of the exercise by the usual organs of the company of the incidents of ownership of the assets of the company does not mean that the company itself has ceased to own beneficially its assets within the meaning of s 80A(1). Power to deal with an asset and matters of ownership or title are not interchangeable concepts' [72].
>
> [72] cf *Blankfield v Federal Commissioner of Taxation* (1972) 127 CLR 610 at [615]–[616].

BENEFICIAL OWNERSHIP/STATUTORY TRUST: ADMINISTRATIONS

53.7 It is less clear if the same beneficial ownership position would apply in relation to administrations.

53.8 The Inland Revenue apparently indicated in 1990[10] that they would not normally regard an administration order as affecting the beneficial ownership tests relating to the various group relationships of a parent company.

53.9 But the position seems to have changed following the changes made in 2003 by the Enterprise Act 2002 to the administration regime in IA 1986. Anthony Davis commented in his book '*Taxation in Corporate Insolvency and Rescue*'[11] that there are features of the reformed regime, such as the power to make distributions under IA 1986, Sch B1, para 65(3) and to dissolve the company under IA 1986, Sch B1, para 84, which bring it closer to liquidation where indisputably beneficial ownership is lost.

7 [2004] 2 AC 398 at [28].

8 [2021] EWCA Civ 535, [2021] 1 WLR 3507 per Vos MR at [36].

9 [2005] HCA 20; 220 CLR 592 (Gleeson CJ, Gummow, Hayne, Callinan and Heydon JJ gave a single judgment. McHugh J agreed in a separate judgement. Kirby J agreed but 'using a path somewhat different from that chosen by the other members of the Court' (see [184]). Discussed in Peacock and Walford, 'A question of trust' (2005) 790 Tax J, 13–14.

10 Davis, *Taxation in Corporate Insolvency and Rescue* (6th edn, Bloomsbury Professional, 2009) at 4.17. Seemingly in a technical release (TR 799) issued by the Institute of Chartered Accountants in England and Wales (ICAEW).

11 Davis, *Taxation in Corporate Insolvency and Rescue* at 4.20.

Anthony Davis stated his view that administration does not automatically have the effect that the company loses beneficial ownership of its assets, 'although there may come a point in some administrations where this does occur'.

53.10 In relation to administrations, in *Harms Offshore AHT 'Taurus' GmbH & Co KG v Bloom*[12] the Court of Appeal held that an administration, like a liquidation, imposes a trust of the assets for the benefit of creditors, and this results effectively in an extra-territorial jurisdiction, which may be exercised (in the discretion of the court) to prevent a creditor taking the benefit of a foreign attachment.

53.11 In *Harms Offshore*[13] Stanley Burnton LJ[14] referred to *In re Oriental Inland Steam Co; Ex p Scinde Railway Co*[15] where Mellish LJ held, in relation to a liquidation:

> 'But, in my opinion, the beneficial interest is clearly taken out of the company. What the statute says in the 95th section is, that from the time of the winding up order all the powers of the directors of the company to carry on the trade or to deal with the assets of the company shall be wholly determined, and nobody shall have any power to deal with them except the official liquidator, and he is to deal with them for the purpose of collecting the assets and dividing them amongst the creditors. It appears to me that that does, in strictness, constitute a trust for the benefit of all the creditors, and, as far as this court has jurisdiction, no one creditor can be allowed to have a larger share of the assets than any other creditor.'

In *Harms Offshore*, Stanley Burnton LJ held:

> '24 It seems to me that the trust the existence of which was established in *In re Oriental Inland Steam Co* was a legal construct created to achieve the equitable distribution of the proceeds of the realisation of the assets of the company wherever situated. As Millett LJ pointed out in *Mitchell v Carter* [1997] 1 BCLC 673, 689, it is a trust which confers no beneficial interest on the creditors, who are the beneficiaries. Their only right is to have the assets of the company dealt with in accordance with the statutory scheme applicable to a company that is the subject of a winding up order. Similarly, the creditors of a company in administration are entitled to have the company and its assets dealt with in accordance with the statutory scheme applicable to such companies. The lack of any material distinction between compulsory winding up and administration is demonstrated by the judgment of Mummery LJ in *In re Polly Peck International plc (No 2)* [1998] 3 All ER 812, 827. If the court has a jurisdiction to protect the assets of a company that is being wound up by the court from foreign attachments and executions, in my judgment it has a similar jurisdiction in the case of a company in administration.'

53.12 It could perhaps be arguable that in an administration this statutory trust (similar to that in a liquidation) only applies for the purposes of preserving assets

12 [2009] EWCA Civ 632, [2010] Ch 187.
13 [2009] EWCA Civ 632, [2010] Ch 187 per Stanley Burnton LJ at [16] and [17].
14 With whom Ward LJ and Sir John Chadwick agreed.
15 (1874) LR 9 Ch App 557 at [559].

and not more generally (at least until the administration becomes a distributing administration under the changes to IA 1986 made by the Enterprise Act 2002) which is more like a liquidation.[16]

53.13 Before 2003 the caselaw[17] in relation to limitation periods for claims against a company in administration were similarly held not to be subject to the same moratorium on time running as applies to liquidations. But it now seems better to consider that a distributing administration should be treated for these purposes as the same as a liquidation, both for beneficial ownership purposes and limitation periods.[18]

BENEFICIAL OWNERSHIP: RECEIVERSHIPS

53.14 Conversely, in relation to administrative receiverships, the rule is that although control of the charged assets (in practice likely to be all the assets of the company) passes from the directors to the receivers,[19] they act as agents of the company (even though they are appointed by the relevant security holder and tending to act both in the company's and the charge holder's interests[20]).

53.15 Receiverships have for tax purposes been treated as different to liquidations, with beneficial ownership of the company's assets remaining with the company.[21]

53.16 In *English Sewing Cotton Co Ltd v Inland Revenue Commissioners*[22] Lord Greene MR stated (albeit obiter):

> 'It has never been suggested to my knowledge, and it cannot be suggested on principle, that the appointment of a receiver by a mortgagee affects the beneficial ownership of the shares.'

16 See eg: *Revenue and Customs Commissioners v Football League Ltd* [2012] EWHC 1372 (Ch) (David Richards J) at [102]. Cited in Anderson, *The Framework of Corporate Insolvency Law* (OUP, 2017) at 8.40.

17 *Re Cases of Taff Wells Ltd* [1992] Ch 179 (HHJ Paul Baker QC) at [190B], *Re Maxwell Fleet and Facilities Management Ltd* [1999] 2 BCLC 721 (Jules Sher QC) at [725/7], *Re Cosslett (Contractors) Ltd* [2004] EWHC 658 (Ch) (Patten J) and *Re Leyland Printing Co Ltd* [2010] EWHC 2105 (Ch), [2011] BCC 358 (HHJ Hodge QC) at [11].

18 Eg on limitation periods, Anderson, *The Framework of Corporate Insolvency Law* (OUP, 2017) at 8.40 to 8.42.

19 Eg *Moss Steamship Co Ltd v Whinney* [1912] AC 254 per Lord Atkinson at [263], *Gomba Holdings UK Ltd v Homan* [1986] 1 WLR 1301 (Hoffmann J) at [1305] and *Silven Properties Ltd v Royal Bank of Scotland plc* [2004] 1 WLR 997, CA per Lightman J at [26] and [27].

20 *Silven Properties Ltd v Royal Bank of Scotland plc* [2004] 1 WLR 997, CA. Recently cited in *Devon Commercial Property Ltd v Barnett* [2019] EWHC 700 (Ch) (HHJ Matthews) at [27] and *Farnborough Airport* [2019] EWCA Civ 118 per Henderson LJ at [54].

21 This seems to be the view of HMRC – see Company Taxation Manual at CTM06030.

22 [1947] 1 All ER 679, CA. See the discussion by Davis in *Taxation in Corporate Insolvency and Rescue* (6th edn, Bloomsbury Professional, 2009) at 3.3 and 3.4. *English Sewing Cotton* was followed in Australia by the High Court in *Dalgety Downs Pastoral Co Pty Ltd v Federal Commissioner of Taxation* [1952] HCA 54, 86 CLR 335 at [341].

English Sewing Cotton was cited by Buckley LJ the Court of Appeal in *Swiss Bank Corporation v Lloyds Bank Ltd*:[23]

> 'Accepting that such a transaction would confer on Lloyds a proprietary equitable interest in the securities, it would clearly not, in my opinion, constitute Lloyds an "owner" of the securities: see in this connection *English Sewing Cotton Co. Ltd. v.* [1947] 1 All E.R. 679. An equitable beneficial interest in property, if it be less than an absolute interest, is less than equitable (i.e. beneficial) ownership.'

53.17 Beneficial ownership of shares is also not affected by the grant of an option to purchase shares (at least until it is exercised) – *J. Sainsbury Plc. v O'Connor (Inspector of Taxes)*.[24]

APPLICATION OF A BENEFICIAL OWNERSHIP RULE?

53.18 If the beneficial ownership rule were to be applied to assessing association or control under s 435, this would mean that subsidiaries of the insolvent company (in administration or liquidation) would cease to be controlled by (or associated with) it. In our example above, if B Co went into liquidation, it would seem that B Co would cease to be beneficial owner of its assets, including the shares in OpCo. It would be the liquidator of B Co who exercised the voting rights in relation to the shares in OpCo, rather than B Co. So B Co would cease to control OpCo.

53.19 Shareholders in the insolvent company would perhaps still like to control it (as they hold the voting power even though shareholder meetings may be uncommon in a liquidation or administration). In our example above, if B Co went into liquidation, it would seem that A Co would still be the beneficial owner of the shares in B Co and so arguably could remain in control of B Co.

53.20 In *Box Clever/Granada*,[25] the UT held that appointment of administrative receivers over a parent company did not mean that the parent ceased to have control of the subsidiary. The UT noted at [190] that:

> 'There was no change in the beneficial ownership of those shares simply because of the appointment of the Administrative Receivers.'

53.21 The Insolvency Act definition of control in s 435(10) does not, of course, use the term 'beneficial ownership' in relation to relevant voting power. Instead

23 [1982] AC 584 at [600]. On appeal to the House of Lords, the CA decision was upheld, but the House of Lords did not refer to *English Sewing Cotton*. Both *English Sewing Cotton* and *Swiss Bank Corporation* have been followed in Australia: *Commissioner for State Revenue v Victoria Gardens Developments Pty Ltd* [2000] VSCA 233 at [34].

24 [1991] 1 WLR 963, CA.

25 *Granada UK Rental & Retail Ltd v The Pensions Regulator* [2018] UKUT 164 (TCC) (Rose J, HHJ Herrington and Ian Abrams).

it refers to an ability to exercise (or control the exercise) of 'one-third or more of the voting power at any general meeting of the company' – s 435(10)(b).

53.22 On appeal in *Box Clever/Granada*,[26] the Court of Appeal did not comment on the beneficial ownership point, instead noting, in relation to a holding by a parent (THSP) in an employer (TUK), at [130]:

> 'In the present case, it would doubtless have been the Administrative Receivers rather than THSP's directors who would have decided how the company's shares in TUK should be voted had there been a general meeting on 31 December 2009. That, however, is neither here nor there. The Administrative Receivers would have been voting in THSP's name and on its behalf. It was THSP that was "entitled to exercise" the voting power and it is, accordingly, to be taken as having had control of TUK and so an associate of it.'[27]

53.23 The Court of Appeal was considering only the position on an administrative receivership, not a liquidation or administration. An administrator is the agent of the company as well (IA 1986, Sch B1, para 69).

53.24 This is all rather unclear. The control provisions in s 435(10) do not seem to be designed to deal with an insolvency position (despite being found within the Insolvency Act 1986). This lack of clarity, reinforces the argument to use an approach that looks at the practicalities of the situation (see comments on interpretation at Chapter 4 above), rather than just seek to construe the text of s 435(10).

26 *Granada UK Rental & Retail Ltd v The Pensions Regulator* [2019] EWCA Civ 1032.

27 The Court of Appeal went on to comment (obiter): 'That the Administrative Receivers were also, presumably, associates of TUK is immaterial.' Whether insolvency practitioners can also be associated or connected is an interesting issue, but outside the scope of this chapter.

54

'Control' in other contexts: Tax law

54.1 The Corporation Tax Act 2010 (CTA 2010) defines 'control' for some purposes in s 450(2) as:

> 'A person ('P') is treated as having control of a company ('C') if P: (a) exercises, (b) is able to exercise, or (c) is entitled to acquire, direct or indirect control over C's affairs.'

Section 450(3) then goes on to expand this definition to include other potential controls.

54.2 The courts have made it clear that the usual definition of 'control' would mean control at general meeting level, but that this is extended by the later provisions. In *PGPH Ltd v Revenue and Customs Commissioners*[1] Judge Falk (as she then was) considered the issue of whether an individual was 'connected' with a developer within CTA 2010, s 1122, which refers to 'control' as defined in CTA 2010, ss 450 and 451.

54.3 Judge Falk referred to various decisions on s 450(2) and its predecessors, including *R v Inland Revenue Commissioners, ex parte Newfields Developments Ltd,*[2] *Kellogg Brown & Root Holdings (UK) Ltd v HMRC*[3] and *Steele (Inspector of Taxes) v European Vinyls Corp. (Holdings) BV.*[4] She also referred to the decisions of the Upper Tribunal and Court of Appeal in *UBS AG v HMRC; Deutsche Bank Group Services (UK) Ltd v HMRC.*[5]

54.4 Judge Falk summarised the position:

> '[149] In *Newfields* Lord Hoffmann referred at [10] to what is now s 450(2) (then the opening words of s 416(2) Income and Corporation Taxes Act 1988) as

1 [2017] UKFTT 782 (TC), [2017] STI 2284 (Judge Sarah Falk) at [149].
2 [2001] UKHL 27, [2001] STC 901.
3 [2010] EWCA Civ 118, [2010] STC 925.
4 [1995] STC 31 (Lightman J) at [51], [1996] STC 785, CA at [794-5].
5 [2013] STC 68; [2014] STC 2278. In *PGPH* Judge Falk noted that the Court of Appeal's decision in *UBS* was reversed by the Supreme Court, but on other grounds.

describing "a concept of control which reflects its meaning in ordinary speech", which is then "enormously widened" by subsequent subsections. Lord Scott referred to the same provision as prescribing a "test of actual control", with subsequent provisions describing other situations where a person is taken to have control, even where another person has control under another part of the test, such that control could be attributed to several different people (paragraphs [41] and [42]). In *Kellogg* Lord Neuberger MR (as he then was) referred at paragraph [34] to these comments in *Newfields* as confirming the approach of giving the opening part of s 416(2) its ordinary meaning, not an artificially narrow meaning because of the scope of the following subsections. In *Steele* Lightman J concluded at first instance at page 51 that "control over the company's affairs" referred to control at general meetings rather than at board level, and this was upheld by the Court of Appeal ([1996] STC 785 at 794-5). In *UBS* the Upper Tribunal referred to these comments in *Steele* and concluded that they were binding on it and had not been implicitly overruled by House of Lords in *Newfields* (paragraphs [117] to [124] in the Upper Tribunal decision). In the Court of Appeal decision in *UBS* it was noted at [92] that HMRC accepted that control in s 416(2) meant control at shareholder level, although the conclusion reached was that in the *Deutsche Bank* appeal the Upper Tribunal had taken the wrong approach in overturning the First-tier Tribunal's finding that the control test was not satisfied on the facts.'

54.5 It is clear from these cases that, absent an expanded definition, the question of 'control' under CTA 2010, s 450 would usually look at the voting power position, requiring a majority of votes.

54.6 A differently worded definition of 'control' applies for certain purposes under CTA 2010, s 1124. In *Farnborough Airport Properties Co v Revenue and Customs Commissioners*[6] the Court of Appeal held that a receiver[7] appointed over all the assets of the company had the effect that the company in receivership was de-grouped for the purposes of CTA, s 152. This was because 'control' (as defined in CTA 2010, s 1124) had passed away from the shareholders and so s 154(2) applied.

54.7 *Farnborough Airport* is noticeable in that it deals with a position where an insolvency process had started (the other tax cases referred to above do not deal with an insolvency).

54.8 But the definition of 'control' in CTA 2010, s 1124(2) differs from that in the Insolvency Act 1986 (IA 1986), s 435(10) in that control is defined in s 1124 to mean:

> 'in relation to a body corporate ('company A') the power of a person ('P') to secure … by means of the possession of voting power … that the affairs of company A are conducted in accordance with P's wishes'.

6 [2019] EWCA Civ 118, [2019] 2 All ER 435, [2019] 1 WLR 6720, [2019] STC 517. Noted by Reilly and Harrop, 'Farnborough Airport: Losing control' (2019) 1436 Tax Journal, 12 (22 March).

7 Seemingly the equivalent of an administrative receiver. The relevant company was incorporated in the Cayman Islands and so outside the UK – see [18].

54.9 Unlike s 435(10)(b), in s 1124(2):

(a) no specific percentage of 'voting power' is specified.

(b) there is no reference to how the voting power is measured – s 1124(2) does not refer to 'at any general meeting'; and

(c) the definition includes the requirement that the voting power allows P to 'secure' that 'the affairs of company A are conducted in accordance with P's wishes'. There is a similar (but not identical) requirement in relation to 'affairs' in the other control definition in CTA 2010, s 450.

54.10 In *Farnborough Airport*,[8] Henderson LJ considered the final limb of s 1124(2) was of 'crucial importance' in deciding whether or not the shareholder of the company in receivership still had s 1124 control. He did not find the decision easy, but held that under the tax legislation something more than just holding share capital was required. Henderson LJ held:

> '[64] .... A telling initial point, as it seems to me, is that section 154 of CTA 2010 only applies in the first place if the two companies concerned would otherwise be members of the same group: see subsection (1). In other words, one starts from a situation where one company is the 75% subsidiary of the other, or (as here) both are 75% subsidiaries of a third company. The definition of "75% subsidiary" in section 1154 depends on ownership of at least 75% of the subsidiary's ordinary share capital, and section 151(4) introduces the further requirement of a corresponding beneficial entitlement to dividends and distributions on a winding up. In those circumstances, the parent company will already have underlying shareholder control of the subsidiary, which to my mind strongly suggests that the requirement of control in Effect 2 in section 154(3) must have been intended by Parliament to go further. If HMRC's submissions are correct, that is indeed the case, because of the need to establish that the affairs of the company are conducted in accordance with the shareholders' wishes. On the appellants' case, by contrast, that further requirement is either ignored or treated as an automatic consequence of the possession of a majority shareholding or voting power.
>
> [65] In agreement with [Counsel for HMRC], I consider that the final limb of section 1124(2) is of crucial importance, both as a matter of ordinary language and because the test is formulated in terms of an ability to bring about an end result by specified means. By choosing to incorporate this definition for the purposes of section 154, Parliament must be taken to have intended this separate requirement to be replicated for the purposes of Effect 2.'

54.11 Henderson LJ went on to distinguish the decision of the House of Lords in *Pilkington Bros Ltd v Inland Revenue Commissioners*,[9] which dealt with the Finance Act 1973, s 29 (the predecessor to CTA 2010, s 154[10]). The House of Lords had held, by a majority, that the control of Pilkington's shareholders was,

8 [2019] EWCA Civ 118, [2019] 2 All ER 435 per Henderson LJ at [64] to [66]. Floyd and Baker LJJ agreed with Henderson LJ.

9 [1982] 1 All ER 715, HL.

10 See *Farnborough Airport* [2019] EWCA Civ 118, per Henderson LJ at [20] and [21].

collectively, enough potentially to give common control over another company. In *Farnborough Airport*,[11] Henderson LJ noted that *Pilkington* did not involve an insolvency process and that the ultimate decision turned on whether relevant arrangements were in existence. Henderson LJ also relied on the Scottish decision in *IRC v Lithgows*[12] (which also turned on a limb in the tax legislation dealing with securing that 'the affairs of company A are conducted in accordance with P's wishes').

54.12 In *Box Clever*, the Court of Appeal was referred to various tax cases, but ultimately held (at [126]) that they did not cast 'any real light on how s 435 IA 1986 should be interpreted.'

11 *Farnborough Airport* [2019] EWCA Civ 118 per Henderson LJ at [66] and [23].
12 1960 SC 405, (1960) 39 TC 270, Ct of Sess.

55

'Control' in other contexts: Employment law

55.1 Continuity of employment for statutory purposes can depend on being employed by an 'associated' employer. Employment Rights Act 1996 (ERA 1996), s 321 defines the term 'associated' for this purpose:

> 'For the purposes of this Act any two employers shall be treated as associated if (a) one is a company of which the other (directly or indirectly) has control, or (b) both are companies of which a third person (directly or indirectly) has control; and 'associated employer' shall be construed accordingly.'

55.2 The term 'control' is not further defined for this purpose, but caselaw has looked to the ability to control more than half the votes attaching to shares in a general meeting. In *Secretary of State for Employment v Newbold*[1] the Employment Appeal Tribunal held:

> 'In the law affecting companies, control is well recognised to mean control by the majority of votes attaching to shares, exercised in general meeting. It is not how or by whom the enterprise is actually run. Control rests in those who by the constitution of the company can say to the management, "Thou shalt do this; thou shalt not do that; thou art no longer the management". If authority is needed, it is to be found in *Inland Revenue Commissioners v Bibby* (1945) 1 AER 667; *Barclays Bank Ltd v Inland Revenue Commissioners* [1959] Ch 659.'

55.3 Notwithstanding this, the EAT has in some cases considered that sometimes it would be necessary to look at practical control rather than theoretical matters. In *Tice v Cartwright*,[2] the EAT held:

> 'the word "control" in section 231 of the Employment Rights Act 1996 is dealing with practical rather than theoretical matters. No doubt the question of voting control is central in the context of company law. However, we consider that in the employment protection field it is legitimate to give the words a purposive interpretation consistent with the intention of Parliament as described by Popplewell J in *Harford v Swiftrim Ltd* [1987] ICR 439.'

1 [1981] IRLR 305 at [12].
2 [1999] ICR 769, 773–774.

55.4 In *Da Silva v Composite Moldings & Design Limited*[3] the Employment Appeal Tribunal took the view that the entry into voluntary liquidation of the first employer company did not mean that a new employer (with the same main shareholder as the first company), who hired the employee after the start of the liquidation, was not an associated employer under ERA 1996, s 321. Arguably this involved just a temporary cessation of work,[4] but it seems tricky to allow this to cover a gap where there is a change in employer – see *Services for Education (S 4E Ltd) v White*[5] and ERA 1996, ss 212(3)(b) and 218(1).

3 [2008] UKEAT/0241/08, [2009] ICR 416, EAT.
4 See [2009] ICR 416 at [25].
5 UKEAT/0024/15.

56

Administrative receivership: *Box Clever*

56.1 In 2018 in the *Box Clever* case, *Granada UK Rental & Retail Ltd v The Pensions Regulator*[1] the Court of Appeal considered the position under the Insolvency Act 1986 (IA 1986), s 435(10) in relation to the requirement for an association at the relevant date for the test of the issue of a Financial Support Direction (FSD) under the Pensions Act 2004 (PA 2004). *Box Clever* is discussed in chapter 36 above.

ITV and its subsidiaries had owned a 50% shareholding in a joint venture company, Box Clever Technology Limited (called 'BxC Tech' in the judgment). BxC Tech had various wholly-owned subsidiaries, some of which were also employers in relation to an occupational pension scheme.

56.2 The subsidiaries (and employers) each entered into administrative receivership during 2003 to 2004. Some years later, the Pensions Regulator sought (in 2011) to use its statutory moral hazard powers under PA 2004 to issue an FSD against ITV. The time limit for the issue of an FSD meant that the relevant test of whether or not an employer was 'insufficiently resourced' needed to be carried out at a relevant date, which was fixed by the Pensions Regulator as 31 December 2009.[2] If an FSD were to be issued against ITV, it would need to be shown that ITV was an associate of an employer at that date.

56.3 ITV argued that as at 31 December 2009 it was no longer associated with the employers, on two grounds: (a) the debenture in favour of a bank (mortgaging the shares in the subsidiaries) meant that voting power had passed to the bank; and (b) the entry of various companies in the chain into administrative receivership meant that control of the shares in relevant subsidiaries had passed to the administrative receivers.

1 *Granada UK Rental & Retail Ltd v The Pensions Regulator* [2019] EWCA Civ 1032, [2020] ICR 747, [2019] Pens. LR 20 on appeal from [2018] UKUT 164 (TCC), [2018] All ER (D) 16 (Jun) (Rose J, HHJ Herrington and Ian Abrams).

2 Time limits in PA 2004 as originally enacted used to mean that the relevant date must not be more than two years before the relevant determination by the Determinations Panel. This time scale has since been amended so that the relevant date must now be within the period of two years before the issue of the relevant warning notice by the Pensions Regulator.

56.4 The Court of Appeal held that the terms of the mortgages did not pass voting control away from the relevant Box Clever companies to the bank (or security agent) – see Chapter 38 above. On the second argument, the Upper Tribunal had held (at [190]) that the administrative receivers of the parent (THSP) acted as the agent of the company over which they were appointed – IA 1986, s 44(1)(a). The administrative receivers of the THSP took the place of the directors of THSP and:

> 'became the body with the ultimate authority to deal with the company's assets and the rights attached to them, including the right to exercise the voting power over the shares held in TUK [the employer] on behalf of THSP'.

56.5 The Court of Appeal went on to state that there was no change in the beneficial ownership of the relevant shares because of the appointment of the administrative receivers. Accordingly the arguments of ITV based on agency issues failed. The Upper Tribunal had previously concluded (at [192]) that:

> 'the Targets controlled the voting rights in the shares in TUK as at the "look-back" date of 31 December 2009 and hence they were associated with TUK for the purposes of s 43(6) PA 2004'.

56.6 The Upper Tribunal had also noted that it was common ground in *Box Clever* that the s 435 tests are technical. It held:

> '[123]. It was also common ground that the test of association and control prescribed by s 435 is a technical test to be applied by the application of the statutory provisions properly construed. This means that the question whether a person is "entitled to exercise, or control the exercise" of the relevant voting power is not to be determined by reference to the extent to which the Targets were able to or actually did influence the way any of the companies within the Joint Venture carried on their business. That continued to be the position in respect of all times after the appointment of the Administrative Receivers. In any event, by 31 December 2009, the date at which the association and control issues are to be determined, there was no business left within the Joint Venture to influence.'

57

Look at term being defined?

57.1 The decision of the Court of Appeal in *Box Clever/Granada* (upholding the Upper Tribunal) was quite extreme for ITV. In reality following the appointment of administrative receivers, the former shareholder (parent) loses all actual control or influence over the business and actions of the employer company.[1] More shareholder interest may remain if there was any prospect of an exit from the administrative receivership (other than by another insolvency process) with a return to the shareholders (ie the relevant charge holder being paid in full), but this seems not to have been the case in the *Box Clever/Granada* case. Despite this the UT (and the Court of Appeal) held that ITV was still an associate of an employer at a date some five years after the employer had entered administrative receivership.

57.2 But, as discussed above, the 'control' test in the Insolvency Act 1986 (IA 1986), s 435(10) can be seen as a technical test, seemingly divorced from concepts of actual control – thus holding over one third of the voting rights at a general meeting is enough to confer control, even though in practice it may well not in reality (eg if another shareholder holds over 50% of the votes).

57.3 It still seems to be arguable that the courts should be influenced by the terminology used, here the term 'control' is being defined. Despite the wording in the definition, it is appropriate to interpret the provisions bearing in mind what is being defined.

57.4 Clearly the term can be defined as Parliament wishes – so it is noticeable that holding just one third or more of the voting power will give s 435(10) control. If this had not been expressly stated in the definition, it is likely that the courts would have construed control to require a majority of the voting power.

57.5 Clear words used in a definition need to be respected by the courts. But this still leaves open the question of interpretation of s 435(10) where it is not clear. How should the courts approach its interpretation?

1 See eg *Farnborough Airport* [2019] EWCA Civ 118, [2019] 2 All ER 435 per Henderson LJ at [34], [54], [60], [61] and [66].

57.5 *Look at term being defined?*

It seems clear that the concept being defined – here 'control' – can and should be used as an interpretation factor. The further away from actual real control the situation is the more the courts may be inclined towards the more realistic or consistent construction. The House of Lords cases on interpretation mentioned at Chapter 4 above, including *MacDonald v Dextra Accessories Ltd*[2] and *Oxfordshire County Council v Oxford City Council*,[3] lend some support to this approach potentially apply.

This approach does not seem to have been raised in *Box Clever*. The Court of Appeal decision does not deal with it.

2 *MacDonald (Inspector of Taxes) v Dextra Accessories Ltd* [2005] UKHL 47, [2005] 4 All ER 107 at [18].

3 [2006] UKHL 25, [2006] 2 AC 674 at [82].

58

Liquidation: *Linter Textiles*

58.1 The terminology used in the Insolvency Act 1986 (IA 1986), s 435(10)(b) is very similar to that used in the Australian tax statute, which was considered by the High Court of Australia in *Linter Textiles.*[1] The High Court considered that the wording of s 80A(3) of the Income Tax Act 1936 (Cth) meant that 'control' of a parent company over its subsidiary was lost when the parent company entered liquidation. This was the case even though the High Court considered that the parent retained 'beneficial ownership' of the shares in the subsidiary.

58.2 Section 80A(3) stated[2] that a loss could not be surrendered:

> '... unless the Commissioner is satisfied, or considers that it is reasonable to assume, that:
>
> (a) at all times during the year of income the voting power in the loss company was, either directly or through one or more interposed companies, trustees or partnerships, controlled, or capable of being controlled, by a person not being a company, or by 2 or more persons not being companies, who, either directly or through one or more interposed companies, trustees or partnerships, controlled, or was or were capable of controlling, the voting power in the loss company at all times during the year in which the loss was incurred'.

58.3 Both s 435(10)(b) and the Australian s 80A refer to 'voting power' (and do not go on to use the UK tax 'wishes' limb in *Farnborough Airport*[3] (noted at 54.6 above): 'the affairs of company A are conducted in accordance with P's wishes').

58.4 In *Linter Textiles*, the High Court considered that the entry of the intermediate parent company (Linter Group) into liquidation meant that control

1 *Commissioner of Taxation v Linter Textiles Australia Ltd* [2005] HCA 20, 220 CLR 592. For a discussion of the differences between *Linter Textiles* and *Ayerst*, see Heydon, Leeming and Turner, *Meagher Gummow & Lehane's Equity Doctrines and Remedies* (5th edn, Lexis Nexis Butterworths, 2015) at [4-115].

2 [2005] HCA 20 at [72].

3 *Farnborough Airport Properties Co v HMRC* [2019] EWCA Civ 118, [2019] 2 All ER 435.

of the 'voting power' over the shares in the subsidiary (Linter Textiles) had been lost. The majority[4] held:

> '[83]. The Commissioner submits that, on the making of the order for the winding up of Linter Group on 12 April 1991 and at all times thereafter, the voting power in Linter Textiles ceased to be controlled, or to be capable of being controlled, by those persons being the Goldberg family who, before the making of the winding-up order, had been in that position. They no longer could control the exercise of the voting power of Linter Group in its wholly owned subsidiary Linter Textiles. It is unnecessary for this purpose to determine whether, within the meaning of par (a) of s 80A(3), that control had passed to, and was vested in, the liquidator of Linter Group. The Commissioner need only establish the negative proposition that the control was not that of the Goldberg family.
>
> 84. These submissions should be accepted. Counsel for the taxpayer sought to outflank them by putting to one side the inconvenient turn taken by the facts when Linter Group was ordered to be wound up. The submission was that the "control" and capacity to control spoken of in par (a) of s 80A(3) was not to be confused with a present ability to exercise the voting rights. Rather, there was an assumption to be made that a general meeting of Linter Textiles was called and voting was in accordance with the articles of that company.'

58.5 McHugh J gave a separate judgment agreeing in the result with the majority and looking in more depth at s 80A(3). He noted that the reference in the section to 'voting power' meant that it was looking at the actual control, rather than the rights attaching to the shares as such. This is in line with the conclusion of Lewison J in *Unidare*[5] on the same point. McHugh J held:

> '[147] … the text of s 80A(3) directs the inquiry not at the rights attaching to shares, but rather at the actual control or capacity to control exercisable by the person or persons in relation to the voting power in the loss company.'

McHugh J went on to consider previous Australian caselaw on control:

> '165. The Commissioner contended that shareholders control a company through the exercise of voting power in the company. Control of voting power has traditionally been understood as the ability to carry an ordinary resolution at a general meeting of shareholders[145]. The Commissioner contended that, by reason of the winding up order made against Linter Group, the voting power in Linter Textiles ceased to be controlled by the Goldbergs and the Goldbergs ceased to have the capacity to control the voting power in Linter Textiles.'
>
> [145] See *W P Keighery Pty Ltd v Federal Commissioner of Taxation* (1957) 100 CLR 66 at [85] per Dixon CJ, Kitto and Taylor JJ, McTiernan J agreeing; *Kolotex Hosiery (Australia) Pty Ltd v Federal Commissioner of Taxation* (1973) 130 CLR 64; *Kolotex Hosiery (Australia) Pty Ltd v Federal Commissioner of Taxation* (1975) 132 CLR 535 at [551]–[552] per Barwick CJ.

4 Gleeson CJ, Gummow, Hayne, Callinan and Heydon JJ.

5 *Unidare plc v Cohen* [2005] EWHC 1410 (Ch), per Lewison J at [54] and [58].

'166. In *Kolotex Hosiery (Australia) Pty Ltd v Federal Commissioner of Taxation* [146] Mason J considered the meaning of "voting power in the company" in the context of ss 80A(1)(c) and 80C(1)(b)(i) of the 1936 Act (as to whether shares in the company carried between them the right to exercise not less than two-fifths of the voting power in the company). The facts of the case required his Honour to consider the effect of voting rights attaching to an office, as well as voting rights attaching to shares in the taxpayer company. (The articles of association of the taxpayer company conferred voting rights on the "Governing Director".) Mason J held that the words "voting power in the company" in ss 80A(1)(c) and 80C(1)(b)(i) as they then stood signified "the *entire voting power in the company*"[147]. They included any voting rights attaching to an office, and "not merely that voting power which is attached to shares" in the company. His Honour noted authorities to the effect that "capacity to control a company resides with the shareholders who by virtue of the voting power attaching to their shares are able to control the company in general meeting."[148] But his Honour considered that those authorities were "neither decisive nor persuasive, in relation to the question now under consideration." [149] He said that the capacity to control a general meeting is central to the concept of control of a company and that capacity rests on majority voting power, regardless of the source of that voting power[150].'

[146] (1973) 130 CLR 64 at [77]; aff'd on appeal in *Kolotex Hosiery (Australia) Pty Ltd v Federal Commissioner of Taxation* (1975) 132 CLR 535.

[147] *Kolotex* (1973) 130 CLR 64 at [77] (emphasis added).

[148] *Kolotex* (1973) 130 CLR 64 at [77], citing *B W Noble Ltd v Commissioners of Inland Revenue* (1926) 12 TC 911 at [926] per Rowlatt J; *Inland Revenue Commissioners v J Bibby & Sons Ltd* [1945] 1 All ER 667 at [670] per Lord Macmillan. In these cases the issue was the voting rights attaching to the shares. There was no issue as to voting rights attaching to an office.

[149] *Kolotex* (1973) 130 CLR 64 at [77].

[150] *Kolotex* (1973) 130 CLR 64 at [77].

'167. Mason J's decision is authority for the proposition that, for the purposes of determining who has control of a company (for income tax deduction purposes), it is permissible to look beyond the voting power attaching to shares. It is also permissible to consider any other voting power conferred on persons by the company's articles of association. But *Kolotex* is not directly in point because the focus of the inquiry under s 80C differed from the inquiry that has to be undertaken under the present s 80A(3)(a). Mason J was not required to look beyond the loss company's articles of association to ascertain the voting power in the loss company. In particular, he was not required to consider whether external events had brought about the result that the voting power in the company was no longer "controlled" by the persons on whom the formal voting power was conferred by the company's articles of association.

168. In *W P Keighery Pty Ltd v Federal Commissioner of Taxation* [151], this Court held that a company was "capable of being controlled" by a person where two conditions existed. First, the person is "able to dictate the decisions of the general meeting, through a preponderance of voting power which either is vested in him or is subject to his command." Second, the person has a "presently existing

power of control." Dixon CJ, Kitto and Taylor JJ (McTiernan J agreeing) said the expression "capable of being controlled" means[152]:

> "possessing, as a present attribute, a liability to be controlled. And a liability to be controlled by one person … involves … that there is one person who holds, or has a right to command, the major portion of the existing voting power".'
>
> [151] (1957) 100 CLR 66 at [85], [86] per Dixon CJ, Kitto and Taylor JJ (McTiernan J agreeing).
>
> [152] *W P Keighery* (1957) 100 CLR 66 at [86].

'169. Their Honours went on to say that "capable of being controlled"[153]:

> "connotes the existence of either one person whose enforceable and immediately exercisable rights enable him to control, or a number of persons whose enforceable and immediately exercisable rights enable them, if they act in concert, to control."

In other words, a person has the capacity to control the voting power in a company at any particular time if, at that time, the person has "enforceable and immediately exercisable rights" that enable such control. In *Federal Commissioner of Taxation v Sidney Williams (Holdings) Ltd* [154], Dixon CJ, Kitto and Taylor JJ, with whom McTiernan J agreed, construed the expression "capable of being controlled" as meaning "a liability to a lawful control by the exercise of legal or equitable rights or powers which persons are shown to possess", not "a possibility of being wrongfully subjected to de facto control by persons acting in breach of the rights of others." In *Federal Commissioner of Taxation v Casuarina Pty Ltd*, this Court also held that a liability to lose control in the future did not contradict the present existence of a capacity to control[155].'

> [153] *W P Keighery* (1957) 100 CLR 66 at [87].
>
> [154] (1957) 100 CLR 95 at [112].
>
> [155] (1971) 127 CLR 62 at [92] per Walsh J, Barwick CJ, Owen and Gibbs JJ agreeing.

McHugh J then considered the role of general meetings and 'contributories', noting that general meetings could still be held (and could be convened by requisition), but that they had no power to direct the liquidator. McHugh J held:

'173. The statutory regime provided that the court "may" have regard to the contributories' wishes in relation to all matters pertaining to the winding up of the company. Moreover, the court might direct that meetings of contributories be convened for the purpose of ascertaining those wishes. But the contributories could not control the company in any real sense. Although the court "may" have regard to the contributories' wishes (and "shall" have regard to the number of votes conferred on the contributory by the company's constitution), it was not compelled to act on the contributories' wishes[162]'.

> [162] Companies Code, s 431, Corporations Law, s 547.

'174. Hence, the making of the winding up order in relation to Linter Group had the consequence that the shareholders in Linter Group were no longer able to exercise 'control' of and no longer had the "capacity to control" the voting power in Linter Textiles. The shareholders no longer had enforceable and immediately exercisable rights enabling such control. By reason of the winding up order, the Goldbergs, through various interposed entities, could not carry and were not capable of carrying an ordinary resolution at a general meeting of shareholders of Linter Textiles. They had no control or potential control of the company in any meaningful sense.

175. It is true that the statutory scheme permitted at least one-tenth in value of the contributories of Linter Group to require the liquidator of Linter Group to convene a general meeting of contributories. The liquidator was required to have regard to any resolutions passed by the contributories at such a meeting. However, the liquidator was not compelled to comply with those resolutions. If those resolutions directed the liquidator to convene a general meeting of the shareholders of Linter Textiles, for example, the liquidator of Linter Group would have been required to have regard to that resolution, but would not have been compelled to comply with it. The Goldbergs therefore would not have controlled the voting on the shares in Linter Textiles, if a general meeting of Linter Textiles were held.'

58.6 McHugh J concluded that the liquidator of the parent (Linter Group) controlled the voting power in the subsidiary (Linter Textiles). And this applied whether or not the shares were still registered in the name of Linter Group, rather than being vested in the liquidator.

'176. If anybody had control of the voting power in Linter Textiles, arguably it was the liquidator of Linter Group. In any event, upon the making of the winding up order in relation to Linter Group, the Goldbergs were not able to satisfy the test in s 80A(3)(a) of the 1936 Act in relation to Linter Textiles. The concept of "control" of, or the "capacity to control", the voting power in Linter Textiles contemplates the existence at a particular point in time of enforceable and immediately exercisable rights enabling such control. That requires consideration of any matters or facts that then bear on the existence of those rights, such as the appointment of a liquidator under the corporations law. Once the winding up order in respect of Linter Group was made, the Goldbergs were unable to satisfy the test in s 80A(3)(a) in relation to Linter Textiles.

177. It is true that the Supreme Court of New South Wales made no order vesting the property of Linter Group in the liquidator. But that omission has no bearing on the question of the "control" of, or the "capacity to control", the voting power in Linter Textiles.'

58.7 In *Linter Textiles*, Kirby J also agreed, but on slightly different grounds.

'214 …. For there to be control over, or capacity to control, the voting power in a company at any particular time, it is necessary that there must be enforceable and immediately exercisable rights enabling such control to be effected[220]. As the Commissioner argued, where a company is in liquidation, shareholders can have no such rights and no such control or capacity of control.'

[220] *W P Keighery Pty Ltd v Federal Commissioner of Taxation* (1957) 100 CLR 66 at [87]. See also *Federal Commissioner of Taxation v Casuarina Pty Ltd* (1971) 127 CLR 62 at [93].

58.8 Care needs to be taken in construing statutory provisions in one statute by comparison with a decision on another statutory provision, even if identically worded and even if in the same jurisdiction.[6] But it is a powerful argument that the analysis in *Linter Holdings* should not apply also to the 'control' position under s 435(10)(b). The Australian statute involves similar wording on 'control' and 'voting power'.

58.9 The Court of Appeal in *Box Clever*[7] did also focus on the position of the registered holder of shares as being the person entitled to exercise the voting power, holding, at [129]:

> 'As we see it, a person registered as the holder of shares carrying a third or more of the total votes attaching to the relevant company's issued shares, and so as between himself and the company 'entitled to exercise … one third or more of the voting power', is also to be considered to be so entitled within the meaning of s.435(10)(b) IA 1986 and, hence, an associate of the company.'

58.10 *Linter Holdings* (a liquidation case) was not referred to in the *Box Clever* decisions.

6 Eg Woolf J in *Walters v Babergh District Council* [1983] 82 LGR 235 'It is always dangerous to look to decisions on similar words in different Acts of Parliament as aids to interpretation.' See ch 4 above.

7 *Granada UK Rental v Pensions Regulator* [2019] EWCA Civ 1032.

59

Summary of position on 'voting power' in insolvency

59.1 This chapter seeks to summarise the position.

ADMINISTRATIVE RECEIVERSHIPS

59.2 There is only one reported UK case on 'control' under the Insolvency Act 1986 (IA 1986), s 435(10) in an insolvency situation, namely *Box Clever/Granada*. It only looks at the position in an administrative receivership, although it does deal with an AR at both the employer and intermediate holding company level. The Court of Appeal clearly held that s 435 control remained with the intermediate holding company and the ultimate shareholder.

59.3 Despite this, it seems, at the very least, to be arguable that the courts should give more weight to the term being defined (namely control) and that it is odd to extend this to apply in an AR where the receiver exercises the powers of the directors and is not in any sense under the control of the company's shareholders or directors. Clearly the receiver is the agent of the company and normally appointing an agent to control shares (or business) would not amount to control passing away from the directors (or shareholders) to the agent. But, as was argued before the UT in *Box Clever*, the agency of a receiver is not an ordinary agency. The directors (and company) cannot remove the receiver or give binding directions.

59.4 However, this argument was rejected by the UT, pointing out (at [190]) that the receiver remained the agent of the company (IA 1986, s 44(1)(a)) and that beneficial ownership of the company's assets did not change.

59.5 In any event the vast majority of formal insolvencies are now not administrative receiverships, but instead administrations or liquidations. In such cases, the decision in *Box Clever/Granada* is clearly distinguishable, primarily on the same grounds as the caselaw on beneficial ownership, namely that a statutory trust is in place over the business and assets of the insolvent company and this is sufficient to cease control for s 435 purposes.

LIQUIDATIONS

59.6 For liquidations, this seems logical given:

(a) The statutory trust: *Ayerst* and *Linter Textiles*;

(b) The cessation of beneficial ownership: *Ayerst*; and

(c) Voting power cessation: *Linter Textiles*.

ADMINISTRATIONS

59.7 For administrations, the position should be the same as for liquidations, at least for an administration which becomes a 'distributing' administration. Before this, it is more arguable that a statutory trust (and change of beneficial ownership) does not apply and so more arguable that control remains.

59.8 An administrator is the agent of the company in exercising his or her functions under IA 1986, Sch B1 (see Sch B1, para 69). So in that respect an administrator is similar to an administrative receiver. But the combination of the potential statutory trust and the fact that the administrator's role is created by statute (and not by contract) points towards an administration being treated in the same way as a liquidation.

60

Application to examples

60.1 Going back to the questions asked earlier in relation to the example (see Chapter 49 above) – what happens to the Insolvency Act 1986 (IA 1986), s 435 control if one or more of the companies in our example enter a formal insolvency process in the UK? For example if:

Example 1: OpCo (the employer) enters liquidation, do A Co and B Co remain in 's 435 control' of (and so associated with) OpCo, despite the fact that in practice control of the business and affairs of OpCo now rests with its liquidator?

> There is no direct caselaw on this, but for the reasons given above, the better view is that the liquidation of OpCo breaks s 435 control by OpCo's shareholders. This means that A Co and B Co cease to be in s 435 control of OpCo.

Example 2: B Co (the holding company of OpCo) enters liquidation, does B Co (and hence A Co) cease to be in s 435 control of OpCo on the basis that beneficial ownership (and effective control) of B Co's assets, including the shares in OpCo, passes to B Co's liquidator (to hold on statutory trust)?

> There is no direct caselaw on this, but for the reasons given above, the better view is that the liquidation means a cessation of s 435 control by B Co of its assets, including the shares in OpCo. This means that A Co and B Co cease to be in s 435 control of OpCo.

Table 1 – OpCo insolvency

60.2 In particular, what happens if OpCo enters a formal UK insolvency process? Who remains 'associated' or 'connected' with OpCo?

Potential Target	Before insolvency	After OpCo entering insolvency:		
		OpCo liquidation	**OpCo administration**	**OpCo administrative receivership**
B Co	B Co controls OpCo by virtue of its shareholding in OpCo – s 435(10)(b). B Co is associated with OpCo – s 435(7).	OpCo liquidator takes control of the business and affairs of OpCo B Co ceases to have s 435 control of OpCo	OpCo administrator takes control of the business and affairs of OpCo B Co probably ceases to have s 435 control of OpCo. This is even more likely once the administrator serves notice of distributions.	OpCo AR takes control of the business and affairs of OpCo If *Box Clever* is followed, B Co retains control of OpCo. (but if B Co goes into insolvency too, see Table 2 below)
A Co	A Co similarly controls B Co and so also controls OpCo. Both A Co and B Co are associated with OpCo – s 435(7).	As for B Co	As for B Co (but if B Co goes into insolvency too, see Table 2 below)	As for B Co (but if B Co goes into insolvency too, see Table 2 below)
X	X is associated with OpCo by virtue of being a director of OpCo – s 435(4) and (9). X is also connected with OpCo – s 249	Arguable that X ceases to be a director in a court liquidation and so ceases to be associated with OpCo. In a voluntary liquidation, X remains a director and so remains associated with OpCo	X remains a director and so remains associated with OpCo	X remains a director and so remains associated with OpCo

Potential Target	**Before insolvency**	**After OpCo entering insolvency:**		
		OpCo liquidation	**OpCo administration**	**OpCo administrative receivership**
Y	Y is *not* associated or connected with OpCo, unless some other association not stated above can be found (eg if Y were a shadow director of OpCo – s 249 – or was someone who had 'control' of A Co)	No change	No change	No change
T Co	T Co looks to be controlled by OpCo, by virtue of OpCo's shareholding in T Co. This seems to mean that T Co is associated with OpCo, despite the exclusions in some provisions in s 435 for pension scheme trustees – see s 435(5).	Statutory trust of OpCo's assets means that T Co probably ceases to be controlled by OpCo T Co may cease to be associated or connected with OpCo (unless there is another connection – eg one of T Co's directors is also a director of OpCo)	Once the administrator serves notice of distributions, statutory trust of OpCo's assets means that T Co probably ceases to be controlled by OpCo T Co may cease to be associated with OpCo (unless there is another connection – eg one of T Co's directors is also a director of OpCo)	OpCo AR takes control of the business and affairs of OpCo If *Box Clever* is followed, OpCo retains control of T Co.

Table 2 – B Co insolvency

60.3 What happens to A Co and B Co if B Co (the parent of OpCo) enters a formal UK insolvency process, but Op Co does not? Does either of them remain 'associated' or 'connected' with OpCo? The position of the directors and T Co should remain the same as in Table 1.

Potential Target	**Before insolvency**	**After B Co (but not Op Co) entering insolvency:**		
		B Co liquidation	**B Co administration**	**B Co administrative receivership**
B Co	B Co controls OpCo by virtue of its shareholding in OpCo – s 435(10)(b). B Co is associated with OpCo – s 435(7).	B Co liquidator takes control of the business and affairs of B Co B Co ceases to have s 435 control of OpCo	B Co administrator takes control of the business and affairs of B Co B Co probably ceases to have s 435 control of OpCo. This is even more likely once the administrator serves notice of distributions.	B Co AR takes control of the business and affairs of B Co If UT in *Box Clever* is followed, B Co retains s 435 control of OpCo.
A Co	A Co similarly controls B Co and so also controls OpCo. Both A Co and B Co are associated with OpCo – s 435(7).	B Co liquidator takes control of the business and affairs of B Co A Co ceases to have s 435 control of B Co and OpCo	B Co administrator takes control of the business and affairs of B Co A Co probably ceases to have s 435 control of B Co and OpCo. This is even more likely once the administrator serves notice of distributions	B Co AR takes control of the business and affairs of B Co If *Box Clever* is followed, B Co retains s 435 control of OpCo and hence A Co retains s 435 control of Op Co

61

Summary on impact of insolvency on Control

61.1 It is not uncommon to find statutes that do not deal expressly with the position on insolvency and how the relevant provisions may take effect. It is perhaps less common to find that the Insolvency Act itself does not deal with an insolvency position very well.

61.2 As mentioned above, this seems to be because, as originally enacted, the IA 1986, s 435(10) control definition was used to look at control before the start of formal insolvency (eg in relation to avoidance of antecedent transactions). The problems arise when the Insolvency Act definition is used in other contexts, in particular by the pensions legislation in relation to the wide ranging moral hazard provisions.

PART 11

MAIN CONCLUSIONS ON CONTROL

62

Section 435(10) control is important

62.1 Insolvency Act 1986 (IA 1986), s 435(10) is a complex sub-section with very little reported caselaw on it. Falling within the test can determine if persons are within scope for moral hazard orders under the Pensions Act 2004 and can determine whether or not a particular investment is 'employer-related' (getting this wrong can be a criminal offence).

62.2 Control though voting power – s 435(10)(b):

(a) this looks at who controls votes at a (probably) hypothetical meeting – *Unidare.*

(b) If the Court of Appeal decision in *Kellogg* the tax case (on similar wording) were to be followed, then non-associates may be aggregated for the purposes of whether two companies have common 'control'. But this still may not mean that the individual shareholders themselves individually have control (and so may not be associated with the underlying company).

(c) *Kellogg* is not a binding precedent in relation to s 435 – a later court is not obliged to follow the decision.

62.3 Control through directors – s 435(10)(a):

(a) Looks similar to the shadow director definition in s 251. Any 'directions or instructions' need to be habitual.

(b) The Court of Appeal decision in *Deverell* on the 'shadow director' provisions (in s 251) indicates that 'advice' can still amount to 'directions or instructions' – these are the same words as appear in s 435(10)(a).

(c) Again *Deverell* is not a binding precedent in relation to s 435(10)(a) and in our view the better position is that simple advice from a professional adviser should not be enough to confer s 435(10)(a) control, even though (unlike s 251) there is no express exclusion in s 435.

(d) It is clear under s 251 that domination of just one director is not enough to make the person a shadow director. There must be a majority of the board involved. The wording in s 435(10)(a) is different, but in our view it would be illogical if it were enough if the person just "dominated" one director.

62.4 Section 435(10) is a key provision for pension lawyers. Unfortunately there is very little case law and it is difficult to construe and as noted above, two decisions of the Court of Appeal on similar wording in other statutes or sections are better distinguished and not followed.

PART 12

WHO IS NOT CONNECTED OR ASSSOCIATED?

63

Not connected or associated?

63.1 In the absence of any other potential connection or association, it is possible to point to some people who are *not* connected or associated (without more) in relation to a company:

(a) advisors;

(b) bankers;

(c) lawyers;

(d) contracting parties (eg the purchaser of a business from the company), creditors;

(e) advisors to pension scheme trustees.

63.2 But any of those categories could become associated (or connected) if they fell within another category in the tests – eg had 'control' over a company or became associated with a director of a company.

64

Purchasers of companies or businesses

64.1 What happens in a corporate transaction – ie a purchase of 100% of the shares in a company (Target) or an acquisition of a business?

There are at least five situations:

64.2

1. The Purchaser buys shares in Target with its own DB pension scheme

- The purchaser will on and following the purchase become associated with the Target (and its subsidiaries) because it will have 'control'. So a moral hazard order is possible against Purchaser in relation to the Target scheme.
- The Seller will cease to have control of Target (so potentially a notifiable event). The Pensions Regulator could still issue a moral hazard order against the Seller in relation to the Target scheme (within six years for a CN and two years for an FSD) after the Seller has ceased to be associated or connected.

64.3

2. The Purchaser buys shares in Target and the Seller's group retains a DB scheme (with on-going actives). Target was an employer in Seller's scheme but ceases to participate on or before the completion of the sale (and pays any relevant s 75 debt)

- Target ceases to be an employer in relation to Seller's scheme (on the sale)[1] 112. The Regulator could still make a moral hazard order against Target in relation to Seller's scheme within the time periods noted above, running from the date of the sale.
- Purchaser becomes associated with Target, but not while it is an employer in Seller's scheme. So no moral hazard order possible against Purchaser

1 This is why the assumption about there being on-going actives is important. If the scheme had been frozen, then Target would (if it had been among the last employer of actives) remain an employer.

in relation to Seller's scheme (unless Purchaser is connected or associated with Seller in some other way).

This seems right. It seems to be difficult to argue that Purchaser becomes associated with Target before the sale completes (Seller normally retains voting power over Target and restrictions on actions etc are not likely to be enough to make Purchaser a shadow director).

The extended definition of employer for the purposes of the moral hazard powers is unlikely to mean that Target could be deemed to remain an employer after completion (when it ceases to participate). The deemed employer provisions for former employers[2] generally do not apply provided the s 75 debt has not been demanded or has been paid.

64.4

3. The Purchaser buys shares in Target and the Seller's group retains a DB scheme (with on-going actives). Target was an employer in Seller's scheme and continues to participate for an interim period after sale (and then pays any relevant s 75 debt)

- Target ceases to be an employer in relation to Seller's scheme (at the end of the interim period).[3] The Regulator could still make a moral hazard order against Target in relation to the Seller's scheme within the one year and six-year time periods noted above, running from the end of the interim period.
- Purchaser becomes associated with Target on the sale and is associated during the interim period while Target is an employer in Seller's scheme. So a moral hazard order is possible against Purchaser in relation to Seller's scheme.

This risk of the Purchaser becoming in this way associated with an employer (Target) in Seller's scheme is one reason why interim periods are much less common than before.

64.5

4. The Purchaser buys shares in Target and the Seller's group retains a DB scheme (with on-going actives). Target is not an employer and has never been an employer in Seller's scheme

- Target ceases to be associated with the Seller's group on the sale. The Regulator could still make a moral hazard order against Target in relation to the Seller's scheme within the time periods noted above after the sale.

2 See eg, reg 15 of the Pensions Regulator (Financial Support Directions etc) Regulations 2005 (SI 2005/2188).

3 This is why the assumption about there being on-going actives is important. If the scheme had been frozen, then Target would (if it had been among the last employer of actives) remain an employer.

- Purchaser becomes associated with Target, but not while it is an employer in Seller's scheme. So no moral hazard order is possible against Purchaser in relation to Seller's scheme (unless Purchaser is connected or associated with Seller in some other way).

64.6

5. The Purchaser buys a business from the Seller. Employees transfer under Tupe. Seller's group retains a DB scheme

- Purchaser does not become associated or connected with Seller as a result just of the Tupe transfer. So no moral hazard order is possible against Purchaser in relation to Seller's scheme (unless Purchaser is connected or associated with Seller in some other way).

The position would be different if Purchaser participated in Seller's Scheme (eg for an interim period) after the Tupe transfer. This risk of the Purchaser becoming an employer in Seller's scheme is one reason why interim periods are much less common than before.

PART 13

CVAS AND IVAS – CONNECTED CREDITORS[1]

1 This Part is derived from part of a paper '*CVAs and Pensions*' given by David Pollard and Tom Robinson to the APL in May 2019.

65

Connected creditors

65.1 Where there is a voluntary arrangement, whether corporate or individual:

(a) the proposal must state how those creditors who are associates of (or connected with) the debtor are to be treated;[2]

(b) the statement of affairs must include details of debts owed to or by associates of (or persons connected with) the debtor;[3]

(c) votes of any creditors who are connected with the debtor must be left out of account in counting votes for resolutions of creditors.[4]

65.2 If the company has any occupational pension scheme (OPS), it may be important to decide whether or not any claim in relation to the OPS is one from a person who is 'connected' or not. The votes of connected creditors count in the usual way for the primary 75% majority test. But the issue of connection goes to the second voting test for approval of a CVA – ie that the CVA fails if more than 50% of the total value of the unconnected creditors vote against.[5]

65.3 The notice sent by the nominee to creditors and members also needs to give details of how creditors connected with the company will be dealt with.[6]

65.4 The nominee will need to decide if the scheme votes are those of a creditor who is connected with the company or not. Often the occupational pension scheme can be a major unsecured creditor (or contingent or future creditor). This gives rise to three issues:

(a) Is the relevant creditor the OPS trustee?[7] – the answer to this is yes.

(b) Is the OPS trustee connected with the company? – it can be.

2 IR 2016, rule 1.3(2)(c)(ii) for a CVA and rule 5.3(2)(c)(ii) for an IVA.
3 IR 2016, rule 1.5(2)(e) for a CVA, rule 5.8(3)(e) for an IVA.
4 IR 2016, rules 1.19(4) and 5.18(4).
5 IR 2016, rule 15.34(4).
6 IR 2016, rule 2.3(1)(f)(ii).
7 Ie the trustee company if this is the sole trustee. Otherwise all the trustees acting together (the 'trustee board').

(c) Does it make any difference if the pension scheme is in a PPF assessment period (under the Pensions Act 2004 (PA 2004)) so that power over the votes of the OPS is held by the PPF – PA 2004, s 137?

65.5 The decision is for convenor or chair to make – Insolvency (England and Wales) Rules 2016 (IR 2016), rule 15.34(5)(a):

> '(5) For the purposes of paragraph (4)—
>
> (a) a creditor is unconnected unless the convener or chair decides that the creditor is connected with the company;'.

CVA NOTICE AND MEETING

65.6 Running alongside the pensions notice process, the nominee will arrange to send out notice of the CVA proposal and the relevant meetings (or the other relevant approval process) of members and creditors – Insolvency Act 1986 (IA 1986), s 3. The relevant proposal must contain specified information (so far as known to the CVA proposer) – IR 2016, rule 2.3(1).[8] Various items will need to deal with pensions, including:

> (e) the nature and amount of the company's liabilities.
>
> (f)(i) how preferential creditors[9] will be dealt with.
>
> (f)(ii) how creditors connected with the company will be dealt with (this can include the pension scheme – see Chapter 70 below).
>
> (x) any other matters that the proposer considers appropriate to enable members and creditors to reach an informed decision on the proposal.

VOTING MAJORITIES

65.7 The CVA is approved by the creditors' decision if *both*:[10]

(i) 75% in value of those creditors who vote, vote to approve; and

(ii) it is not the case that 'more than half of the total value of the unconnected creditors vote against it'.

65.8 The test under (i) looks at the majority as a percentage of the total value of creditor claims actually voted, but the test at (ii) is rather more convoluted and is less clear in only looking at the relevant majority (in value) as a percentage of the unconnected creditors who are actually admitted to vote, as compared

8 A summary is set out in '*Kerr & Hunter on Receivership and Administration*' (Robinson and Walton, 21st edn, 2020, Sweet & Maxwell) at 16–18.

9 Employees and the pension scheme trustees can be preferential creditors.

10 IR 2016, rule 15.34(3) and (4).

to the (presumably potentially lower number) of unconnected creditors who actually vote.

65.9 IR 2016, rule 15.34(5)(c) defines, for this purpose, the 'total value of the unconnected creditors' (ie the divisor used in working out the relevant majority under (ii) above) as being 'the total value of those unconnected creditors whose claims have been admitted for voting'. This looks to be a cross-reference to the provisions for admission (or rejection) of claims by the convenor or chair under the previous rule, IR 2016, rule 15.33.

65.10 It is unclear why this connected creditor test at (ii) refers to creditors 'admitted for voting' as compared to the reference to the terminology of those actually 'voting' which is used in the primary 75% test under (i). In practice there may be no difference – creditor claims are generally only admitted for the purpose of voting, although it does perhaps leave it open for abstentions to count towards the divisor.

65.11 If the test at (ii) were instead a test that looked at the total number of unconnected creditors who could potentially have voted (or been admitted), this would make this test an easier hurdle for a CVA proposal to pass – in order for the CVA proposal to fail it would require more than half of the unconnected creditors in total (ie not just those admitted or voting) to vote against.

65.12 In relation to (ii), dealing with unconnected creditors, IR 2016, rule 15.34(5) provides that 'a creditor is unconnected unless the convener or chair decides that the creditor is connected with the company'. The term 'connected' is not defined expressly in IR 2016, but there is an official 'Note'[11] in IR 2016, rule 1.2(2) stating that where the term 'connected' is used of a person in relation to a company, the term is defined in IA 1986, s 249.

65.13 The position on connected creditors is discussed further at chapter below in relation to the position of the trustees/pension scheme.

65.14 These provisions in IR 2016 refer to a creditor as being connected with the CVA company (or as being 'unconnected' unless the chair decides that the creditor is connected with the company.[12]).

11 See the 'Note' at the beginning of rule 1.2:

> '[Note: the terms which are defined in rule 1.2 include some terms defined by the Act for limited purposes which are applied generally by these Rules. Such terms have the meaning given by the Act for those limited purposes.]'

This use of official 'non-legislative' Notes is flagged in the Explanatory Memorandum to the IR 2016 (at paras 3.1 and 3.2).
Notes in legislation can be tricky to construe – see eg: *R (on the application of Maughan) v HM Senior Coroner for Oxfordshire* [2020] UKSC 46 discussing the status of a note in the Coroners (Inquests) Rules 2013.

12 IR 2016, rule 15.34(5).

65.15 As mentioned above, if the only link is that a director of the trustee company is also an employee of the CVA company, this mean that the pension trustee company is not connected with the CVA company (although the CVA company is connected with the pension trustee company). IR 2016, rule 15.34(5) provides that 'a creditor is unconnected unless the convener or chair decides that *the creditor is connected with the company*'. So it seems that in this case the emphasised words clearly refer to the need for the pension trustee company to be connected with the CVA company (rather than the CVA company being connected with the pension trustee company) so that the pension trustee company is an unconnected creditor for these purposes. See further chapter 66 below.

66

Pension trustee as connected or unconnected in a CVA

66.1 As discussed in Chapter 65 above, the nominee will need to decide if the votes of a pension scheme are those of a creditor who is connected with the company or not.

66.2 Often the occupational pension scheme can be a major unsecured creditor (or contingent or future creditor). This gives rise to three issues:

(a) Is the relevant creditor the OPS trustee?[1] – the answer to this is yes, even where the PPF controls how the votes are cast – see below.

(b) Is the OPS trustee connected with the company?

(c) Does it make any difference if the pension scheme is in a PPF assessment period (under the Pensions Act 2004 (PA 2004)) so that power over the votes of the OPS is held by the PPF – PA 2004, s 137?

66.3 The situation will differ depending on whether the trustee is:

(a) a trustee company (this is now much more common); or

(b) a group of individual trustees (who may include a trustee company among their number).

PENSION TRUSTEE COMPANY

66.4 As discussed in Chapter 29 above, a trustee company acting as a trustee of an occupational pension scheme of the CVA company (as employer) will be connected with the CVA company if:

(a) The company (or an employer or director) is a beneficiary under the pension trust and the exclusion in the Insolvency Act 1986 (IA 1986), s 435(5) does not apply; or

1 Ie the trustee company if this is the sole trustee. Otherwise all the trustees acting together (the 'trustee board').

(b) The trustee company is otherwise an associate of the CVA company; or

(c) It is an associate of a director (or shadow director) of the CVA company.

Limb (a): s 435(5) exclusion

66.5 IA 1986, s 435(5)[2] provides for a trustee of a trust to be an associate of another person if the beneficiaries of the trust include that other person (or an associate of that other person).

66.6 But for the pension scheme exclusion, s 435(5) would practically always mean that a pension trustee would be an associate of the employer company:

(i) if the trust includes the company (or an associate of the company) as a beneficiary. This will be quite likely, for example if the company has rights under the trust (eg to surplus on a winding-up); or

(ii) if any associate of the company (for example an employee or director of the company[3]) are members of the trust.

But s 435(5) has a pension scheme exclusion. It is expressly stated not to apply to a trustee of a pension scheme.

66.7 The term 'pension scheme' is not defined in s 435(5), but almost certainly will include an 'occupational pension scheme' under the pensions legislation – see Chapter 29 above, discussing *Granada Group Ltd v Law Debenture*[4] but a decision on different legislation: Companies Act 1985 (CA 2005).

Limb (b): Trustee company otherwise an associate?

66.8 Looking at limb (b), in practice, a pension trustee company, even within the exclusion in s 435(5), will often still be an associate of the CVA company, because one of the other grounds in s 435, outside s 435(5), will apply. An example would be if the trustee company is under the 'control' of the CVA company (or under common control of an entity that controls the company and the trustee company) – IA 1986, s 435(10)[5].

66.9 If the trustee company is (for example) in the same group of companies as the CVA company[6] (eg is a wholly-owned subsidiary of the CVA company),

2 See chs 28 and 29 above.

3 Employees: IA 1986, s 435(4). Directors: IA 1986, s 435(9) and (4).

4 *Granada Group Ltd v The Law Debenture Pension Trust Corporation Plc* [2016] EWCA Civ 1289, [2017] 2 BCLC 1 at [45].

5 See Parts 7 to 10 above.

6 It is quite common for the shares in a sole purpose trustee company to be held by the employer company (or another group company). The other model is for the shares to be held by the trustee company directors (or for the trustee company to be a company limited by guarantee). See Pollard, *The Law of Pension Trusts* (OUP, 2013) at 4.31.

then the trustee company will be an associate of the CVA company by virtue of the common control through the shareholdings. The impact of the grant of security over some or all of the shareholdings (eg in favour of a third party lender) or any of the companies entering a formal insolvency process (eg administration) can be complex.[7]

66.10 It could be argued that the exclusion of pension trustees from s 435(5) is wide enough not just to cover the specific trust provision in s 435(5), but also generally to mean that a pension trustee is not associated with the employer company under any of s 435 – see Chapter 29 above.

66.11 But it is unlikely that such an expanded argument would succeed. In relation to s 435, the point was argued in *Re Thirty-Eight Building Ltd*,[8] but not decided.

66.12 A similar (but not identical) provision in CA 2005, s 254, was applied in relation to a member of a charitable company in *Children's Investment Fund (UK) v Attorney General.*[9] Vos C held that it did not matter that the relevant transfer was to a charitable company that would hold the proceeds on a charitable trust that would not benefit the member of the company.

Limb (c): Trustee company connected because it is an associate of a director (or shadow director) of the CVA company

66.13 Looking at limb (c), a pension trustee company will be connected with the CVA company if it is an associate of a director (or shadow director) of the CVA company – s 249.

66.14 In practice, directors of the CVA company are most likely to be individuals.[10] In this case, the pension trustee company will be associated with an individual (who is also a director of the CVA company) if (for example) the individual is also a director of the pension trustee company.[11]

7 See ch 35 above.

8 [1999] 1 BCLC 416, [1999] OPLR 319 (Hazel Williamson QC). See ch 29 above. The judge commented at p 423h:

> 'I should make it clear that my decision is not intended to be of wider application than the facts of this case. In particular, I make no decision as to whether the exception in s 435(5)(b) would still apply in the absence of the fifth respondent as a trustee of the scheme, ie if the trustees had been only the first four respondents, who are all 'persons connected with the Company', and the beneficiaries had also been the very same connected persons.'

9 [2017] EWHC 1379 (Ch), [2018] Ch 371 (Vos C) at [96] and [97].

10 See ch 21 above.

11 IA 1986, s 435(9) treating directors in the same way as employees and so associated with the company of which they are directors (under s 435(4)).

66.15 It would *not* be enough to make the pension trustee company connected with the CVA company:

(a) if one (or more) of the pension trustee company directors was an *employee* of the CVA company; nor

(b) if they were a director or employee of another group company (eg the parent company of the whole group).

The connected status only applies under s 249 limb if the individual with whom the pension trustee company is associated is also a director (or shadow director) of the CVA company.

66.16 It is likely to be much more difficult in practice to work out if a person is a shadow director[12] of the CVA company. If a person is a shadow director of the CVA company, then if the trustee company is an associate of that person (eg that person is also a director of the trustee company), then the trustee company will be connected with the CVA company. It is also conceivable that a company could be found to be a shadow director of the CVA company.

INDIVIDUAL OPS TRUSTEE BOARD AS A CONNECTED CREDITOR

66.17 Individual trustees (together acting as a pension trustee board) will together be the relevant creditor in relation to any debts owed to the pension scheme. This seems to mean means that the trustee board will be a connected person with the CVA company only if each of them is connected with the CVA company – *Re Thirty-Eight Building Ltd.*[13]

IMPACT OF PPF POWERS UNDER PA 2004, S 137 ON CONNECTION?

66.18 The Pensions Act 2004, s 137 provides that during a PPF assessment period the Board of the PPF takes over 'the rights and powers of the trustees or managers of the scheme in relation to any debt (including any contingent debt) due to them by the employer'.

66.19 The better view[14] is that, if s 137 applies, it does not mean that the pension trustee ceases to be the creditor for CVA purposes. The PPF does not become the creditor in place of the trustee.

12 As defined in IA 1986, s 251. See ch 22 above.

13 [1999] 1 BCLC 416, [1999] OPLR 319 (Hazel Williamson QC). See the discussion in ch 29 above.

14 Pollard '*Corporate Insolvency: Employment and Pension Rights*' (7th ed, 2021, Bloomsbury Professional) at ch 85. Also David Pollard and Tom Robinson '*CVAs and Pensions*' APL talk (May 2019).

66.20 The consequence of this is that whether the pension scheme should be treated as being a connected creditor (or not) of the CVA company involves looking at the status of the trustee board. If the pension trustee is connected then so is the pension scheme debt, even if the relevant voting power in relation to the CVA is exercised by the PPF on behalf of the trustee (and to the exclusion of the trustee). It should make no difference to the status of the pension scheme debt that the PPF is not connected (or even if arguably the PPF was itself connected[15]).

66.21 An appeal against the decision of the chair that a creditor is (or is not) connected can be made under IR 2016, rule 15.35 by the creditor, another creditor, the CVA company, or one of its shareholders.

15 Eg through its publicly owned status – or perhaps through its investment shareholdings.

Appendix A

Insolvency Act 1986, ss 249 and 435 and linked legislation

INSOLVENCY ACT 1986 (AS AMENDED)

249 'Connected' with a company

For the purposes of any provision in this Group of Parts, a person is connected with a company if—

(a) he is a director or shadow director of the company or an associate of such a director or shadow director, or

(b) he is an associate of the company;

and 'associate' has the meaning given by section 435 in Part XVIII of this Act.

PART XVIII, INSOLVENCY ACT 1986

Interpretation

435 Meaning of 'associate'

(1) For the purposes of this Act any question whether a person is an associate of another person is to be determined in accordance with the following provisions of this section (any provision that a person is an associate of another person being taken to mean that they are associates of each other).

(2) A person is an associate of an individual if that person is—

(a) the individual's husband or wife or civil partner,

(b) a relative of—

(i) the individual, or

(ii) the individual's husband or wife or civil partner, or

(c) the husband or wife or civil partner of a relative of—

(i) the individual, or

(ii) the individual's husband or wife or civil partner.

(3) A person is an associate of any person with whom he is in partnership, and of the husband or wife or civil partner or a relative of any individual with whom he is in partnership; and a Scottish firm is an associate of any person who is a member of the firm.

(4) A person is an associate of any person whom he employs or by whom he is employed.

(5) A person in his capacity as trustee of a trust other than—

(a) a trust arising under any of the second Group of Parts or the Bankruptcy (Scotland) Act 2016, or

(b) a pension scheme or an employees' share scheme ...,

is an associate of another person if the beneficiaries of the trust include, or the terms of the trust confer a power that may be exercised for the benefit of, that other person or an associate of that other person.

(6) A company is an associate of another company—

(a) if the same person has control of both, or a person has control of one and persons who are his associates, or he and persons who are his associates, have control of the other, or

(b) if a group of two or more persons has control of each company, and the groups either consist of the same persons or could be regarded as consisting of the same persons by treating (in one or more cases) a member of either group as replaced by a person of whom he is an associate.

(7) A company is an associate of another person if that person has control of it or if that person and persons who are his associates together have control of it.

(8) For the purposes of this section a person is a relative of an individual if he is that individual's brother, sister, uncle, aunt, nephew, niece, lineal ancestor or lineal descendant, treating—

(a) any relationship of the half blood as a relationship of the whole blood and the stepchild or adopted child of any person as his child, and

(b) an illegitimate child as the legitimate child of his mother and reputed father,

and references in this section to a husband or wife include a former husband or wife and a reputed husband or wife and references to a civil partner include a former civil partner and a reputed civil partner.

(9) For the purposes of this section any director or other officer of a company is to be treated as employed by that company.

(10) For the purposes of this section a person is to be taken as having control of a company if—

(a) the directors of the company or of another company which has control of it (or any of them) are accustomed to act in accordance with his directions or instructions, or

(b) he is entitled to exercise, or control the exercise of, one third or more of the voting power at any general meeting of the company or of another company which has control of it;

and where two or more persons together satisfy either of the above conditions, they are to be taken as having control of the company.

(11) In this section 'company' includes any body corporate (whether incorporated in Great Britain or elsewhere); and references to directors and other officers of a company and to voting power at any general meeting of a company have effect with any necessary modifications.

251 Expressions used generally

In this Group of Parts[1], except in so far as the context otherwise requires—

> ....
>
> 'director' includes any person occupying the position of director, by whatever name called;
>
> ....

SHADOW DIRECTOR – AMENDED DEFINITION IN S 251, IA 1986 (FROM 25 MAY 2015)

'shadow director', in relation to a company, means a person in accordance with whose directions or instructions the directors of the company are accustomed to act[, but so that a person is not deemed a shadow director by reason only that the directors act—

(a) on advice given by that person in a professional capacity;

(b) In accordance with instructions, a direction, guidance or advice given by that person in the exercise of a function conferred by or under an enactment (within the meaning given by section 1293 of the Companies Act 2006);

(c) in accordance with guidance or advice given by that person in that person's capacity as a Minister of the Crown (within the meaning of the Ministers of the Crown Act 1975)[2].

1 Note that 'this Group of Parts' does not include s 435.
2 In definition 'shadow director' words from ', but so that' to 'Ministers of the Crown Act 1975)' substituted by the Small Business, Enterprise and Employment Act 2015, s 90(1).

OTHER LEGISLATION

Section 1293 Companies Act 2006

1293 Meaning of 'enactment'

In this Act, unless the context otherwise requires, 'enactment' includes—

(a) an enactment contained in subordinate legislation within the meaning of the Interpretation Act 1978 (c 30),

(i) an enactment contained in, or in an instrument made under, a Measure or Act of the National Assembly for Wales,

(b) an enactment contained in, or in an instrument made under, an Act of the Scottish Parliament, and

(c) an enactment contained in, or in an instrument made under, Northern Ireland legislation within the meaning of the Interpretation Act 1978.

Ministers of the Crown Act 1975

8 Interpretation, consequential amendment and repeals

(1) In this Act—

.....

'Minister of the Crown' means the holder of an office in Her Majesty's Government in the United Kingdom, and includes the Treasury, the Board of Trade and the Defence Council.

Modified application

IA 1986 applies, with modifications, to:

- Limited liability partnerships: see the Limited Liability Partnerships Regulations 2001 (SI 2001/1090), reg 5, Sch 3 (as amended by SI 2005/2114, art 2(18), Sch 18, Pt 1, para 3). See Chapter 32 above.
- a body which holds a licence issued by the Law Society which is in force under the Legal Services Act 2007, Part 5: see the Legal Services Act 2007 (Designation as a Licensing Authority) (No 2) Order 2011 (SI 2011/2866), art 8(1), (2), Sch 2.
- Charitable incorporated organisations: see the Charitable Incorporated Organisations (Insolvency and Dissolution) Regulations 2012: (SI 2012/3013), reg 3, Schedule, para 1(1)(a), (f), (2), (3).
- Industrial and Provident Societies and Credit Unions: see the Industrial and Provident Societies and Credit Unions (Arrangements, Reconstructions and Administration) Order 2014 (SI 2014/229), art 4(c), Sch 3.

Insolvency Act 1986, s 436

(1) In this Act, except in so far as the context otherwise requires (and subject to Parts VII and XI)—

....

'associate' has the meaning given by section 435;

'body corporate' includes a body incorporated outside Great Britain, but does not include—

(a) a corporation sole, or

(b) a partnership that, whether or not a legal person, is not regarded as a body corporate under the law by which it is governed;

'employees' share scheme' means a scheme for encouraging or facilitating the holding of shares in or debentures of a company by or for the benefit of—

(a) the bona fide employees or former employees of—

(i) the company,

(ii) any subsidiary of the company, or

(iii) the company's holding company or any subsidiary of the company's holding company, or

(b) the spouses, civil partners, surviving spouses, surviving civil partners, or minor children or step-children of such employees or former employees;

(2) The following expressions have the same meaning in this Act as in the Companies Acts—

.....

'holding company' (see sections 1159 and 1160 of, and Schedule 6 to, that Act);

......

'subsidiary' (see sections 1159 and 1160 of, and Schedule 6 to, that Act)

Interpretation Act 1978

Section 6 Gender and number

In any Act, unless the contrary intention appears,

......

(c) words in the singular include the plural and words in the plural include the singular.

IA 1986, ss 249 and 435

Schedule 1

'Civil partnership' means a civil partnership which exists under or by virtue of the Civil Partnership Act 2004 (and any reference to a civil partner is to be read accordingly).

'Person' includes a body of persons corporate or unincorporate.

SCOTTISH LEGISLATION

Bankruptcy (Scotland) Act 2016 (asp 21)

229 Meaning of 'associate'

(1) For the purposes of this Act, any question whether a person is an associate of another person must be determined in accordance with the following provisions of this section.

(2) Subsection (1) is subject to section 230(1).

(3) And any reference, whether in the following provisions of this section or in regulations under section 230(1), to a person being an associate of another person is to be taken to be a reference to their being associates of each other.

(4) A person (in this subsection referred to as 'A') is an associate of a natural person (in this subsection referred to as 'B') if A is—

(a) B's spouse or civil partner,

(b) a relative of B or of B's spouse or civil partner, or

(c) the spouse or civil partner of such a relative.

(5) A person (in this subsection referred to as 'C') is an associate of any person (in this subsection referred to as 'D') with whom C is in partnership and of any person who is an associate of D.

(6) A firm is an associate of any person who is a member of the firm.

(7) For the purposes of this section, a person (in this subsection referred to as 'E') is a relative of a natural person (in this subsection referred to as 'F') if E is F's brother, sister, uncle, aunt, nephew, niece, lineal ancestor or lineal descendant treating any relationship of the half-blood as a relationship of the whole-blood and the stepchild or adopted child of someone (in this subsection referred to as 'S') as S's child.

(8) References in this section to a spouse or civil partner include references to a former spouse or civil partner and a reputed spouse or civil partner.

(9) A person (in this subsection referred to as 'G') is an associate of any person whom G employs or by whom G is employed.

(10) For the purposes of subsection (9), any director or other officer of a company is to be treated as employed by the company.

(11) A company is an associate of another company if—

(a) the same person has control of both, or if a person (in this subsection referred to as 'H') has control of one and persons who are H's associates have control of the other, or

(b) a group of two or more persons has control of each company and the groups either—

(i) consist of the same persons, or

(ii) could be regarded as consisting of the same persons by treating (in one case or more) a member of either group as replaced by a person of whom that member is an associate.

(12) A company is an associate of another person (in this subsection referred to as 'J') if—

(a) J has control of it, or

(b) J and persons who are J's associates together have control of it.

(13) For the purposes of this section, a person (in this subsection referred to as 'K') is taken to have control of a company—

(a) if the directors of the company, or of another company which has control of it, (or any of them) are accustomed to act in accordance with K's directions or instructions, or

(b) if K is entitled to exercise, or control the exercise of, ⅓ or more of the voting power at any general meeting of the company or of another company which has control of the company.

(14) Where two or more persons together satisfy either of the conditions mentioned in subsection (13), they are taken to have control of the company.

(15) In subsections (10) to (14), 'company' includes any body corporate (whether incorporated in Great Britain or elsewhere).

230 'Associates': regulations for the purposes of section 229

(1) The Scottish Ministers may by regulations—

(a) amend section 229 so as to provide further categories of persons who, for the purposes of this Act, are to be associates of other persons, and

(b) provide that any or all of subsections (4) to (15) of that section (or any subsection added to that section by virtue of paragraph (a))—

(i) is to cease to apply, whether in whole or in part, or

(ii) is to apply subject to such modifications as they may specify in the regulations.

(2) The Scottish Ministers may in the regulations make such incidental or transitional provision as they consider appropriate.

Appendix B

Company Law Review Steering Group (2000)

SHADOW DIRECTOR

The statutory definition of 'shadow director makes it clear that a person is only a shadow director if 'the directors as a whole' are accustomed to act in accordance with the relevant directions etc. Caselaw extends this to a majority of the board – *Ultraframe v Fielding*, but it is not enough for shadow director purposes if only a minority of the board is 'controlled' – *Smithton Ltd v Naggar*.

The Company Law Review Steering Group consultation document '*Modern Company Law For a Competitive Economy: Developing the Framework*' (March 2000) asked the question (3.11 at page 20) if this should be changed to refer to any one or more of the directors? Should this be limited to public companies?

Response in later condoc (p55)

In its later consultation document "Completing the Structure: A consultation document from the Company Law Review Steering Group"[1] – November 2000, the Steering Group responded:

> **Modern Company Law: Completing the Structure**
>
> 4.6 The current law treats as a shadow director, and thus subject to many of the obligations of a de jure director, a person in accordance with whose directions or instructions the directors are accustomed to act (section 740(2)). We asked whether this definition should be extended so that it would be sufficient if a person "pulled the strings" of just one director, rather than of the board as a whole. There was a slight majority of responses against this idea. Opponents stressed the uncertain and unpredictable effect that the extension would have in financial and complex corporate relations where the appointment of a nominee, or partly representative, director (sometimes with a mandate which operates only in certain, often critical, circumstances) is a frequent, perfectly acceptable, means of protecting parties'

1 URN 00/1335 http://webarchive.nationalarchives.gov.uk/20061209054628/http://www.dti.gov.uk/bbf/co-law-reform-bill/clr-review/page25080.html.

positions. The point was made that "shadow director" is something of a misnomer as the policy is to catch the person who normally controls the board as a whole, and thus the company, rather than a particular director. It was however widely argued that there should be wider disclosure in annual reports or elsewhere of the existence of such relationships.

4.7 We are not wholly convinced that such disclosure requirements would be effective. Shadow directors are required now to be registered under section 288 and, perhaps not surprisingly, this is rarely done. However the position may be different in the case of a pure disclosure requirement and we are inclined to adopt this approach. We therefore propose that disclosure of relationships of influence or control between a director and another person or body should be required to be disclosed as part of the requirements concerning governance to be imposed under the authority of the Companies Commission Ð see Chapter 12. By making this a matter for rules we hope to ensure that the requirement is developed flexibly and effectively in response to levels of compliance and avoidance. The application of the shadow director concept to each provision relating to directors will need to be determined in detail as the legislation is prepared. We are however inclined to suggest that the proposed statement of directors' duties and all the provisions of Part X should apply to shadow directors as they apply to directors 56.

Appendix C

Similar terms in other legislation

CHARITIES ACT 2011

Charities Act 2011

117 Restrictions on dispositions of land: general

(1) No land held by or in trust for a charity is to be conveyed, transferred, leased or otherwise disposed of without an order of—

(a) the court, or

(b) the Commission.

But this is subject to the following provisions of this section, sections 119 to 121 (further provisions about restrictions on dispositions) and section 127 (release of charity rent charges).

(2) Subsection (1) does not apply to a disposition of such land if—

(a) the disposition is made to a person who is not—

(i) a connected person (as defined in section 118), or

(ii) a trustee for, or nominee of, a connected person, and

(b) the requirements of—

(i) section 119(1) (dispositions other than certain leases), or

(ii) section 120(2) (leases which are for 7 years or less etc.),

have been complied with in relation to it.

Charities Act 2011 s 118:

(1) In section 117(2) connected person, in relation to a charity, means any person who falls within subsection (2)—

(a) at the time of the disposition in question, or

(b) at the time of any contract for the disposition in question.

(2) The persons are—

(a) a charity trustee[1] or trustee for the charity,

(b) a person who is the donor of any land to the charity (whether the gift was made on or after the establishment of the charity),

(c) a child, parent, grandchild, grandparent, brother or sister of any such trustee or donor,

(d) an officer, agent or employee of the charity,

(e) the spouse or civil partner of any person falling within any of paras (a) to (d),

(f) a person carrying on business in partnership with any person falling within any of paras (a) to (e),

(g) an institution which is controlled—

(i) by any person falling within any of paras (a) to (f), or

(ii) by two or more such persons taken together, or

(h) a body corporate in which—

(i) any connected person falling within any of paras (a) to (g) has a substantial interest, or

(ii) two or more such persons, taken together, have a substantial interest.

(3) Sections 350 to 352 (meaning of child, spouse and civil partner, controlled institution and substantial interest) apply for the purposes of subsection (2).

350 Connected person: child, spouse and civil partner

(1) In sections 118(2)(c), 188(1)(a), 200(1)(a) and 249(2)(a), "child" includes a stepchild and an illegitimate child.

(2) For the purposes of sections 118(2)(e), 188(1)(b), 200(1)(b) and 249(2)(b), where two people are not married to, or civil partners of, each other but live together as if they were a married couple or civil partners, each of them is to be treated as the spouse or civil partner of the other.

351 Connected person: controlled institution

For the purposes of sections 118(2)(g), 157(1)(a), 188(1)(d), 200(1)(d) and 249(2)(d), a person controls an institution if the person is able to secure that the affairs of the institution are conducted in accordance with the person's wishes.

1 The term 'charity trustee is widely defined in s 177:

"In this Act, except in so far as the context otherwise requires, "charity trustees" means the persons having the general control and management of the administration of a charity."

This will include the directors of a company acting as a charity trustee – William Henderson and Jonathan Fowles *Tudor on Charities* (10th ed, 2015, Sweet & Maxwell) at 17-001.

352 Connected person: substantial interest in body corporate

(1) For the purposes of sections 118(2)(h), 157(1)(b), 188(1)(e), 200(1)(e) and 249(2)(e), any such connected person as is there mentioned has a substantial interest in a body corporate if the person or institution in question—

(a) is interested in shares comprised in the equity share capital of that body of a nominal value of more than one-fifth of that share capital, or

(b) is entitled to exercise, or control the exercise of, more than one-fifth of the voting power at any general meeting of that body.

(2) The rules set out in Schedule 1 to the Companies Act 2006 (rules for interpretation of certain provisions of that Act) apply for the purposes of subsection (1) as they apply for the purposes of section 254 of that Act ("connected persons" etc.).

(3) In this section "equity share capital" and "share" have the same meaning as in that Act.

FINANCIAL SERVICES AND MARKETS ACT 2000

FSMA 2000, ss 422 and 422A

422 Controller

(1) In this Act "controller", in relation to an undertaking ("B"), means a person ("A") who falls within any of the cases in subsection (2).

(2) The cases are where A holds—

(a) 10% or more of the shares in B or in a parent undertaking of B ("P");

(b) 10% or more of the voting power in B or P; or

(c) shares or voting power in B or P as a result of which A is able to exercise significant influence over the management of B.

(3) For the purposes of calculations relating to this section, the holding of shares or voting power by a person ("A1") includes any shares or voting power held by another ("A2") if A1 and A2 are acting in concert.

(4) In this section "shares"—

(a) in relation to an undertaking with a share capital, means allotted shares;

(b) in relation to an undertaking with capital but no share capital, means rights to share in the capital of the undertaking;

(c) in relation to an undertaking without capital, means interests—

(i) conferring any right to share in the profits, or liability to contribute to the losses, of the undertaking; or

(ii) giving rise to an obligation to contribute to the debts or expenses of the undertaking in the event of a winding up.

(5) In this section "voting power" —

(a) includes, in relation to a person ("H")—

- (i) voting power held by a third party with whom H has concluded an agreement, which obliges H and the third party to adopt, by concerted exercise of the voting power they hold, a lasting common policy towards the management of the undertaking in question;
- (ii) voting power held by a third party under an agreement concluded with H providing for the temporary transfer for consideration of the voting power in question;
- (iii) voting power attaching to shares which are lodged as collateral with H, provided that H controls the voting power and declares an intention to exercise it;
- (iv) voting power attaching to shares in which H has a life interest;
- (v) voting power which is held, or may be exercised within the meaning of sub-paragraphs (i) to (iv), by a controlled undertaking of H;
- (vi) voting power attaching to shares deposited with H which H has discretion to exercise in the absence of specific instructions from the shareholders;
- (vii) voting power held in the name of a third party on behalf of H;
- (viii) voting power which H may exercise as a proxy where H has discretion about the exercise of the voting power in the absence of specific instructions from the shareholders; and

(b) in relation to an undertaking which does not have general meetings at which matters are decided by the exercise of voting rights, means the right under the constitution of the undertaking to direct the overall policy of the undertaking or alter the terms of its constitution.

(6) For the purposes of this section, an undertaking "B" is a controlled undertaking of H if any of the conditions in section 89J(4)(a) to (d) (read with section 89J(5)) is met (reading references in those provisions to A as references to H).

422A Disregarded holdings

(1) For the purposes of section 422, shares and voting power that a person holds in an undertaking ("B") or in a parent undertaking of B ("P") are disregarded in the following circumstances.

(2) Shares held only for the purposes of clearing and settling within a short settlement cycle are disregarded.

(3) Shares held by a custodian or its nominee in a custodian capacity are disregarded, provided that the custodian or nominee is only able to exercise voting power attached to the shares in accordance with instructions given in writing.

(4) Shares representing no more than 5% of the total voting power in B or P held by an investment firm are disregarded, provided that it—

(a) holds the shares in the capacity of a market maker (as defined in article 2.1.6 of the markets in financial instruments regulation);

(b) has a Part 4A permission to carry on one or more investment services and activities;

(c) neither intervenes in the management of B or P nor exerts any influence on B or P to buy the shares or back the share price.

(5) Shares held by a qualifying credit institution or investment firm in its trading book are disregarded, provided that—

(a) the shares represent no more than 5% of the total voting power in B or P; and

(b) the voting power is not used to intervene in the management of B or P.

(6) Shares held by a qualifying credit institution or an investment firm are disregarded, provided that—

(a) the shares are held as a result of performing the investment services and activities of—

(i) underwriting shares; or

(ii) placing shares on a firm commitment basis; and

(b) the qualifying credit institution or investment firm—

(i) does not exercise voting power represented by the shares or otherwise intervene in the management of the issuer; and

(ii) retains the holding for a period of less than one year.

(7) Where a management company (as defined in section 237(2)) and its parent undertaking both hold shares or voting power, each may disregard holdings of the other, provided that each exercises its voting power independently of the other.

(8) But subsection (7) does not apply if the management company—

(a) manages holdings for its parent undertaking or a controlled undertaking of its parent undertaking;

(b) has no discretion to exercise the voting power attached to such holdings; and

(c) may only exercise the voting power in relation to such holdings under direct or indirect instruction from—

(i) its parent undertaking; or

(ii) a controlled undertaking of the parent undertaking.

(9) Where an investment firm and its parent undertaking both hold shares or voting power, the parent undertaking may disregard holdings managed by the investment firm on a client by client basis and the investment firm may disregard holdings of the parent undertaking, provided that the investment firm—

(a) has permission to provide portfolio management;

(b) exercises its voting power independently from the parent undertaking; and

(c) may only exercise the voting power under instructions given in writing, or has appropriate mechanisms in place for ensuring that individual portfolio management services are conducted independently of any other services.

(9A) Shares acquired for stabilisation purposes in accordance with the market abuse regulation and Commission Delegated Regulation (EU) No. 1052/2016 of 8 March 2016 supplementing Regulation (EU) No. 596/2014 of the European Parliament and the Council with regard to the regulatory technical standards for conditions applicable to buy-back programmes and stabilisation measures are disregarded, provided that the voting power attached to those shares is not exercised or otherwise used to intervene in the management of B or P.

(11) For the purposes of this section, an undertaking is a controlled undertaking of the parent undertaking if it is controlled by the parent undertaking; and for this purpose the question of whether one undertaking controls another is to be determined in accordance with section 89J(4) and (5).

TAXATION OF CAPITAL GAINS ACT 1992

TCGA 1992, s 286

286 Connected persons: interpretation.

(5) A company is connected with another company—

(a) if the same person has control of both, or a person has control of one and persons connected with him, or he and persons connected with him, have control of the other, or

(b) if a group of 2 or more persons has control of each company, and the groups either consist of the same persons or could be regarded as consisting of the same persons by treating (in one or more cases) a member of either group as replaced by a person with whom he is connected.

(6) A company is connected with another person, if that person has control of it or if that person and persons connected with him together have control of it.

(7) Any 2 or more persons acting together to secure or exercise control of a company shall be treated in relation to that company as connected with one another and with any person acting on the directions of any of them to secure or exercise control of the company.

(8) In this section "relative" means brother, sister, ancestor or lineal descendant.

CORPORATION TAX ACT 2010

Corporation Tax Act 2010

1122 "Connected" persons

(1) This section has effect for the purposes of the provisions of the Corporation Tax Acts which apply this section (or to which this section is applied).

(2) A company is connected with another company if—

(a) the same person has control of both companies,

(b) a person ("A") has control of one company and persons connected with A have control of the other company,

(c) A has control of one company and A together with persons connected with A have control of the other company, or

(d) a group of two or more persons has control of both companies and the groups either consist of the same persons or could be so regarded if (in one or more cases) a member of either group were replaced by a person with whom the member is connected.

(3) A company is connected with another person ("A") if—

(a) A has control of the company, or

(b) A together with persons connected with A have control of the company.

(4) In relation to a company, any two or more persons acting together to secure or exercise control of the company are connected with—

(a) one another, and

(b) any person acting on the directions of any of them to secure or exercise control of the company.

(5) An individual ("A") is connected with another individual ("B") if—

(a) A is B's spouse or civil partner,

(b) A is a relative of B,

(c) A is the spouse or civil partner of a relative of B,

(d) A is a relative of B's spouse or civil partner, or

(e) A is the spouse or civil partner of a relative of B's spouse or civil partner.

(6) A person, in the capacity as trustee of a settlement, is connected with—

(a) any individual who is a settlor in relation to the settlement,

(b) any person connected with such an individual,

(c) any close company whose participators include the trustees of the settlement,

(d) any non-UK resident company which, if it were UK resident, would be a close company whose participators include the trustees of the settlement,

(e) any body corporate controlled (within the meaning of section 1124) by a company within paragraph (c) or (d),

(f) if the settlement is the principal settlement in relation to one or more sub-fund settlements, a person in the capacity as trustee of such a sub-fund settlement, and

(g) if the settlement is a sub-fund settlement in relation to a principal settlement, a person in the capacity as trustee of any other sub-fund settlements in relation to the principal settlement.

(7) A person who is a partner in a partnership is connected with—

(a) any partner in the partnership,

(b) the spouse or civil partner of any individual who is a partner in the partnership, and

(c) a relative of any individual who is a partner in the partnership.

(8) But subsection (7) does not apply in relation to acquisitions or disposals of assets of the partnership pursuant to genuine commercial arrangements.

1123 "Connected" persons: supplementary

(1) In section 1122 and this section—

"company" includes any body corporate or unincorporated association, but does not include a partnership (and see also subsection (2)),

"control" is to be read in accordance with sections 450 and 451 (except where otherwise indicated),

"principal settlement" has the meaning given by paragraph 1 of Schedule 4ZA to TCGA 1992,

"relative" means brother, sister, ancestor or lineal descendant,

"settlement" has the same meaning as in Chapter 5 of Part 5 of ITTOIA 2005 (see section 620 of that Act), and

"sub-fund settlement" has the meaning given by paragraph 1 of Schedule 4ZA to TCGA 1992.

(2) For the purposes of section 1122—

(a) a unit trust scheme is treated as if it were a company, and

(b) the rights of the unit holders are treated as if they were shares in the company.

(3) For the purposes of section 1122 "trustee", in the case of a settlement in relation to which there would be no trustees apart from this subsection, means any person—

(a) in whom the property comprised in the settlement is for the time being vested, or

(b) in whom the management of that property is for the time being vested.

Section 466(4) of ITA 2007 (which applies for the purposes of the Corporation Tax Acts as a result of section 1169 below) does not apply for the purposes of this subsection.

(4) If any provision of section 1122 provides that a person ("A") is connected with another person ("B"), it also follows that B is connected with A.

1124 "Control"

(1) This section has effect for the purposes of the provisions of the Corporation Tax Acts which apply this section (or to which this section is applied).

(2) In relation to a body corporate ("company A"), "control" means the power of a person ("P") to secure—

(a) by means of the holding of shares or the possession of voting power in relation to that or any other body corporate, or

(b) as a result of any powers conferred by the articles of association or other document regulating that or any other body corporate,

that the affairs of company A are conducted in accordance with P's wishes.

(3) In relation to a partnership, "control" means the right to a share of more than half the assets, or of more than half the income, of the partnership.

ss 450 and 45

450 "Control"

(1) This section applies for the purpose of this Part [Part 10, Close Companies].

(2) A person ("P") is treated as having control of a company ("C") if P—

(a) exercises,

(b) is able to exercise, or

(c) is entitled to acquire,

direct or indirect control over C's affairs.

(3) In particular, P is treated as having control of C if P possesses or is entitled to acquire—

(a) the greater part of the share capital or issued share capital of C,

(b) the greater part of the voting power in C,

(c) so much of the issued share capital of C as would, on the assumption that the whole of the income of C were distributed among the participators, entitle P to receive the greater part of the amount so distributed, or

(d) such rights as would entitle P, in the event of the winding up of C or in any other circumstances, to receive the greater part of the assets of C which would then be available for distribution among the participators.

(4) Any rights that P or any other person has as a loan creditor are to be disregarded for the purposes of the assumption in subsection (3)(c).

(5) If two or more persons together satisfy any of the conditions in subsections (2) and (3), they are treated as having control of C.

(6) See also section 451 (section 450: rights to be attributed etc).

451 Section 450: rights to be attributed etc

(1) This section applies for the purposes of section 450.

(2) A person is treated as entitled to acquire anything which the person—

(a) is entitled to acquire at a future date, or

(b) will at a future date be entitled to acquire.

(3) If a person—

(a) possesses any rights or powers on behalf of another person (A), or

(b) may be required to exercise any rights or powers on A's direction or behalf,

those rights or powers are to be attributed to A.

(4) There may also be attributed to a person all the rights and powers—

(a) of any company of which the person has, or the person and associates of the person have, control,

(b) of any two or more companies within paragraph (a),

(c) of any associate of the person, or

(d) of any two or more associates of the person.

(5) The rights and powers which may be attributed under subsection (4)—

(a) include those attributed to a company or associate under subsection (3), but

(b) do not include those attributed to an associate under subsection (4).

(6) Such attributions are to be made under subsection (4) as will result in a company being treated as under the control of 5 or fewer participators if it can be so treated.

Index

[all references are to paragraph number]

www.ingramcontent.com/pod-product-compliance
Ingram Content Group UK Ltd.
Pitfield, Milton Keynes, MK11 3LW, UK
UKHW051931150926
475560UK00005B/346

9 781526 519597